Walter Murdoch

Walter Murdoch, 1959
Pen and wash drawing by Louis Kahan

JOHN LA NAUZE

Walter Murdoch

A BIOGRAPHICAL MEMOIR

MELBOURNE UNIVERSITY PRESS
1977

First published 1977

Printed in Australia by
Wilke and Company Limited, Clayton, Victoria 3168
for Melbourne University Press, Carlton, Victoria 3053
U.S.A. and Canada: International Scholarly Book Services, Inc.,
Box 555, Forest Grove, Oregon 97116
Great Britain, Europe, the Middle East, Africa and the Caribbean:
International Book Distributors Ltd (Prentice-Hall International),
66 Wood Lane End, Hemel Hempstead,
Hertfordshire HP2 4RG, England

National Library of Australia Cataloguing in Publication data

La Nauze, John Andrew, 1911–
  Walter Murdoch.
  Index.
  ISBN 0 522 84119 8.
  1. Murdoch, Walter Logie Forbes, 1874–1970. I. Title.
A824

Amid a world of sceptred sham
   Be this my humble aim, at least;
To seem the sort of beast I am,
   And not some other sort of beast.

WALTER MURDOCH

CONTENTS

ILLUSTRATIONS

PREFACE

This is a short book about a long-lived man whose name and writings were familiar throughout Australia for much of the twentieth century. I call it a 'memoir'. Applied to a biographical narrative, that word implies that the author has had some personal knowledge of the man or woman who is its subject. Since I have found it impossible to avoid a personal mode of writing, I should explain the extent of my acquaintanceship with Walter Murdoch. As a schoolboy growing up in South Perth in Western Australia I knew him by sight, as I knew most of my elders in what was still a village-like community, and I looked on him with some awe, for professors were not then fourpence a bunch. Later, I was for three years one of his 'English' students at the University of Western Australia. After I departed permanently in 1931 from Perth we corresponded, from time to time, for nearly forty years. I invariably called on him when I revisited that pleasant city.

It would be pretentious to claim intimate friendship with a man to whom my personal attitude was always that of pupil to teacher, even when some of his opinions on particular matters seemed to me to be obstinately eccentric, but I did know him for a long time. Readers must allow for my prejudices if I honour his memory in the spirit expressed by another of his pupils, Paul Hasluck, who said when Murdoch died, 'he would have found us a little foolish if we shied away from laughter and affection. We will not honour him by being over-solemn.'

Some years ago, with the approval of Murdoch's family, I appealed through the press for copies of his letters and other documents relating to him to be deposited in the National Library of Australia. At that time I had no intention of writing about him. The responses from many people who knew him only through his writings made me think that they might care to know more about him personally, and that there was a good deal that I did not know myself. Before long I found that I would need to write a book rather than a biographical essay.

To mention the names of all the people who have helped me with reminiscences or who have made documents available is impossible here. I have space only to thank them collectively: correspondents unknown to me personally, private friends, Murdoch's colleagues, officers of libraries, archives and universities. To Murdoch's family—his daughters Catherine King and Anne Vanzetti, and his wife Barbara Murdoch—mere thanks are inadequate, when I consider how they have patiently answered my hundreds of questions over the years, knowing that they would not see a word of the book before it was published. I wonder that they still (as I think) remain my friends. My able 'assistants' at different times—Elizabeth Nurser, Amanda Gordon, Christopher Connolly—became my colleagues and teachers. Lois Simms was not only a skilled typist but a shrewd detector of errors. In particular but important ways I am indebted to D. Abbott, C. Bram, P. J. W. Kilpatrick, B. B. La Nauze, J. D. B. Miller and P. Ryan.

For permission to quote from documents or printed material in their ownership or custody or in which they have rights of various kinds I thank: Messrs Angus and Robertson, publishers; the Australian Broadcasting Commission (through the Deputy General Manager); A. D. Brookes; Mrs J. D. Clarke; F. Strahan, University of Melbourne; the National Library of Australia; the trustees of the State Library of Victoria; A. J. Williams, University of Western Australia; the members of Murdoch's family, named above; and many friends who have freely made available to me letters in their possession. For the use of illustrations I thank: for the frontispiece, Murdoch University and Louis Kahan; for those in the text, Catherine King, Barbara Murdoch, Jean Murdoch, Murdoch University, the National Library of Australia, Kevin Smith, Anne Vanzetti, Peter Walden, Arthur Williams.

Canberra *John La Nauze*

CONVERSIONS

1 mile   1·61 kilometres
1 yard   0·91 metre
1 acre   0·40 hectare

1 pound (£1) Australian is nominally equal to 2 dollars ($2) Australian but this means little in comparisons of the purchasing power of money over time. Expressed in dollars, the 'basic wage' of an adult male worker per week in Melbourne, as determined by the Commonwealth Arbitration Court, was approximately 4.20 in 1907; 7.10 in 1920; 9.00 in 1930; 8.10 in 1940; 13.40 in 1950. Under a different method of determination, the minimum award wage (average of six capital cities) in 1976 was about $100. Salaries of professors in the University of Western Australia, in dollars per annum, were 1800 in 1913, 2000 in 1923, 2000 in 1940, and about 30 000 in 1976.

𝔛 1 𝔛

A SON OF THE MANSE

WALTER MURDOCH, the subject of this memoir, was born in
1874 in Rosehearty, 'a burgh of barony and a small
seaport, in the parish of Pitsligo, district of Buchan,
county of Aberdeen'. It will not be found on a map of Scotland in a
school atlas, but one can start with the city of Aberdeen and follow
the coast as it trends north, then swings around to run west and
define the southern shore of the great indentation of the Moray
Firth. At the turning-point, as it seems to be on a small-scale map, is
Kinnairds Head and nearby the town of Fraserburgh. Four miles to
the west of Fraserburgh on the way along the coast to Banff lies the
little town of Rosehearty.

In official descriptions in the nineteenth century, Rosehearty was
called a 'fishing village', and so it really was: its population in 1841
was 750, and in 1881, when Walter Murdoch left it for ever, 1400. But
'village' is hardly dignified enough for a place which since the 1680s
had been a 'burgh of barony', with certain chartered privileges of
local government granted by an overlord. For a royal burgh, that
overlord would have been the monarch; for this burgh of barony he
had been Alexander, second Baron Forbes of Pitsligo.

The coast, sandy to the east, savage, rocky, dangerous with low
cliffs to the west, had for centuries been a place of shipwrecks. Indeed
the original settlement, it was supposed, had been made in the four-
teenth century by a party of shipwrecked Danes. Inland there were
ruined castles and the sites of ancient churches. In summer it could be
a pleasant place in the long twilight, but when the fierce wind blew

1

from the north it was a reminder that on a line between Rosehearty and the North Pole there lay nothing but sea and ice-floes.

In the 1840s Rosehearty was prosperous by the standards of such villages. Partly, it had sizeable revenues, for a generation earlier an ingenious lawyer had discovered that the shore-dues belonged to its people, not to its 'superior'. But mainly its prosperity came from two things, its harbour and the fish brought into it by forty or more boats—cod, ling, haddock, skate and above all herring. It had always been a fishing village and it seemed then that it would always remain so. The fish, with some grain and potatoes from the small inland farms, were sent out to Glasgow, Edinburgh and London in vessels which brought back Rosehearty's simple requirements of timber, coal and salt.

The fishermen and their families who lived in the 'sea-town' near the harbour in grey stone cottages, gable-ends to the streets, were a close community; not until a century later were Rosehearty folk inclined to marry outside their own people. Beyond the Square, a few hundred yards inland, was the 'new-town', where lived 'traders and business people, also a few farmers, crofters, carters and other such people'. There was a parochial school, whose master had a salary of £34 4s 4d with an allowance of £2 in lieu of a garden, and a few 'private' schools. Market day was Saturday.

A leading inhabitant of the town and parish was the minister of the Church of Scotland, with his stipend (in the 1840s) of nearly £200, his manse, his glebe, and his spiritual influence upon the congregation which met in the handsome seventeenth-century church. But from 1843, though he and his successors in that office might be materially no worse off, their spiritual influence would necessarily be diminished, since to the end of the century and beyond there would now be more than one minister of the Presbyterian persuasion, ordained and inducted to serve the parish of Pitsligo, each of them with his own congregation. In that year, when so many ministers of the Church of Scotland 'came out' to form the Free Church and sign away their livings, laymen of like mind in Pitsligo must have been earnestly busy. Their own kirk-session minutes began and their own Free Church, 'the red Kirkie', was built in Rosehearty in 1844.[1]

From 1846 to 1881 the minister of the Free Church in Pitsligo was the Reverend James Murdoch, born in Stirling on 13 September 1818, the fifth child of Peter Murdoch and his wife Isabella McNie. Peter was variously described as 'iron-monger' and 'merchant', words which come together in the 'Sometime Hardware Merchant' of his will. Born in 1772, he was comfortably off by the time of his death in 1850. His son James is recorded as a matriculated student of the

University of Glasgow, and a member of the Latin class of 1831, but appears not to have taken a degree, though in later life he was regarded as an able and learned man. Clues to his mode of life before we meet him in 1846 are lacking, though it would seem that by 1843 his intentions were to enter the Presbyterian ministry, for his children cherished a legend that he had been the youngest 'minister' to 'come out' at the Disruption. That could not have been literally true, since a 'minister' was one who had been ordained and inducted into his own parish, and James did not attain that status until 1846; moreover he is not listed in the roll of honour of the Free Church in Brown's *Annals of the Disruption*. Yet the legend does seem to reflect more than an ordinary layman's decision to leave the Church of Scotland. Possibly James (like his oldest son later) had been an 'assistant' to a minister, hoping for his own parish, but in 1843 prepared on this matter of principle to sacrifice his prospects in the Scottish church establishment.[2]

A mile or so from Rosehearty was Braco Park, the house and land (today a farm) which in the later eighteenth century had formed part of the estates of Francis Garden, Lord Gardenstone, whose family tree, with its complex system of branches, extended far back into the history of Aberdeenshire and of Scotland; from one twig in the United States came the name of the plant gardenia. An able judge, lord of session and lord of justiciary, he was well known for his amiable eccentricities, which included the keeping of a pig in his bedroom, the consumption of vast quantities of snuff—he used to say that if he had a dozen noses he would feed them all—and the foundation of a model village. He is relevant here because after his succession to the family estates in 1785 he appointed as his 'factor' a relative, William Garden, who came to live at Braco Park. William married Eliza Logie, on her mother's side related to Alexander Forbes, fourth and last Baron Forbes of Pitsligo, the unfortunate elderly Jacobite who for some years after the Forty-five had been hunted throughout that district by the redcoats. Eliza Forbes Garden, born at Braco Park in July 1788, lived to recall for young Walter Murdoch in the 1870s her memories of the illuminations for the victories of Trafalgar and Waterloo. Her brother Francis Garden became an advocate practising in Aberdeen. His daughter Helen Young Garden, born in April 1825, brings us back to James Murdoch.

James may have met Helen Garden in Free Church circles before he came to Rosehearty, for she was a cousin of his contemporary William Garden Blaikie, a rising and later eminent divine, and had other clerical relatives of that persuasion, including her aunt's friend

Dr Davidson of Aberdeen. But in any case Miss Eliza Garden of Braco Park was so distinctly a 'figure' in the parish to which the young minister came in 1846, that he must have met her and her niece soon after his arrival. On 28 September 1848, in the parish of Banchory Devenick near Aberdeen, James Murdoch and Helen Garden were married.[3]

When James Murdoch told the Pitsligo kirk-session in February 1881 that he and his family would be leaving Rosehearty, he was choosing to be a 'senior' (or retired) minister. He was not soon forgotten by those whom he had baptized, married and preached to. After his death a plaque to his memory was placed in the church (now disused) which succeeded the old red Kirkie, and as late as 1906 his presence was still vivid to one who had often heard his admonitions from the pulpit. This anonymous parishioner pictured him as a gifted and scholarly man, of reserved and dignified manner, 'more among the people than of them', but greatly respected and admired. Despite a somewhat harsh and unmelodious voice, he was a powerfully impressive reader of the Scriptures, with a fine articulation and an occasional illuminating use of emphasis 'producing the effect of a louvre window opened in a dark apartment'. His attainments as a scholar were known far beyond Rosehearty; he was (writes our anonymous authority) more than once proposed to fill a professor's chair in the Free Church, but the occasion came too late. A man of liberal mind, he was anxious to see union between the Free and the United Presbyterian Churches, for some years collaborating for this and other purposes with his ministerial colleague in Rosehearty, until events outside their little world brought the project to an end for their generation. Many of his powerful discourses, we are told, would ring in the ears of some of his hearers while life lasted.[4]

We may believe it. Preserved in great libraries is a sermon which James Murdoch must have prepared with particular care, for it was preached before the Free Synod of Aberdeen, connoisseurs of Calvinist preaching and doctrine who were so impressed that they urged him to publish it. The difficult subject was 'Everlasting Punishment'. Speaking to colleagues, James Murdoch was concerned with the technical problem of conveying to their congregations the truth and use of a doctrine which, he admitted, did sound rather terrifying, yet needed constantly to be kept before the mind.

> To all men and women,—to the gentleman and scholar as well as the mechanic and the peasant—to the tender and delicate woman, who will scarce set her foot on mother-earth for very delicateness, equally with her serving-maid, must these awful warnings be displayed, and in unvarnished colours—the terrible strength and simplicity of Bible language.

The slumberers in their congregations must be wakened:

> It is demanded of us to expose and warn these barren fig-
> trees—these wells without water,—to cause these sinners in Zion to
> be afraid, and to surprise these hypocrites with fearfulness. We
> must tell them of the doom of the unprofitable servant. We must
> summon them to cut off the right hand or the right foot, or pluck
> out the right eye, if these offend against holy living, reminding
> them that the Lord has warned us, *once, twice, thrice*, in the same
> brief discourse, and with ever-deepening emphasis, that except we
> shall thus deny ourselves, we shall be cast into hellfire, 'where their
> worm'—each man's worm—'dieth not and the fire is not quenched'.

This was powerful medicine. It was not, as James Murdoch freely
admitted, for 'very frequent' application to a flock by their own 'fixed
pastor'; often he should rather remind them of their duty within a
sentence or two, reserving express and lengthened exposition for
comparatively rare occasions.[5] No doubt he continued to practise
what he preached. Perhaps his son Walter's first sermon, preached at
the age of five when 'playing church' with his brothers and sisters,
reflected, for a childish understanding, the import of one of those
lengthier expositions. It was delivered in four words: 'All people, be
good.'

The old Free Church manse still stands solidly in Rosehearty, a
grey stone house long since given over to private purposes. In some
thirty years of married life there, Helen Murdoch bore fourteen
children: nine boys and five girls. Our concern is with Walter, the
last-born. I give below their names as they were recorded in the
register when their mother died in Melbourne in 1905 at the age of
nearly eighty.* Eight had died before her. Four of these had certainly
died of tuberculosis, which seems likely also to have caused or has-
tened the deaths of two others. The legend that the other two—both
girls, buried in Rosehearty—had died of 'eating green gooseberries'
may (so medical scientists tell me) be disregarded; substitute
'appendicitis', or the coincidental eating of contaminated food or . . .
But tuberculosis (phthisis, or consumption, they called it) haunted
that family. One other child, whose death from the disease was daily
expected, recovered to live into her seventies. Of those who never

---

* Helen Murdoch died in Camberwell near Melbourne on 1 April 1905. The form
for the registration of deaths required the listing of issue in order of birth, with names
and ages. The information was probably supplied by Helen Murdoch's oldest son
Patrick. I give in parentheses years of birth instead of his figures for actual ages, and put
Andrew in his proper place in the order. The list runs: Patrick John (1850), Francis
Garden (1852), James (1853) dead, Eliza Jane (1855), William Garden (1856) dead,
Ivon Lewis (1858) dead, Andrew Crystall (1859) dead, Helen Nora (1861), Keith
Arthur (1862) dead, Isabella Agnes (1863) dead, Hugh (1865) dead, Grace Young
(1867), Amelia (1870) dead, Walter Logie Forbes (1874).

contracted it (or more likely in whom its attack was arrested early), one lived to eighty-two, two to ninety, and one to nearly ninety-six. In extreme old age the last of these, still remembering with affection the brothers whom consumption had taken when he was a child, would speak with a kind of savage sadness of the ravages of the 'curse of Scotland' in that time.

Walter Logie Forbes Murdoch was born on 17 September 1874. 'Walter' was the name of one of his father's uncles; 'Logie' was the surname of Helen Murdoch's grandmother, and her aunt was Eliza Forbes Garden. The child was baptized on 11 October by the Reverend (and very learned) Dr William Garden Blaikie, by now professor of apologetics and pastoral theology at New College, Edinburgh. So much is firmly recorded in the baptismal register of the parish of Pitsligo. Beyond that, Walter's childhood in Scotland must be recovered almost entirely from what he himself wrote, or told others, in later years, for it is one of the penalties (or advantages) of living to extreme old age that when death comes no one alive will have known you when you were young. If his visual memories of Rosehearty in the years round about 1880 were sharpened in middle and old age by two brief visits to his birthplace, most of his recollections of events clearly go back directly to his first eight years.

We learn a little more about his father. His wide reading included contemporary journals: he had, for instance, taken the *Cornhill* from the beginning. With learned clerical friends he greatly debated theology, being a 'specialist' (but this may have come from his oldest son Patrick) on the Latitudinarians. To his children he read English and Scottish literature in general, but especially Burns—surely from an expurgated version, thought Walter, but on reflection he was not so sure, for if his father might have frowned on Burns the man, he would have laughed with him too. He was a good parish priest; when the men in overdue vessels were known to be safe, the news would immediately be reported to him by the fisher-folk who knew he would be anxious, and he always impressed upon them that it was essential to take whisky with them to sea. His fault was over-smoking, said the son who was rarely himself seen without a pipe during seventy years.[6]

In Walter Murdoch's various reminiscences there is less about his mother. She had literary tastes and a turn for writing; no doubt she occasionally let it be known in the company of educated Scots that her brother William had married a daughter of the poet James Hogg, the 'Ettrick Shepherd'.[7] Walter mentioned occasionally her simple and strict standards of life and conduct. Thus it would have shocked her, he believed, as much as his father, to think that parents could allow their children to go out into the world like sheep without a shepherd. They should be instructed in a faith to live by. She would have been unmoved by his proposition that how you arrived at your beliefs was more important than what you believed. When he was a very old man he could still see his mother, in the distant Rosehearty days, regularly writing to Aberdeen, to Australia, to New Zealand, to South Africa, to the children who had left home, and could see himself, a small boy, trudging to the post office with her letters. Whatever, he wondered, could she have found to write about? But he should have reflected that when he wrote to his own children he never lacked subject matter.

When Walter was born, his older brothers had left home or would soon do so. Patrick John, the first-born, a graduate of the University of Aberdeen and New College, Edinburgh, was ordained in 1878 as minister of the parish of Cruden, some twenty miles north of Aberdeen, and his brother James was by then pursuing his medical studies at Edinburgh. So young Walter saw some of his brothers only when they came back for holidays. But there were still children at home, and an atmosphere of family affection that he treasured as an old man. There survives a book compiled by James and Ivon and dedicated 'by the artists' to their brothers and sisters as a new year's present for 1877. Coloured crayon-and-wash pictures illustrate deliberately artless verses irreverently ascribed to a large range of English poets; the kind of artefact that helps faintly to recreate a type of family life, and a household in which there were more books on the shelves than *The Ten Years' Conflict*, the four volumes of the *Annals of the Disruption*, and various sets of 'Works' which Walter vaguely remembered but never himself read.

He was thankful for memories of winter snow and snowballing, and in other seasons strawberries and gooseberries, though apricots and peaches he never saw when he was young. He remembered the bearded fishermen who would hoist him to their shoulders, the anxious women assembled at the harbour as the little fishing smacks straggled in one by one after a stormy night, and the solid masses of gleaming silver herring in the holds when the hatches were removed. There were picnics in summer along the rocky coast, with sandwiches and hard-boiled eggs. A favourite spot was the cave, a mile or two to the west, where the last Baron Forbes of Pitsligo was believed to have hidden from the redcoats. On one picnic occurred the incident which Walter was later to think of as a parable of Scotland. Some of the party, with the food hamper, had already squeezed through the narrow entrance into the cave when a buxom young woman became stuck, and could move neither forward nor backward. The elders among those still outside deliberated, and came to the practical

Scottish conclusion that since nothing could be done immediately and emaciation should solve the problem within at most a few days, they themselves should return home to have a meal, and they would have done so had she not, by a supreme effort, just then extricated herself.[8]

A son of the manse necessarily had memories of Sunday mornings in church. To join in the enthusiastic singing of the metrical version of the 124th Psalm was fun, but the Shorter Catechism he learned by rote. 'As a small boy', he once wrote, 'I could have rattled you off answers to anything you wanted to know about justification, sanctificaton, adoption, effectual calling and other mysteries of religion.' He thought that the process did him no harm, even if it did him no good. But in fact in later life it did have its uses, for he could always remind theological critics that he was brought up on the Shorter Catechism; moreover he had been compelled, and with more positive pleasure to himself, to acquire a thorough knowledge of the Bible which did stay with him, to the benefit of (among other things) his prose and possibly that of some of his pupils. Perhaps his father was also distantly responsible for some of those ideas about organized religion which in later years were not to please all of his son's readers. Walter Murdoch was apt to say that 'at a very early age' he became aware of the 'evils' of divisions between Christian churches. Even in Rosehearty there were three of them, each supposing itself to be looking down upon the others. Somewhere outside there were people called Episcopalians who believed in bishops, and that was being half-way to Rome. One can imagine the Reverend James's explaining that these divisions did exist and were, for those outside the Free Church, unfortunate. One can hardly suppose that young Walter at that time drew for himself the conclusion of his later years, that what mattered was not their differences but the essential Christianity which they all claimed to profess.

The Education (Scotland) Act of 1872 made it the legal duty of parents 'to provide elementary education in reading, writing and arithmetic' for all their children between the ages of five and thirteen. The parish schools of Scotland, whether independent or Free Church, were transformed into 'public' schools under a Board of Education, and attendance was to be compulsory. But Walter never went to school in Scotland; the Reverend James (like his son after him) did not believe in formal education at too early an age, and presumably private 'education' in the home of a minister was sufficient to satisfy H.M.'s Inspector that the provisions of the act were in Walter's case sufficiently met. He gained his elements mainly from his sister Lizzie, his senior by some twenty years. She taught him to read, and before

they all left Scotland his father had begun to teach him Latin, pulling
his hair when he didn't know his declensions. He first went to school
in England at the age of eight, probably at least as well informed as
his contemporaries there except for his illusion that the supreme hero
of all time was Robert the Bruce, and next to him James Douglas.

Walter Murdoch was a small boy when he left Scotland for ever.
When he died, he was one of the oldest of all Australians of his time.
What, beyond a few memories of childhood, did he bring with him
from the land of his birth? He did retain some traces of Scotland, or at
any rate Aberdeenshire, in his speech. To his distress he had almost
forgotten the dialect of the schoolboys who spoke to him when he
revisited Rosehearty after fifty years' absence, but in his own educated Australian accent there was a slight burr or deepening of the 'r'
which perhaps went back to the language of his infancy. It may be
that he took some care to preserve it.

The most considerable asset was the mere fact, if he chose to assert
it, of being a Scot. When it suited him, as an Australian of twenty or
fifty or eighty years' standing he would produce this extra trump, this
Joker in the pack. He could admit that his habit of 'preaching' was an
incurable legacy from those useful if unidentified ancestors, his
'Covenanting forefathers', and his readers would forgive him. There
seems to be no English-speaking country in which Scottish ancestry is
not a flexible but always positive asset, and Walter Murdoch knew it
very well. He would assert that he could detect in his mind no
affection for Scotland comparable with that which he felt for Australia—unless he heard the Scots criticized by members of other and
inferior races.

When the doctors in Scotland told Walter's parents that he would
be lucky to live to the age of forty, they were doubtless forecasting
fatalistically the onset of the 'constitutional' disease to which the
family had what they would have called a 'tendency'. Consumption
was already visibly affecting some of them. There was no known cure,
but sometimes it seemed to be arrested in mild and sunny climates.
On 8 February 1881 James Murdoch told the kirk-session that owing
to the state of his health, and the health of his family, he proposed to
leave them in order to go to New Zealand. The family tradition is
clear that by 'health' he must have meant the fact or fear of tuberculosis in the children, though his own illness had other causes.

If James Murdoch had been contemplating emigration simply to a
'healthy' British colony, he might in any case have thought first of
that Antipodean paradise, for a minister of his persuasion would
know of the province of Otago and its capital Dunedin, more Scottish
than Scotland and founded as a Free Church settlement. But there

was a particular reason. His son James, now fully qualified in medicine, had himself left for New Zealand together with his younger brother Ivon. Presumably the intention was to follow them when they were sufficiently settled; in the event it was nearly three years before the Murdoch family sailed, and then not for New Zealand but for Australia. It is not hard to account for the change of plan. Ivon—that 'nice boy' as he remained in Walter's memory—had reached New Zealand only to die. James decided to leave for Victoria, where by 1883 he had become medical officer at the hospital in Echuca, on the river Murray, and then his youthful brother Hugh also arrived in Australia, and was now working on a sheep station near Balranald in New South Wales.

Meanwhile the Murdochs had moved south, living before their final departure from England mainly between two 'health resorts', St Leonards near Hastings and (for six-month periods) Arcachon near Bordeaux, where British visitors came for the mild climate and the medicinal air of the nearby pine forests. At Hastings Walter first went to school. He retained some memories from this time of picnics on the downs, of a visit to an exhibition of performing fleas, and of an American who spoke about 'that wizard Edison' and wore a glittering electric bulb in place of a tie pin. But his most vivid recollection came from the Arcachon days: his lying on the floor of a little shop, his nose broken in a fall from a bolting donkey, and friendly faces around him while a woman fed him teaspoonfuls of sugared water. It was then, he thought, that he fell in love with France for life.[9]

When the *Potosi* left London for Melbourne on 20 August 1884, all the Murdoch family—parents and children—now remaining in Britain were on board. One son was in South Africa; two others were already in Australia; another, the only Murdoch ultimately to return to Scotland to live, was one of the ship's officers. With the Reverend James were his wife, three daughters—Eliza, Grace and Helen—and Walter. But before them on the passenger list were the Reverend Patrick Murdoch, his wife and two infants, for earlier that year James's oldest son had accepted a call to the Presbyterian church in West Melbourne. Why the commissioners in Scotland had sounded him out and duly suggested his name to that church I do not know, but I suspect that moved by family affection he may already have let it be known in church circles that he would be willing to accept a call from Victoria.

Thus Walter's tenth birthday occurred at sea. The voyage gave him the lasting impression that a passage through the Red Sea at that time of the year was to be avoided. Over forty years later he begged his daughter, then in England, to avoid it. 'When *we* came', he wrote, 'it was dangerous; then there were no fans in the cabins, no ices, and very stuffy little cabins even in the 1st class. Still, no 1st-class passenger went down to it; the trouble was all in the 2nd and the steerage. In the steerage, they died.'[10]

On 3 October 1884 the *Potosi* arrived at Melbourne. A few days later the Reverend Patrick Murdoch was inducted as minister of the West Melbourne Presbyterian church, then standing on the northeastern corner of the intersection of William and Lonsdale Streets. Fifty years later still, when the church was removed stone by stone to a site in Box Hill, he was to lay the foundation stone.

The new minister had been provided with one of a set of terraced houses off nearby a'Beckett Street, while his father took lodgings at 6 Victoria Parade, within easy walking distance. James Murdoch did not have much time to consider where he might live more permanently in this metropolis of the south, the end of the quest for his family's health. He had not been well on the voyage. On 29 October 1884 he died. The 'cause of death' was hepatitis; the 'rank or profession' of the deceased was entered as 'Minister of the Gospel'.

2

SCHOOLBOY TO SCHOOLMASTER

WHEN THE BLOW of James Murdoch's death fell upon the family, there must have been prompt legal aid from their new Melbourne friends, for probate of his will was sworn on 11 November 1884. It had been drawn a year earlier when he was living in Sussex at St Leonards-on-Sea. His estate was entirely 'personal', consisting (except for his gold watch and the furniture still in bond) of money already deposited in two banks in Melbourne. Its value was sworn at £3432, and there may have been a little more to come later, together with something from the Free Church's Widows' and Orphans' Fund. The estate was left in trust with James's widow, his sons Patrick and Francis and his daughter Eliza, with some immediate legacies to Patrick and Eliza, and other provisions for such of his daughters as should marry, but mainly, under the administration of his widow, 'for providing home and suitable maintenance for herself and for my son Walter Logie Forbes Murdoch until he is of the age of twenty-one years, and for my unmarried daughters, and for every other purpose affecting their comfort and welfare'. His books were divided between four sons: Patrick was to have his 'theological, critical and philosophical books', Francis (the sailor) his poetical books, James (the doctor) his historical books, and Andrew (the son in South Africa) his *Encyclopaedia Britannica*. But was the last of these actually sent, one wonders, for years later Walter wrote:

> I once had to face the problem of getting rid of an eighth [1853–60] edition of the *Encyclopaedia Britannica*. None of my friends would take it as a gift, no second-hand bookseller would look at it; I could not afford house-room for it . . . In the end I hit on the idea of using

it for the top of a V-shaped drain I was constructing in the garden . . .[1]

James Murdoch's will goes some way towards the solution of what
was still a puzzle to his son Walter in old age—there must have been
some money, he knew, for a house was later built for his mother, and
until 1893 they were relatively 'well-to-do' by the standards of a
careful Scottish family, if not those of Scottish businessmen in the
boom years now beginning in Melbourne. He supposed that the
assets must have been his mother's, and no doubt they partly were, for
after her aunt's death in 1879 she would have had a share in the
property of Braco Park. Walter could not understand how a minister
with a large family could have saved any significant sum, and he
dismissed as probably a family joke a legend that his father had
owned a public house in Stirling. In fact, the will of Peter Murdoch of
Stirling does show that in 1850 he left considerable property in town
land to his surviving children—James and a sister—and among the
assets was rent due by an innkeeper. James must have realized such
property as he still held when he departed from Scotland for ever, and
the £3000 left to his widow after the deduction of Patrick's and
Eliza's immediate shares, if invested with good Scottish advice in
Melbourne in the later 1880s, would for some years have provided a
very useful addition to whatever assets of her own were held by Helen
Murdoch.[2]

The family was not long in lodgings. Hawthorn, eastward from the
city, had some evident advantages as a pleasant suburb beyond the
Yarra river, 'healthy and attractive', and within easy reach by railway of Patrick's church and house. In the 1850s successful men in
business and the professions had begun to build 'mansions' in that
area, and had been followed more modestly by the middling sorts of
people. The railway from the city (1861) had recently been extended
farther east to the neighbouring suburb of Camberwell, providing
further stations within Hawthorn itself. Not far from one of these,
Glenferrie station, 'Ellen' Murdoch is shown in the directory for 1886
as occupying a house at the corner of St Columbs street and Oxley
road and, perhaps as important to her as the station, practically
around the corner from the Presbyterian church and manse in Glenferrie road. They had probably moved before the beginning of the
school year in 1885.*

---

* Names of streets and suburbs will mean little to most readers, but I give them
because Victorians to whom Walter Murdoch's writings were once a regular feature of
life may like to know where he grew up. Most of the various houses in which he lived
until he finally left Melbourne in his late thirties, all in the Hawthorn-Kew-Camber-
well area of respectable Melbourne, were still standing in the mid-1970s.

For two years, 1885–6, Walter went to a school in Hawthorn which he remembered as 'primitive', followed by four years at a newly established school in Camberwell, now rapidly being built up as the land boom expanded. Camberwell Grammar School, opened in 1886, assembled for its first year in the rented Sunday school of the Anglican church of St John in Burke road, moving the following year to a site in Fermanagh road, Prospect Hill, where it remained throughout Walter's time.[3]

In 1889, the year in which Walter qualified for matriculation at the age of fifteen, he was dux of the school. The rolls do not survive, but it seems that he must have stayed on for another year, since he spent only 1891 in his last school, Scotch College. The change was prompted with one purpose in his (or more likely Patrick's) mind, the improvement of his classics in preparation for the university. Founded in the early 1850s by what was then the Free Church Presbytery of Victoria, Scotch College with its high reputation for scholarship was the inevitable choice as an intellectual finishing school for a son of the manse.

There is little to tell about Walter's schooldays. He once described himself as an 'undistinguished boy at various schools', remembering perhaps that in those days to be dux at Camberwell Grammar was one thing, but to reach the standard of the top classics class at Scotch was another. There are some scattered recollections. He was no athlete but regarded himself as a fair gymnast. His collection of British birds' eggs was envied. Few boys like getting up in the morning and he missed trains; too often the master's greeting was, 'Well, sir, late as usual!' He revelled in Scott's *Marmion* and was excited by Burton's *Pilgrimage to El-Medinah and Meccah*. The favourite recent books among schoolboys were Anstey's *Vice-Versa* (1882) and Stevenson's *Treasure Island* (1882). At Camberwell Grammar, with two friends, he brought out for a while a monthly school paper and had the thrill of writing his first editorial. At Scotch College he won a prize for an essay on Australian federation—not a surprising subject to be set in the year (1891) of the first federal convention—but possibly, he thought, because he was the only competitor. The awesome headmaster Alexander Morrison had however himself read the essay, and the prize he chose for Walter was Macaulay's *History of England* which, he said, if diligently studied might teach him some day how to write.[4]

Walter remembered the boredom of history as taught in his time (and long, long beyond his time): 'niggling details of various pieces of legislation which were quite meaningless to us, or large sweeping generalizations—such as the Decay of the Feudal System—which meant rather less than nothing. Every now and then a human being intruded into this land of shadows'. In senior classes the boys read adventure stories under their desks instead of paying attention to the warfare between the Rockingham and Bedford Whigs. His recommendation in later life, to remove all history books from schools and replace them with lots of brief biographies, is explicable.

During these years, 1885–91, there were important changes in the situation of the immigrant Murdoch family. Patrick's Aberdeen University friend James Climie had come as minister to the Trinity Presbyterian church at Camberwell in 1886 and died within a year, apparently another victim of 'the curse of Scotland'. So movingly did Patrick preach at his funeral that he was 'called' with one voice to replace his friend, and was glad to accept the call. He was inducted on 30 August 1887. By the energetic efforts of his congregation a manse next to Trinity church in Riversdale road was purchased, and occupied by him and his own family in December 1888. In due time he was to see the small wooden building of his church replaced by the substantial structure with its spire still familiar to residents of Camberwell and to the incessant motorists who now pour through the Camberwell junction. It was probably when her eldest son was called to Trinity church that Helen Murdoch decided or was induced to move to Camberwell. By 1890 she was living in her own newly built two-storey house in Riversdale road, half a mile or so from her son's manse. It stands there today, ugly and sturdy, in the built-up road where then it stood without neighbours. Henceforth, and in a sense even today, Camberwell would be to the family 'Murdoch country'.

These years in which Walter was becoming, if not yet an Australian, at least a Victorian, saw the greatest and most notorious boom in Australian colonial history. It was the era of 'Marvellous Melbourne, the Metropolis of the Southern Hemisphere, the Chicago of the South, the Paris of the Antipodes'—so the historian of that extraordinary time sardonically lists some of the labels which contemporary Melburnians were happy to see applied to themselves.[5] It is unlikely that the Murdochs were tempted to imitate their more experienced fellow-Scots, promoters or followers, who eagerly led or joined 'the rush to be rich'. Land speculation, or attendance at champagne auctions, was hardly in their line. But the boom may have raised the cost of building Helen Murdoch's house. When they arrived in Melbourne, one of similar size and appearance was advertised 'to be built for £1,050'. In the next four years the orchards and open paddocks of Camberwell were being rapidly subdivided for building, and visitors 'heard on every side the sound of the hammer and the tapping of bricks'.[6]

In his last year at school Walter must have travelled daily to the city by train, for Scotch College still remained on its original urban site and would do so for many years to come. In future, at least during term, he would be living away from home. At the end of 1891 he added second-class honours in Greek and Latin to his qualifications for matriculation. In 1892 he entered the University of Melbourne as an undergraduate in residence at—again inevitably—Ormond College.

The university grounds, opened in 1855 on a wasteland site a mile north of the city, had been transformed into a pleasant space of lawns and trees and lake separating several blocks of buildings, the most impressive of them the curiously isolated Wilson Hall with its decorated pinnacles. Farther north were the three residential colleges founded by the Anglican, Presbyterian and Methodist Churches, each on its own ten acres. Ormond, the Presbyterian college named after its greatest benefactor, rose threateningly into the sky to culminate in the high weird tower that brought tears of nostalgia or apprehension to graduates of Glasgow University. Outside, it looked like 'a forbidding baron's castle'; inside, the high dark spaces of its corridors struck visitors with a gloomy foreboding. Here, though cheerfully enough, Walter spent much of his time for the next three years.

He was between seventeen and eighteen years of age, very solemn-looking in a formal photograph of about this time, with light-coloured hair (actually reddish-brown) parted on the left, light (grey-blue) eyes, and regular features defying particular description—one can only say 'a fresh-faced youth'. In a college group taken a few years later he is seen with the moustache which in various forms and despite changing general fashions he was to wear all his life. To his university teachers and to the college servants he was 'Mr Murdoch'; to his friends he would be 'Murdoch'. Ormond imposed no denominational tests, but as the son of a deceased Presbyterian minister he may have been eligible for special bursaries though, since the college records appear to have vanished, there is no way of confirming his statement that he actually finished his course with a credit balance. Out of term he would have returned to Camberwell, and if the food at Ormond in his time was comparable to that of the 1960s, he must in term have been happy to visit his mother on Sundays, accompany her to church and return home to a good midday dinner.

It seems natural that Murdoch should have entered upon the first year of the degree of Bachelor of Arts but there is a slight mystery about his course, for he said and wrote in old age that his elders had intended him for Medicine, and did not imply that he had objected. Though it was common enough for students to begin an Arts degree

which could later overlap with Law, to do so before Medicine would
have meant a long-lasting and expensive burden for Helen Murdoch.
Perhaps Murdoch was given a year in which to make up his mind. At
any rate he did well in Arts. With Latin, Greek, English and French
as 'supporting' subjects, he chose to specialize in the philosophy
'group', gaining first-class honours in logic and philosophy in the final
examination after his third year, 1894. He took out his Bachelor of
Arts degree at the end of 1895.

Meanwhile calamity had fallen upon thousands of families in
Victoria, including the widowed Helen Murdoch and her still
dependent daughters and son. Long afterwards Murdoch professed
to remember the Easter Sunday, 2 April 1893, when after church he
heard a friend of his mother's say that her husband knew that the
Commercial Bank would not open after the recess: had Helen Murdoch withdrawn her money? She had not. The family waited with
apprehension. On the evening of 4 April it was announced to the
press that the imposing Commercial Bank had suspended payment.[7]

The sorry story of the Victorian bank smash of 1893 has been told
by several able historians and it need not be repeated here. Some
banks in Victoria never closed their doors. Others, including the
Commercial, did survive after long processes of reconstruction,
though for many years the effect upon thousands of shareholders or
depositors was as if they had lost their assets for ever. So it seems to
have been for the Murdochs, but there was something wrong, if not
with Murdoch's distant recollection, at least with the implications he
drew from it. His mother may have had a current account at the
Commercial Bank, which would have meant immediate distress, but
(so the foremost authority on these matters informs me) she was never
among the bank's shareholders, as perforce she would have been
under the reconstruction scheme if she had held a fixed deposit.[8] The
loss of the family's capital may nevertheless be related indirectly to
the fall of the Commercial in various plausible ways—most readily
perhaps to the spate of other failures that followed in its wake. What
matters here is that whereas the family income had been some £400 a
year, they now (as Murdoch put it) had to earn what money they had.
Murdoch was anxious to pick up scholarships; in the 1890s we find his
sister Grace advertising herself as a teacher of music, and his sister
Eliza (Lizzie) running a genteel laundry in Camberwell specializing
in goffering lace, while at one time the house in Riversdale road
appears to have been let. It was the end of any prospect of a medical
career for Murdoch if, as he implies, the family had still hoped he
would pursue one. 'There are probably still people alive', he reflected
in old age, 'who would not be alive if I had been their physician.'

The three university colleges had developed in the 1880s a vigorous community life. Alexander Leeper, warden of Trinity, had introduced Oxford's tutorial system; college lectures supplemented, or for some students largely replaced, the official university lectures; college men dominated the honours lists. They had as well their own social life, and the fragmentary records show that Murdoch took his part in it. In 1892 he won the Literary and Debating Society's essay competition. He was an occasional speaker at impromptu speech nights and in debates, and honorary secretary in 1894, when he was auditor of the Students' Club and a member of the Common Room Committee.[9] His room-mate in Ormond was Jim Legge, a friend from Scotch College days who went on to the Presbyterian ministry. So did Fred Oxer, somewhat older, whom they came to know as a friend in their third year when he was already a theological student. A good scholar and oarsman, he possessed a curious qualification in one who was later to become not only a prominent minister but a professor of theology in Ormond's Theological Hall, for before he entered the university he had won the gold medal for the best student at the Melbourne College of Pharmacy. Mr Felton, a leading drug manufacturer, had secured Fred's apprenticeship to a pharmaceutical chemist after hearing from his widowed mother that the boy was fond of 'chemistry', and the faithful son had done what his mother wished, though his real interest was divinity. Another friend, an engineering student from Ballarat, was Adam Baird, whom Murdoch was later to know for many years as head of a large retail business in Perth—'my oldest friend in Western Australia—in the world, I might have said', he wrote when Baird died in 1954.[10]

In those days, and for many years afterwards, there were few or no assistants in faculties of Arts; the professor took all lectures himself. If he were incompetent or lazy, he could wreck a subject for a generation as J. S. Elkington, successor to the celebrated W. E. Hearn in the chair of history and political economy, was well on the way to doing by this time. But Murdoch was fortunate in his teachers. E. E. Morris, who professed English, French and German—all three—was a man of diverse talents, literary as well as linguistic, and a pleasant host in his house in the university grounds. T. G. Tucker, the classicist, still in his early thirties, was not only an able and established scholar but a fine teacher and lecturer. Henry Laurie, the philosopher, was not even a graduate. He had been a promising student in philosophy and logic at the University of Edinburgh when (another delicate Scot) he was advised to emigrate for the sake of his health. After years as the editor of a country newspaper, he was appointed lecturer in logic and in 1886 the first professor of mental and moral philosophy, a surprising appointment which was to prove well justified.

Murdoch took his 'major' with Laurie, five courses in all. Where his other teachers spoke with the accents of Oxford and Cambridge, Laurie, a red-bearded Scot in his fifties, outwardly shy but friendly to those he knew well, spoke Murdoch's native tongue as he must have heard it when there were learned visitors to the Free Church manse in Rosehearty. If Murdoch had an intellectual father, it was Laurie. There is more than a conventional tone in the public tribute of 'regard, respect and gratitude' which he paid to his old teacher on his retirement at the end of 1911. He wrote first of 'the personal affection—there is no other phrase for it—with which he inspired the members of his classes year by year', and then went on to describe

> the work which, quietly, unobtrusively, but with consummate skill, Professor Laurie has for thirty years been performing in our midst . . . He who teaches men and women to think does a work of quite incalculable value. The worth of Professor Laurie's work consisted not in any facts which he hammered into his students, nor in any doctrines, nor in any conclusions; it consisted of an attitude, a method. It was possible to be a student of his for three years without discovering to what philosophic creed he subscribed. He knew that it was not his business to present us with a set of ready made conclusions but to teach us to arrive at conclusions for ourselves. Every year there has gone forth from his class-rooms into the world a little company of young men and women trained to think; to review with a large tolerance every idea that might be set before them; to accept nothing and to reject nothing without calm and dispassionate reflection.[11]

Long after he had forgotten even the philosophic jargon of that time, Murdoch recalled with gratitude the fun they had had in the course in deductive logic. Laurie would read a passage from a newspaper leader and call upon a student by name to stand up and say what kind of a fallacy the writer had perpetrated. It was a good introduction to philosophy itself, thought Murdoch; they had to examine statements carefully and they came later to realize that what was 'difficult' about the great philosophers was the complexity of their thinking, not their language, if you worked hard to understand it.[12]

His first-class honours in logic and philosophy in 1894 brought to an end Murdoch's formal education, except that he had still to pass an examination in mathematics at the end of 1895. In those days there was, for an honours graduate, no nonsense about presenting a research thesis for the Master's degree. As in Oxford and Cambridge still, you waited for a few years, you paid your money and you were (by reason of your 'maturity') a Master, as Murdoch became in December 1897.

Though the university had provided the formal part of his higher education, he always maintained that two other institutions were in their own ways as important to him in his youth. One was the Public Library which was then, even relatively, a great library for its time, though its growth was soon to be stunted for many years by the savage economies of the depression. Within easy walking distance from Ormond, it was a haven for an earnest student who was quickly becoming a besotted reader beyond the demands of his university courses. But there was also another 'public library' which played a distinct role in Melbourne—Cole's Book Arcade, the greatest book-shop in Australia or, as Murdoch then thought, in the world: 'A Million Books to choose from' seemed to him, and to many another reader, probably to be an understatement. Mr Cole, the self-educated student of evolution and advocate of the federation of the world, 'allowed and even encouraged the public to read books without buying them. He seemed to have designed the place, with its quiet alcoves, as a paradise for browsers; you could browse for hours at a time and no one would come and ask you what your intentions were.'[13] As well, there was an orchestra in the afternoon, and at one period monkey and cockatoo cages. Here, from the shilling-tray and the second-hand department upstairs, Murdoch and others began to collect the libraries that became part of themselves.

As the time for his final examinations approached, he must have had considerable apprehensions about his future. Victoria was now suffering for its sins, new building had ceased, large numbers of houses were empty, general employment had fallen sharply during his years at the university, the neglected gardens of the university grounds were visible evidence of the rigid economy which was the government's remedy for a depression as dismal as the boom years had been exhilarating. Where would a Bachelor of Arts find employment?

A teaching position at the university was not to be expected even in prosperous times. Men simply did not then enter the university on the assumption that if they did well they might hope to enter academic life in Australia. Some did, of course, in the end, but opportunities were so few that one could not talk of an 'academic profession'. If you took a degree in Arts, you were looking to school-teaching in private or public ('independent') schools, for as yet there were no state secondary schools, or to becoming a clergyman, or to proceeding further to qualify as a lawyer. Murdoch would doubtless have gone schoolteaching if a post had been available, but in 1895 few schools were likely to have vacancies on their staffs. He was 'lucky' (he said) to get a job as a tutor for a year on a sheep station near Beaufort, a small town some thirty miles west of Ballarat, at £40 a year with keep. So much, in the 1890s, for first-class honours in philosophy.

Once the 'Fiery Creek Diggings', Beaufort still had gold mines, but it was also a 'centre' in classical pastoral country. In scattered recollections of his year as a tutor Murdoch never identified the sheep station where he had lived, but in fact it was Eurambeen, a property held from 1860 to the present day by members of the Beggs family. His eleven-year-old pupil, Balcombe Beggs, the son of R. G. Beggs, had been left motherless and had been reared by his grandmother, wife of the original pioneer Francis Beggs. Whether Murdoch had answered an advertisement, or whether (more likely) the family had made private enquiries about a tutor through friends in Melbourne, I do not know.[14]

Occasionally Murdoch recalled incidents of his year at Eurambeen. He made some friends, including a young boundary-rider from the next station, with whom he would make Sunday excursions on horseback. Once they discovered a deserted village where Murdoch saw something strange and new—empty beer casks with rows of a black, rectangular substance tacked inside. This was plug-tobacco, the legendary additive to beer which was said to aid the transfer of the shearers' wages to the publican's pocket in the least possible time. All his life Murdoch remembered a particular blazing hot day, when his pupil came running to tell him that a roaring grass-fire was upon them. The shingle-roof of the stone-walled woolshed was in danger, and in the shed was the year's clip. The men ran and climbed and passed up buckets of water in the disciplined scurry of those who knew their job, the roof was saved, and after quaffing pannikins of weak whisky-and-water they fell, instantly as it seemed, dead asleep upon the ground.[15]

These and similar experiences were later to be reflected in some of Murdoch's critical writing. In that year Murdoch had seen sheep-shearing and sheep-washing at first hand. He had seen the beer-shanties where the shearers spent their wages, and nearby the wretched humpies where the small selectors and their families lived. So when he wrote of Lawson's stories that 'to anyone who has seen something of the life Mr Lawson describes, these sketches of his contain some of the most poignant things in literature', he was referring to himself. Of course he had not lived, but only seen, that life. He had his own room at the station and, so far as his memories reflect that aspect of his first year of employment, it seems that he was contented enough. And so apparently was his pupil, whose youngest daughter recalled eighty years later that her father had often mentioned Mr Murdoch.[16]

Murdoch could now claim some experience in teaching. After passing his examination in mathematics at the end of 1895, he was admitted to his degree and could now look around for a position as a regular schoolmaster. There could still have been little choice; he again felt himself lucky to receive the 'dazzling offer' of a position as a junior master at the Hamilton Academy on £80 a year, with board.

Hamilton, the 'metropolis' of the southwestern pastoral district of Victoria, was a very different place from Beaufort. It had the apparatus of a real town—churches with spires, 'many fine shops', public buildings, a racecourse, gas lighting, a mechanics institute with a library of 18 000 volumes—and (it was said in 1888) it was 'certainly not to be excelled for the magnitude and excellence of its educational institutions', one of which was the Hamilton Academy, so named after the Edinburgh 'Academy'. It had been opened in 1870 by James Begg, yet another young Scot whose university course at Glasgow (nearly completed, as he was understandably to emphasize) was interrupted by consumption and the inevitable doctor's orders to proceed without delay to a warmer climate. At the Academy, a handsome building at the entrance to the town, Murdoch spent the year 1896. Though few of the pastoralists were directly involved in Melbourne's boom and crash, they had troubles of their own in the 1890s, and no doubt Mr Begg too had his worries about the finances of the Academy which looked to their children for its pupils. He was an enemy of extravagance, as Murdoch recalled: he would 'shout across the table at any of us who seemed to be putting too much treacle or golden syrup on our bread', and the junior masters were required to assist him with such non-academic tasks as killing sheep and hanging up the carcasses beside the outhouse where they slept.[17] For Murdoch his time there was an episode which he was prepared to admit had occurred, but he would rarely describe it. Many years later, from something written by Sir John Latham, he found that his old friend had followed him as a master. 'What staggers me', he wrote, 'is that though I have known you for about 65 years, I only learned today that you had ever been near Hamilton Academy. Do you agree with my estimate of old Jimmy Begg? It is a great satisfaction to me that he got you £10 cheaper than he got me. It is significant that anybody who taught at that seminary tends to conceal the fact, even unto 60 years.'[18]

Early in December 1896 Murdoch wrote to Fred Oxer in the

facetious, familiar way of an old friend aged twenty-two to congratulate him on his first ministerial appointment and (incidentally) on his engagement to be married. He would be back in Melbourne soon. But 'I don't know how you knew I was in the same boat—are you sure it shouldn't be the same *ward?*—as yourself.'[19] His formal engagement may have been recent but he had long since known that he would marry Violet Hughston.

When Helen Murdoch moved with her family to Riversdale road, Camberwell, Johnstone Hughston was living in the same road in a house which they would pass on their way to Patrick Murdoch's church. Trained as a civil engineer and surveyor, he came of a Scottish-Irish family now settled in Canada. He had travelled extensively in the United States, where his first wife died, and practised as a surveyor in New Zealand and Victoria. His second wife was Kathleen Wilson, daughter of a Northern Irish farmer who had arrived in Victoria in 1841 and done well. From surveying, Hughston had turned to schoolteaching to express in practice the ideas about education that he had first conceived in Boston under the influence of the teachings of Emerson and Alcott. The Hughstons had moved around a good deal in the country and in suburban Melbourne, but the family name was now long to be associated with Camberwell. Their youngest child, Violet, had been born in 1872.[20]

The Murdoch children always believed that their father met Violet Hughston at church, and that they were 'walking out' together while he was 'still in short pants'. This may well be true. If they first met in 1889 or 1890, he would still have been a schoolboy, and the 'short pants' of those days would have been the knee-length knickerbockers and stockings (also, suitably adapted, then worn by the mighty adult heroes of Australian rules football) which a modern schoolboy might well envy in a Melbourne winter, though he might have different ideas about 'walking out'. In November 1949 Murdoch wrote of their 'unmarred companionship' of, 'counting the years of our engagement, about 57 years'. It seems rather unlikely that they were, with their families' blessings, 'officially' engaged as early as 1892 or 1893, when Walter, not yet twenty, was without prospects, but perhaps they had their 'understanding', in the language of the day. When he decided after his return from Hamilton to create his own 'prospects', it may well have been the Hughstons who, by precept or example, encouraged him to do so.

Violet Hughston's older sister Annie had been encouraged by her father to take up teaching. In due time she became senior mathematics mistress at the celebrated Presbyterian Ladies' College in Melbourne; lately she had conducted a school of her own at

Camperdown in the country. Her brother William was also a schoolteacher with original ideas about education. In February 1896 Annie Hughston made a formidable entry into 'that competitive branch of late-Victorian industry, female education', formidable because she was an able woman concerned, as P.L.C. was concerned, with more serious educational aims than the teaching of accomplishments to young ladies. In the new school which they named 'Fintona', after the Irish village in which their mother was born, she was at first assisted by her brother; and the teacher of music, drawing and painting was Violet Hughston, who left at the end of 1897 to become the wife of a headmaster.[21]

Whether Murdoch pursued any gainful occupation in 1897 remains obscure. I suspect that he then began to try his hand at verse and short stories for the press, very likely unsuccessfully at first; towards the end of the year he must have been planning to open his own school. But two events are well established: on 22 December he was married to Violet Hughston and on 23 December he took out his Master's degree.

The Melbourne directory for 1898 had an attractive entry, clearly composed in the previous year: 'CAMBERWELL COLLEGE. Fermanagh Rd., Camberwell. 5 mins. from station. Train fares paid. W.L.F. Murdoch B.A.'. Thirty years later Murdoch explained to his daughter, rather sadly in retrospect, why he had settled down so soon into the rut of conventional suburban life—a poor way to start, he thought, for young people, though it might be well enough in middle age. He and Violet were desperately anxious to marry, 'and there was no way but by my being a schoolmaster'.[22] Here was the only profession in which his academic qualifications might be a positive asset.

Some capital must have been needed, but not necessarily much more than would pay the original rent of a suburban house at a time when tenants were still hard to come by. In the school's existence of three years Murdoch was assisted for at least part of the time by his brother-in-law William Hughston and by a Mr Redmond. Long afterwards a boy who began at this school and ended his career as engineer of the Victorian Railways remembered a little about it. Among his fellow-pupils were Patrick Murdoch's sons, Keith, Frank, Alec and Ivan. When the school was given up at the end of 1900, the pupils were transferred 'lock, stock and barrel' to Camberwell Grammar School.[23]

One direct impression of Murdoch's schoolteaching, written in 1911, may be somewhat biased, since it was most likely that of his nephew Keith:

He was one of the pioneers of the modern system of teaching. He believed that a teacher's business was to teach, and not to make his pupils learn, as so many schoolmasters unfortunately did. In all his school work he developed these ideas, so that learning from him was a pleasant business as well as a successful one. Always a student himself, he always understood and appreciated the attitude of mind of those who were striving to learn.[24]

The 'College' was a private day-school. Murdoch himself lived with his family in a cottage in Brinsley road, close to his mother and to his father-in-law—the Australian pattern of the family. A first child, a boy, was born to them in 1898 and died the next year. It was many years before their other children learned that he once had briefly been, and that their mother had not forgotten him. In 1900 another boy, William Garden Murdoch, was born.

There was little profit in the 'College'. Murdoch was soon seeking and to some extent finding supplementary income. Before long his contributions to the press were being consistently published and by the time he left Melbourne in 1901 his name was well known to readers who had never heard of Camberwell College. He was also engaged on another activity traditional in his profession, the writing of a textbook. On the last day of 1900 he wrote to an eminent Victorian (whom he had not yet met) to ask the favour of a preface to a projected text, 'The Australian Citizen'. That was Alfred Deakin, one of the makers of the Australian federation which was now about to be inaugurated. Though he declined, his polite reply showed that he was already a reader of Murdoch's articles. But the book remained for the time unfinished, for its writer had undertaken new duties.

Warrnambool was a pleasant town on the coast, about 170 miles southwest of Melbourne. In those days, as Murdoch recalled, the town was 'absurd enough to try to support three private schools'—the College, the Grammar School and the more recent 'Academy'. He had taken an opportunity to go into partnership with old Mr Scott, the proprietor of the College, an established boarding-school which seemed to offer better prospects than his own 'College'. The headmaster of the Grammar School, 'an eccentric old gentleman who drank too much but was able none the less to remain the chess champion of Victoria', soon induced Scott and Murdoch to take over both his school and himself; then Scott also retired, to leave Murdoch the sole proprietor. Here we see him in a new role—the football coach. Fifty years later he recalled all the faces (but one, he said) in a photograph of the school football team of 1901, the exception being a keen-faced young man standing beside the group, dark-suited, wearing a starched collar, and with a very respectable moustache, though his trousers had already the somewhat unpressed look familiar to other pupils in later years.[25]

Life in the neat white town, the centre of a dairying and farming district, was happy enough. The country around was attractive; there were excursions by pony-and-phaeton, picnics and fishing. But to live in the style appropriate for a headmaster who had to keep up appearances, Murdoch found, was not easily managed on the income yielded by the school to its proprietor. He continued to write for the Melbourne press, he had himself placed on the list of university extension lecturers, and he again sat down to write a school textbook. Experience had now taught him the secret for success in this useful sideline. It was simple: produce a book which will be widely pre-scribed in courses to which most schoolchildren will necessarily be exposed; if it happens to be a fairly good book in itself, so much the better for the children. British history was such a course. In *The Struggle for Freedom*, a manual of English constitutional history, Murdoch had hit upon a formula that would sell 10 000 copies in the first year. Unexpectedly, the little book gave rise to a curious con-troversy. In two pamphlets published by the Catholic Truth Society as *History Falsified* by one James W. Wallace, it was vehemently attacked as an example of anti-Catholic bias. A correspondence in the *Argus* followed. The society, with expressions of regret, withdrew the pamphlets from circulation, while still indicating that in some respects the book, from its point of view, was not entirely satisfactory. Another pamphlet in the series, *The Struggle for Freedom: A Review*, by Ronald Stewart, including a note by Murdoch himself, was now issued. In a tone of civilized discussion the author pointed to some differences of interpretation as Catholics would see them, and to some errors of fact, but on the whole praised a text which would be welcomed in Catholic schools if a few revisions were made. In his 'Note' Murdoch apologized for one error and promised to read and consider some other passages carefully before any second edition should appear. It was not the last controversy about historical textbooks in Australia, nor the last controversy to be provoked by Murdoch's writings, but it ended more amiably than most.[26]

The preface to this admirable condensation of the Whig view of British history was dated 'The College, Warrnambool, October 1903'. At the end of November its author applied for an advertised post of assistant lecturer in English at the University of Melbourne, at £150 per year.

ELZEVIR

THE SCHOOL AT Warrnambool 'was rather a failure and I was jolly glad to get a lectureship at Melbourne, at £150 a year', wrote Murdoch in 1928. He must also have felt himself to be jolly lucky, though doubtless as a Melbourne graduate regretting the general circumstances that had led to the creation of such a lectureship. There were no regular positions of the kind in the university's faculty of Arts, and this one had become available only as a result of a series of calamities. In August 1901 it had been discovered that the university accountant had for years been systematically defrauding his employers. So great were the losses and the scandal that stringent economies were imperative. Hence in January 1902 when Morris, the professor of English, died while on leave in Europe, there was no question of filling his chair. The English classes in 1902 were taken over by the gifted Alexander Sutherland, but he too died in the course of the year. Tucker, professor of classics, who then nobly offered to take the extra burden had to tell the university council in October 1903 that beyond a few lectures a week he must surrender it if the students of classics were not to suffer. His request for an assistant lecturer in 1904 was granted.

Murdoch's application stressed his experience as a teacher, his continued studies of modern English and French literature as reflected in his critical articles for the Melbourne *Argus*, and the fact that he had been invited by 'Messrs Angus and Robertson (Publishers, Sydney) to write for them a History of Australian Literature'. In

Walter Murdoch, about 1904

recommending the appointment, Tucker described him as a man of literary originality and of independence of judgement and an excellent writer: 'his academical training and self-culture have been of a kind well-suited to equip him for the post in question.' In December 1903 Walter Murdoch M.A., aged twenty-nine, was appointed as assistant lecturer in English.[1]

The changes in the status and salary of his position until he resigned at the end of 1911, though important to him at the time, are to others likely to be the least interesting aspect of his life in those years. It is enough to say that 'assistant' was soon dropped from the title, and by 1905, with more work to do, he was a 'lecturer' at a salary of £300 with some extra remuneration for taking evening lectures. But two points about his situation need to be understood. Though

Violet Murdoch, about 1900

soon improved beyond his expectations of 1903, his salary was still relatively low, given his necessary obligations, and that meant, as he remembered, 'hard work to augment one's income so as to be able to live'. And further, his situation was always uncertain, for lecturers held only annual appointments. Where the positions themselves, though not their temporary occupants, were permanently established, there could be some confidence about reappointment. But no lectureship was permanently attached to English. When in time the vacant chair should come to be filled, Murdoch would be without a job unless he were himself appointed to it, and at least in his first few years he could hardly have expected that. So he had to look for some

kind of insurance, and most obviously the maintenance of the journalistic work which already meant that what he wrote for the *Argus*
would be readily accepted.

At the end of 1904 Tucker recorded his appreciation of the 'high
character' and 'great loyalty' of his assistant in the English Department where he still nominally presided. Thereafter the administration was largely left to Murdoch, who could fairly claim in 1911
that for six years he had been 'virtually Acting Professor'. But his
moral if not his formal duties were wider, for to educated people in
Melbourne he *was* the English Department (there was no one else) in
those years when the university was still assumed to be part of such
cultural life as the city had, rather than a kind of professional work-
shop outside it.

His first duty was to construct his lectures. If he would rather have
told students why Ibsen had for him 'shattered the world of convention', or discussed with them the controversial plays of Shaw, it would
not have occurred to him that the first had a place in 'English'
literature, or that the second could be prescribed in university syllabuses before time had confirmed his credentials. He might and did
talk or write about these and other contemporaries to public
audiences, but young university students of English literature should
be required first to consider the unquestioned classics of the language.

So his courses in English, partly inherited from Morris but extended and varied by himself, were of a type found in all Australian
universities for thirty or forty years beyond his time in Melbourne
—'general surveys' of long 'periods', with particular texts for special
study, and with more or less, in his case less, emphasis on
Anglo-Saxon and Middle English. Murdoch was to argue that a
lecturer on 'English' must make up his mind whether he was going to
deal with philology or with literature, for 'if he attempts to deal with
both, one or the other will be, inevitably, mere dabbling'. He was of
course thinking of the case of a sole teacher, without specialist colleagues. He began with some study of Chaucer and proceeded in a
familiar way—always some Shakespeare, and then selected poetry
and prose (mainly essays and criticism, rarely novels) for special
study. The 'periods' for general study ended with the Romantics, but
the prescribed texts extended to the late nineteenth century, the most
'modern' writer in his lists being Robert Louis Stevenson, a writer
unknown in English syllabuses today. Any university syllabus of
former years can be criticized with amusement or wonder in later
times, but the relevant historical question is whether it engaged the
minds of students. In Murdoch's Melbourne years his courses certainly did that. English was a lively subject in the university, and not

less so because its teacher spoke about more than was formally prescribed in the printed syllabus. His students knew that he was better
read in 'modern' literature than they were; indeed, it was often
through his lectures outside the class-room, and above all his weekly
articles in the *Argus*, that they were made aware of contemporary
writing in prose and verse, including the work of Australian writers.
This became much less true in later years. The time would come
when he would solemnly ask students in another university what he
should read to keep up with them, and there would be some who
would proceed earnestly to instruct him.

Like most other university teachers in Australia then and for long
afterwards he had to spread his courses too widely, and there was no
way out of it. What the university required of him gave no time for
the slow and painful exercise of scholarship in its more professional
sense, and I suspect that in any case he was already too fond of
reading for enjoyment to have serious ambitions in that field, even if
sometimes he tried to persuade himself otherwise.

For the Murdochs, living in Melbourne meant living in or near
Camberwell. They were first at Surrey Hills, where in 1904 their first
daughter, Catherine Helen, was born in time to be approved by 'the
old lady', Helen Murdoch, who died in April 1905, twenty years a
widow, yet outliving eight of her fourteen children. The next move, to
a two-storey house in Kew was prompted by a medical opinion that
living on the first storey would somehow help to relieve their young
son's asthma; but for lack of funds the ground floor remained unfur-
nished, sometimes to the surprise of visitors. In 1906 they found
themselves in the house of their own from which most of Murdoch's
letters in these years were written. Torrington avenue, in Canterbury,
ran off Burke road past a large paddock where, by fits and starts
reflecting the state of Murdoch's bank account, one of Violet's
relatives built the house. Still standing, from the outside it looks
roomy enough, but inside it seems to be all hallways. It was a mistake,
Murdoch reflected, to have designed it himself for the sake of saving
an architect's fee; somehow it was always too cold. But to come home
to a cold house after delivering evening lectures in a Melbourne
winter, and then to sit down to write, was an experience confined
neither to him nor to his generation.

Murdoch's activities within the university and his friendships and
associations outside it before he left Melbourne for life, need to be
seen against the background common to all of them, his public
reputation as an expositor and critic of literature. Its beginnings take
us back to the time at the end of the 1890s when he was running his
own school in Camberwell. When he returned from Warrnambool in

1904, his occasional articles in the *Argus* had already made his name well known to discriminating readers such as Alfred Deakin. They, and his multitudinous readers in later years, would have been surprised to learn that he was at that time contemplating the publication of a book of verse.

I shall not linger over the works of Murdoch the poet and Murdoch the writer of stories, who both existed and saw themselves in print, but since Murdoch the critic and essayist did preserve them they may be described briefly.[2] The poet began as a writer of light verse. In 1892 his 'Ballade of Examination Week' was a neat enough example, for a student journal, of an artificial form.[3] When he tackled the sonnet, he very naturally looked to the manner (and the landscape) of the young Keats:

> I know two little rivulets that leave
>   The self-same mountain. One o'er hill and lawn
>   Pursues its quiet course, murmuring on
> Through sedgy plains where osiers interweave,
> And through green woods the autumn's tints relieve . . .[4]

He kept cuttings of such of his early verses as were published, most of them in his schoolmastering years, and around the end of 1903 made a 'fair copy' notebook of some of these and of other manuscript verses of the period. Though he could manage competently the technical business of verse-making, what he had to say in a 'serious' vein tended to read as an exercise 'in the manner of' one or other of the English poets of the nineteenth century; his landscapes, his settings and his poetical sentiments came from literature, not life. He could write graceful enough verse in various stanza forms:

> And so, the year is dying;
>   And so let passion die;
> Time sets new lovers sighing,
>   As we were used to sigh;
> Time sets the old love spinning,
>   And bids the new attend;
> June saw our love's beginning,
>   —December sees it end.

But Swinburne ('A Match') could do it better.

In 'The Climber' an 'old man', ever conscious of the vast burden of human suffering unrelieved by prayers, cries in anger to 'the multitude of stars':

> A bitter jest ye played us,
>   And a sorry gift ye gave,
> When ye sate as kings at the shaping of things,
>   And there was none to save![5]

But Kipling was a better practitioner of such ballad-biblical language. The more 'serious' of these early verses were not deliberate imitations, but their mode is familiar; they could have come from a volume of verse by ... but does it matter? They have the air of pastiche.

This talent for verse-making could be adapted to various purposes—light verse, parody, comment on public affairs. Thus Murdoch wrote poems 'to' England, then engaged in the Boer War, and, like many others, he greeted the imminent advent of the new Australian Commonwealth with verse:

> While yet the trumpet's voice is mute,
>   Before the bells' triumphant peal,
> In solemn silence we salute
>   Our virgin-vestured Commonweal![6]

And so on. But he rightly preferred to include Bernard O'Dowd's sonnet on that theme when in later years he compiled an anthology of Australian verse.

In 1903 he reviewed a little book of poems by Frank Wilmot, a young man whom he did not yet know personally, but whose appearance, as an assistant in Cole's Book Arcade, was familiar to him. It was printed at the writer's own private printing press, and at the end of November Murdoch wrote from Warrnambool to ask for an estimate for the printing of a similar small volume of poems, about forty pages. When to his surprise he learned that for £2 the young printer-poet would agree to print and publish 250 copies, he promised to collect 'from old newspapers and old note-books such verses as I think might pass muster'.[7] Thus the fair-copy notebook, with its careful calligraphy and numbering, is explained. But no such volume was ever published. If it had been, anthologists of the next thirty years might have included one or two of the poems in their collections, for they were quite as 'good' as many they did choose. I do not know why Murdoch did not proceed, but perhaps the man who had now become a kind of official authority on poetry may have felt a little shy, when he looked his poems over, about exposing them to public gaze. He did throughout his life retain and exercise his talent for 'occasional verse', playful or satirical. But it seems evident that by the time he was thirty he had come to realize that if he really had some acquaintance with a muse, she was the muse of comedy. 'I'm not a poet, and I found that out pretty early in life', he said in old age.

We may suppose nevertheless that for some time he thought that he might really be a poet. His few attempts at fiction suggest rather the view of a fluent young man that if others could sell their stories to the journals, so could he, and certainly any supplement to his scanty income as a schoolteacher would have been welcome. He may have been affected by the example or advice of his brother-in-law William Hughston, his senior by five years, a man of ability and originality, who had himself turned his hand to the writing of short stories published under the pseudonym of 'H. Stone'.[8] These were generally set in the Victorian 'bush' country where he had spent his early years, and if their plots were sentimental or melodramatic, their background, unlike the second-hand poetic landscape of Murdoch's 'serious' verse, was authentic.

Three short stories, originally published in the *Argus* by one 'W. L. Forbes', survive in cuttings in Murdoch's papers.[9] The setting of 'Fiction on Myalong Station' faintly recalls his year as a tutor at Eurambeen station in 1895. 'We were on the broad verandah, some playing euchre, others loafing . . .' The men are told that a distinguished young novelist is to visit the station in search of local colour and they are to make sure that he gets it, blood, bushrangers and all. Their temporary chairman outlines plans; he sits down 'amid tumults of applause, and there was a holy, chastened joy in all our hearts'. It is the tone of a Kipling, introducing one of those stories in which 'I' will rush around assisting the clever, strong insiders to humiliate some cad of an outsider. As the visiting novelist, in mortal danger as he believes, is tricked into 'escaping', we may suppose that the story is a kind of parody, with the tables turned on a pseudo-Kipling. 'When the Creek Is in Flood' tells of two brothers, one (from Aberdeen) seeking revenge for a grievous wrong, of a furious chase along a flooded creek, of the death by drowning of the wicked brother, of forgiveness in retrospect. Though 'Jan Kroetz' is set in South Africa, the background may be founded on family letters. Murdoch's brother in South Africa had married a girl of Boer family, and with war imminent had been forced to make a hurried escape with his family from Johannesburg and to endure hardships which led to his death. In Murdoch's story a 'good Boer' protects an English family in the course of a similar agonizing journey and later, after a military action, nurses back to life his wounded English rival for the affections of the daughter of the family. He dies in another battle; the rival says that if more Boers were like him he would see the war as unjust; the girl says that if more Boers were like him there would never have been a war.

Murdoch was still a young man of about twenty-five when he wrote these stories, and it might be supposed that he really thought there was some power in his melodramatic plots. But when we consider that within a year or so he was writing shrewdly and critically about the best English fiction, it seems more likely that in his own stories he was, with tongue in cheek, attempting to turn an honest penny. There are no entries for further stories in his notebook of work published in these years. It was more congenial to read good fiction and to be paid for writing about it.

In his last year at 'The College, Camberwell' Murdoch wrote a 'bit of jaunty polemic' which set him on the road to his true vocation. The *Argus* of 6 May 1899 published an exceptionally long article, 'The New School of Australian Poets, by Walter Murdoch' which, the editor explained, had been submitted in two parts but was better given as a whole. Brightly written, it was a sceptical survey of the claims to be considered as poets of a number of the verse-writers of the 1890s—Paterson, Lawson, Dyson, Boake, Daley, Ogilvie, Brady, Quinn, who were lumped more or less together. Their verse did have a distinctively Australian note, but its technique was derivative, and altogether said nothing not better expressed in prose. You could hardly tell one from another—a proposition supported by the device of presenting a stanza made up of lines from five different writers. It was Murdoch's first article 'except schoolboy things', as he told Vance Palmer long afterwards, and he was now surprised that the *Argus* had published such a thing.[10]

It was designed to irritate, and it did. In the *Argus* its tone and judgements were contested by Edward Dyson and 'Rolf Boldrewood'; more thunderously and effectively, the great A. G. Stephens demolished it in a whole Red Page of the *Bulletin*.[11] This forgotten controversy affected Murdoch in two ways. The editor of the *Argus* was shrewd enough to recognize that a young man who could thus provoke discussion from his seniors was a writer worth watching; from that time the columns of the paper were open to him. And secondly it is evident that he learned something to his advantage. There is more in criticism than pertness; he had made some good points not answered by Stephens, but in a way that was bound to incur the wrath of a skilled journalist who was truly concerned to encourage literary endeavour in Australia; to be taken seriously in denunciation one must also show a capacity to discriminate and to discern the promise of something new and original. When, the next year, he wrote on recent Australian fiction,[12] he began lightly with some banter about popular novelists, but went on to a discriminating comparison of the short stories of A. H. Davis ('Steele Rudd') and Henry Lawson that said much that later critical opinion has endorsed, and concluded with a speculation, supported by examples, about the short story as a fitter medium than the novel for 'the presentment of a new phase of life, a new chapter of civilization'. He had found his own medium. Within a few years he had developed the individual style and manner, the confidence without arrogance, that marks a good professional writer with something of his own to say.

When a man begins to keep a notebook recording dates, titles and payments received for his writing, he has come (we may suppose) to believe that it will continue to yield him at least a supplementary income. Some time in 1902, in a small 'Journal' for keeping accounts Murdoch wrote the heading 'Literature' and retrospectively entered the items for which he had been paid from about 1899 onwards, though the first precise date he recorded was 1 May 1902. The entries, which continue until the end of September 1911, allow us to trace fairly closely the beginning and the firm establishment of his career as a literary journalist—a true professional, though for only one year before his retirement from academic life in 1939 was he ever employed full time in that capacity.

Until the end of 1912 nearly all Murdoch's articles were published in the *Argus*, one of the two morning newspapers which had seemed to be almost synonymous with Victorian colonial life since the 1850's, and still retained much of their sense of power and self-satisfaction in a city that until 1927 was the political capital of the Australian federation inaugurated in 1901. The *Age* had once been the champion of 'radical' or 'liberal' policies, and its principal proprietor David Syme probably believed that it still was. The *Argus* was understood to be the exponent of political and social conservatism. But it is unlikely that young Murdoch sent his early manuscripts to the *Argus* because he preferred its politics; so far as we have hints of his political views at this time, they suggest that he did not. Simply, the literary tone of the *Argus*, the space it gave to 'literary' contributions and, compared with the *Age*, the relative freedom it allowed to writers on topics not overtly political made it a better prospective buyer of the kind of wares he hoped to sell. By December 1900 the editor, himself a man of literary taste and style, could write of Murdoch as 'one of our very best literary men' in a letter of introduction to Alfred Deakin, a man not likely automatically to assume the accuracy of such a description. With varying closeness of attachment, the newcomer was to remain as one of 'our' men for the best part of forty years. Thus 'Walter Murdoch' was by 1904 a name well known to readers of the literary pages of the *Argus*, and during the next ten years he continued to write signed literary articles from time to time, as well as special contributions, such as a notable series on education (1908), which were avowedly direct and earnest expressions of his personal views on a matter of public interest.

It was known to fewer readers than he was also frequently an anonymous contributor to the *Argus*, as book reviewer and leader writer. Though his occasional 'Saturday leader', by convention avoiding politics, was generally 'literary', he sometimes wrote on such subjects as the university jubilee, or a public speech by a prominent university man. The first 'leader' identified in his note book was on Kipling (11 February 1905). Other examples, taken at random from later years, discuss English teaching, criticism, religion. We know that the *Argus*, and especially its Saturday edition, was widely read by 'educated' people in and beyond Victoria, even those who had no sympathy with its political attitudes. From 1904 to 1913 Murdoch, in one guise or another, was the author of much of what they read in it about old and new books.

'*BOOKS AND MEN*. By ELZEVIR.' The heading first appeared in the *Argus* of Saturday 3 June 1905, in that form, though the title was later to be set in roman type. 'Books and Men' was not a new feature of the literary page. From May 1903 until October 1904 a column under that title had appeared at about monthly intervals, at first anonymously and then with the awkward pseudonym 'A Piccadilly Clubman'. Murdoch had been writing for the *Argus* under his own name since 1899, but it is certain that the first author (or authors) of 'Books and Men' did not represent him in another guise, for he entered no payments for such a column in his notebook entries for his articles of that period. On 19 November 1904, seven weeks after the last of the 'Books and Men' articles by the 'Piccadilly Clubman', an anonymous column headed 'Among the Books' appeared. This was by Murdoch, though for that date his notebook entry was 'Books and Men'. He had evidently begun to write a regular article to replace that of his predecessor, and perhaps he or the editor had at first thought that a change of title was called for. But a week later 'Books and Men', still anonymous, was restored, to appear henceforth as a weekly feature until, and after, he became 'Elzevir' in June 1905.

Why 'Elzevir'?* A sentence in some letter or article could at once solve that not very important mystery, but it has not been found. Murdoch was never specially interested in the history of publishing, nor was he a 'collector' of rare or fine books as such. He knew a rarity when he saw one in a second-hand bookshop, and would buy it if it were a bargain, but generally he would have been hoping to find *any* edition of a text he sought, rather than the first or any other particular edition or imprint. 'Books and Men' had been and would be concerned with writing and writers, not with publishing, printing or rare-book collecting. So, we may guess, he adopted 'Elzevir', the

---

* In reviewing the *Oxford Companion to English Literature* (*Argus*, 23 May 1936) Murdoch confessed that he had now discovered the proper spelling, 'Elzevier'.

familiar name of the seventeenth-century Dutch printers, because it was euphonious, because it was vaguely 'bookish', and perhaps because it had a more personal significance. He knew his Scott, and had in fact written on Scott and Burns a few weeks before 'Elzevir' made his appearance. Though Mr Oldbuck, the antiquary, was indeed searching for rarities, Murdoch as student and teacher had also been, and still was, a haunter of second-hand bookshops, equally alert for his own kind of treasures. Looking at his own bookshelves, he could well have understood the feelings of the old antiquary: 'Those little Elzevirs are the memoranda and trophies of many a walk by night and morning . . . How often have I stood haggling on a half penny . . . how have I trembled, lest some passing stranger should chop between me and the prize, and regarded each poor student of divinity that stopped to turn over the books at the stall, as a rival amateur . . .'

If he really supposed that a pseudonym would conceal the identity of the writer of 'Books and Men', Murdoch was soon disillusioned. His style and manner were too characteristic to allow any regular reader to doubt for long that Walter Murdoch, who signed literary articles, and Elzevir who reviewed books every week, were identical. Within a year Deakin was telling him that 'there is no mystery as to Elzevir', and we may assume that long before he republished some of the Elzevir articles under his own name, the pseudonym was a familiar formality, at least to Melbourne readers. But its continued use did have the advantage that when Walter Murdoch wrote in the first person on a public question like educational policy, he could be assumed, as a university teacher, to be claiming some authority; Elzevir, from time to time, might be allowed the indulgence of pulling his reader's leg.

Few forms of publication become so rapidly inaccessible as those which first appear in a daily newspaper. Murdoch did reprint a selection of them in a little book, *Loose Leaves* (1910), but these were not well chosen to illustrate all his qualities as critic and expositor of literature, as they were remembered by his Melbourne contemporaries. Though he was to remain always a 'literary' writer, drawing naturally on his reading for allusions and illustrations, his later essays, known throughout Australia because they were reprinted as books, were mostly essays on things in general. In his Melbourne years his reputation rested mainly on his discussion of contemporary literature. Later readers could not know that the reminiscent essayist had once been a critic well abreast of the literature of his time.

He soon developed an easy conversational style, 'chat' in a sense, but not 'chit-chat'. Though his tone was serious when he had something serious to say, cheerfulness kept breaking in. As Walter

Murdoch he generally wrote on a single topic or author; as Elzevir he would review or mention several new books at a time, though giving most of his space to one of them, or to a general theme provoked by its subject. Thus Walter Murdoch might write an article on Stevenson or Chesterton or the death of Swinburne, but Elzevir's first article reviewed new books on Yeats, on J. H. Shorthouse, on Shakespeare's marriage, and a recent article by Andrew Lang. In the last 'Books and Men' published before he left Melbourne, his main review discussed O'Dowd's *The Bush* but he noticed also Samuel Butler's *Notebooks* and a new edition of Meredith's poems.[13]

A regular column of commentary by the same author necessarily reflects individual prejudices and enthusiasms but if it is well done it may come to be read with pleasure for its own sake, for the reflection of its author's personality as much as for its information. For a decade in Melbourne, Elzevir's *causeries de samedi* were so read. A student of literary taste in Australia will some day disinter them from the files of the *Argus* and will find that he has discovered not only 'material' for his thesis but actually something to read with interest and pleasure. It is not possible fairly to illustrate the method of an Elzevir article short of reproducing one at length, but two extracts from articles of 1909 will recall its manner. Of Chesterton's *Orthodoxy* Elzevir wrote:

> He has succeeded brilliantly; people devour his books who would never dream of opening a theological text-book. He defends orthodoxy with the most agile wit, the quaintest humour. His defect—the defect which forces us to question his sincerity; the defect which separates him from the finest and rarest minds and places him among the commonplace people he abhors—is self-consciousness. You are not quite certain whether he sees the beauty of Christianity; you are certain that he sees the beauty of his defence. And so his endless gambols in front of a mirror become at last infinitely wearisome, and one longs for a little of the steadfastness, the serenity, the repose, and the humility of the loftier spirits. If you wish to realise the difference between a man in love with religion and a man in love with his own presentment of it, take down from your shelf, after reading Mr Chesterton, the late Edward Caird's 'Lay Sermons', and read a few pages. Then go back to Mr Chesterton, and you will find yourself asking the question with which I started, the question to which I confess myself unable at present to reply—Does he mean it?[14]

And of Alfred Noyes's *William Morris*:

> . . . my central objection to this book is that in it the essential thing about Morris's work, its unity, its continuity, is lost sight of. Mr Noyes speaks of him as a poet who happened to devise wallpapers,

as one might speak of a bimetallist who happened also to keep canaries. Mr Noyes speaks of his socialism as it if were an accidental hobby, as a member of Parliament might take up stamp-collecting. Now the first thing to understand about Morris was that all his activities sprang from the same impulse—the desire for beauty. He made poems exactly as he made chairs, he designed wallpapers exactly as he designed utopias, all for the same compelling reason—because he was in revolt against the hideousness of the Victorian era, because he desired to escape—and to carry others with him—into a more beautiful world. The utter unloveliness of modern life—this he realised from the first; and at first he merely sought refuge from it in an imaginary world of poetry. It was, at first, enough for him to escape from reality, into Malory's world, or Froissart's, or Chaucer's, or a world of his own imagining, 'out of space, out of time'. Keats, in exactly the same way, took refuge from reality in a remote ideal world. But Keats was content to abide in that sheltered place till he died; had he lived as long as Morris, who knows what might have happened? Morris, at all events was not content. He was intensely practical, the most practical man that ever wrote poetry; and he sought to realise his ideals. He was a dreamer who wore himself out in the effort to make his dreams come true. To ignore this practical side of the man is to misunderstand his poetry. One has not really caught the meaning of 'Sigurd the Volsung' until one has understood why the man who wrote it was also senior partner in the firm of 'Morris, Marshall, Faulkner, and Co., Fine Art Workmen in Painting, Carving, Furniture, and the Metals'.[15]

Thus for a decade and more 'Walter Murdoch' or 'Elzevir' wrote for—one may guess—a majority of the 'serious' readers of literature in Victoria. Of course it must be a guess, but there is evidence of the wide general appreciation of his articles among such readers, and of their eager interest in his Saturday appearances. It is true that the daily circulation of the *Argus*, then about 70 000, was perhaps half that of its rival, the *Age*, but it is clear that its readership, and especially that of its Saturday issue, was by no means confined to those who favoured its politics. If Sir John Madden, chief justice and lieutenant-governor, regularly looked for his Elzevir, so did Deakin who was in a sense a child of the *Age*.

Murdoch's reviews and commentaries were not concerned only with the literature of England. From time to time he discussed the work of contemporary European writers; Maeterlinck, Tolstoy, Faguet, Anatole France, Turgenev, were among these. But sophisticated readers could look to the overseas reviews for a wider range of discussion of continental literature. More interesting, to those who knew only the Murdoch of later years, is the fact that he gave regular attention to Australian writing. The 'history of Australian literature' commissioned by Angus and Robertson in his Warrnambool days was never published, beyond a series of articles in 1904 (Barrington, Harpur, Wentworth, Deniehy, Marcus Clarke) which presumably reflected an original determination to begin at the beginning, abandoned as the flow of new English books for review began to absorb the whole of his spare time, though his interest in new Australian books also continued. Thirty years later it would be asserted, with some justification, that he lacked qualifications to write about Australian literature, since apparently he knew little about contemporary writing. In his Melbourne years, however, when new Australian writing was for him part of new writing in general, to be assessed by similar criteria, he wrote about it as a real and sensitive critic.

His later readers could not know or judge this. The 'essays' of the 1920s, the foundation of his Australian fame, did of course frequently discuss books and authors, but he tended now to treat new books as pegs on which to hang his own ideas about the varieties of human behaviour, and old books as occasions for sharing familiar pleasures with people less widely read than he was. The Elzevir of 1900–13 was concerned closely with the books and authors themselves, and wrote about them with a different audience in mind, the kind of audience that would wish as much to debate points with him, on a basis of common knowledge, as simply to be instructed or entertained. In the later essays there is a subtle kind of 'talking down' which marks Murdoch the preacher, rather than the critic known to readers of the old *Argus.*

A. G. Stephens is remembered as the outstanding, perhaps the only, significant Australian literary critic of the early twentieth century. Those who are concerned to identify the tone, even the 'souls', of Sydney and Melbourne might be tempted to find a useful contrast between the vigorous and flamboyant 'Red Pagan' of the Sydney *Bulletin* and his counterpart in Melbourne in the same period, Elzevir of the *Argus*, a quieter, more academic writer, ironic where Stephens was sardonic. This would be superficial; physically and temperamentally they were certainly very different men, but it makes little sense to see them as typical products of contrasted environments. The real difference between Sydney and Melbourne, in this context and period, was the existence of the *Bulletin*, and the question to be argued would be whether such a journal would necessarily have failed in Melbourne if J. F. Archibald had launched it there.

But their differences and likenesses as critics are worth noticing a little. Murdoch's later reputation was made when he had largely ceased to write as a critic of current literature, yet a rereading of his

Argus articles of the period 1900–13 could support the claim that there was in Australia at the time a real critic, bound to be less influential and less well-known outside Victoria than Stephens, but one who assessed new writing by standards not inferior to his. Of course Stephens's critical work while he controlled the Red Page, and less effectively afterwards, was his life; Murdoch's was a secondary occupation, treated seriously and performed skilfully, but taking up each week perhaps as much time as his colleague Tucker might have spent on his recreations of 'billiards, golf, rusticating'. And the literary page of the *Argus* was not the Red Page of the *Bulletin*.

Murdoch was the younger by nearly ten years and was by nature and training a man who would necessarily appear 'to have less blood in him' than Stephens. But they had in common a wide acquaintance with English and European literature, and a special knowledge of French; they could both bring more than parochial standards to their assessment of Australian writing. Stephens had effectively dealt with Murdoch's youthful *jeu d'esprit* on the poets of the 1890s; 'he was defending', wrote Vance Palmer in 1941, 'not the actual work of the writers in question, but the creative spirit itself'.[16] The comment was just, but Palmer (who valued Murdoch's later writing highly, and said so) should have stressed how very early this 'early heresy' was. Before long a more mature Murdoch was writing as well as any critic has written about Lawson's stories, and he put his finger on something about his verse as a literary phenomenon. It had no value as poetry, and yet thousands of Australians knew particular verses by heart: 'he has come nearest to giving us genuine folk-songs . . . he is a folk-singer or he is nothing'. And the more mature Murdoch also knew well enough the value of the 'creative spirit' in the literature of a new society:

> I do not pretend to believe that Gordon is a poet of the first rank—or even of the second rank—or that Clarke is a novelist of the order of Flaubert. But I do believe—and believe more and more firmly, as the years go by—that the interpreter of the land in which we live gives us something which neither a Flaubert nor a Dante can give us—something which it is eminently worthwhile getting hold of.[17]

The two men knew something of each other's writings and critical opinions, though it is not certain that they ever met. Murdoch may for a while have continued to smart a little at the memory of Stephens's attack of 1899, for in 1905 he wrote about him severely when it was announced that he was editing an anthology of Australian verse even though it was well known that Bertram

Stevens's anthology was already in the press. This, he said, was a question of literary ethics, 'a plain violation of the unwritten code of honour which prevails all over the literary world.'[18] But he was not a vindictive man. More characteristic was the letter he wrote to Stephens a few months after the association with the *Bulletin* had come to an end. His excuse was that Stephens's own journal, the *Bookfellow*, had quoted sympathetically something Murdoch had written, but it is clear that his real intention was to express as tactfully as possible his considerable respect for the work of a man whose occupation (as it may well have seemed) was gone: 'I wish you, and your excellent little magazine, every possible success: and hope you will not resent my having written to say so'.[19] Yet he was never inclined entirely to acknowledge the validity of the long-lived legend. After reading in 1941 Palmer's recent memoir of the great man, he wrote:

> A.G.S. certainly did a great service to our literature in the days of its teething. He was a clever man with a real regard for letters; but I doubt whether he was ever a real critic or had a profound sense of what is great in literature. You say he under-rated O'Dowd, Furnley Maurice, &c: you don't mention the persons he *over-*rated—Daley, for instance, and (for a time) Arthur Adams. But he did undoubtedly wake people up to a consciousness that there *is* a world of literature.[20]

I have said a good deal more about Murdoch the literary journalist than about Murdoch the lecturer in English. It could be asked—and in the conditions of the 1970s I would certainly wish to ask—whether an academic so well known as a journalist was properly performing his duties in the university that employed him. In 1906 Murdoch's university salary was raised on condition that he delivered evening lectures, and when he asked whether his acceptance would debar him 'from doing such things as the writing of occasional newspaper articles or the writing or editing of books', he was informed definitely that the university council had no such intention. It is well to establish the point, though we may think that in practice he interpreted 'occasional' rather generously. During his academic career in Melbourne and later in Perth his journalism, and the similar activities of his colleagues, had not only the tacit but the formal sanction of his employers.

Security of tenure, provisions for superannuation and financial assistance for travel and research have since given some logical justification for universities to set limits to the 'outside' earnings of members of their staffs. Though the University of Melbourne did not place any such constraints upon Murdoch, in fact what he earned by his journalism in these years does not seem excessive provided that his academic duties were competently performed. We can find from his 'Literature' notebook that from the beginning of 1904 until September 1911 his total income from his books and articles was about £1260. Nearly £670 of this came from royalties on his two textbooks, *The Struggle for Freedom* and *A New Primer of English Literature*, written in collaboration with his colleague Tucker. Thus his journalism in this period brought him about £600, or rather less than £80 a year: not a negligible sum when the average weekly wage of the factory worker was between £2 and £3, but gained at the sacrifice of reasonable leisure in evenings and weekends.

Certainly his students did not feel that he was neglecting them, as they were to testify emphatically in 1911 when he was a candidate for the chair of English. Coming to the university as an evening student, Katharine Susannah Prichard found his lectures so interesting that by 'astute dawdling' she would sometimes contrive to catch the same tram to the city so that she might hear him talk further about literature in his 'easy, quizzical way', and she found that her friends among the day students held him in a kind of affectionate awe.[21] Perhaps a clue to their attitude can be found in a letter which one of them, Nettie Higgins, preserved all her life. She had apparently misread the instructions on her examination paper, and written to Murdoch to explain the distress of an anonymous candidate (in fact herself) who had done just that.

W.M. to Nettie Higgins, 22 November 1905

I suppose the converse (or obverse or whatever logicians call it) of your rule applies, and that examiners must not hold even indirect communication with candidates; I must therefore ask you not to hand on the information I am about to impart to you to the candidate whose distress you have depicted so powerfully, but merely to receive, as a matter of abstract & general interest, the assurance that the ferocity of the examining animal has been exaggerated in popular accounts. So far as I know him, he is mild-mannered and docile. Under illegible handwriting he sometimes grows restive: but he is not put out at all by a little thing like the questions being out of order. In such cases he recognizes that the candidate's order is quite as likely to be the ideal order as his own. If you happen to see the candidate in question will you kindly add a weary examiner's congratulations to those she is sure to receive shortly on the result of her first University Exam?[22]

In the class list for English Part I for 1905 Janet Gertrude Higgins was placed first in the first class.

4

MELBOURNE FRIENDSHIPS

WRITING TO JOHN LATHAM in December 1912 Murdoch said, 'It will be a severe wrench for me to leave Melbourne, which has been very good to me and has given me more than a fair share of those things which I see to be the most valuable things in life; chief among which is friendship.'[1] They had become friends through common association with Ormond College and the university, for Latham as a student-at-law and then a young barrister had been glad to pick up some income from tutoring and lecturing, but they might equally have met in one of the more or less informal groups with overlapping membership that seem to have made up much of the intellectual and cultural life of Melbourne at this time. We find some of the same names wherever we dip. Students who have recently become interested in this network of association[2] could for example begin with the clubs or societies whose membership included Bernard O'Dowd, poet, radical and civil servant, or Ernest Scott, Hansard reporter and historian. They could equally begin with an exploration of the associations of Walter Murdoch, university lecturer and journalist.

To illustrate, in 1904 Murdoch became a member of a private group, the 'Boobooks', who dined together monthly before the reading and discussion of papers on diverse themes from literature to politics.[3] Founded in 1902 by Frederic Eggleston, an earnestly thoughtful young barrister, its name ('Boobook' is a species of owl) reflected their nocturnal habits and the wisdom of their discussions, in the mock-serious ritual that helps to preserve the continuity of such private societies over the years. In Murdoch's time the members

45

included such men as Bernard O'Dowd, Ernest Scott, Robert Garran, John Latham, Harrison Moore, Archibald Strong, T. G. Tucker, Edward Shann, David Rivett and other academic and professional men, mostly graduates, who in one way or another would find some place in the history of their generation. No one who has belonged to some such 'club' will suppose that they always composed their papers with unvaried solemnity; I imagine that only one of Murdoch's three papers—'Paradox', 'Nietzsche', 'The Futility of Philosophy'—was of the kind he would have submitted for a university examination. But I am concerned here with the proceedings of the 'Boobooks' themselves only to point to one example of a cultural or intellectual group in Melbourne at that time, and to notice the names of some of its members.

We could turn to another group, the Literature Society of Melbourne, which for some years from 1905 met monthly in Glenn's Music House in Collins street to hear critical discussions or the reading of original work. A literature society was only too familiar to Murdoch the schoolteacher: 'a small body of men and women who meet periodically to pass judgment on works which they but half understand . . . What is called discussion ensues in which the reader of the paper is eulogized to his heart's content; and the result of it all is either precisely nothing, or what Carlyle would have called "a frightful minus quantity", in the shape of a wasted evening'. But for a while the Literature Society of Melbourne seems to have been something more than that; certainly some of those who took part in it bore names not entirely forgotten today, and they are names we have met already. It was a public society, subscription 5s per annum. Tucker, Murdoch, Strong and O'Dowd were among its presidents. Old Mr Lothian the publisher, who knew them all well, affirmed in the 1970s that there must have been three hundred or more present when Murdoch gave his presidential address in May 1907, 'The Enemies of Literature', preaching 'unwearying war' on 'the dull indifference of the Philistine, on the cocksure materialism of the present-day scientist, on the narrowness of the puritan and the triviality of the dilettante'. Lothian had another memory of that lecture:

> It was a big audience, a big room. One thing I remember about it especially was that in the middle of the lecture someone like a farmer walked down the middle aisle tramping his heavy boots when Murdoch was still speaking . . . I shushed him. Two days later Syme died—the Age man—and that was who it was.[4]

There is something wrong here. Syme died in 1908, but it does sound like him.

Though the Literature Society did not survive for long, it is still remembered in footnotes, for it was as president in 1909 that O'Dowd delivered his manifesto *Poetry Militant.*

Consider now another venture of these years, and the names associated with it. The ghosts of drowned journals haunt Australian literary history, repeating in faint voices some variation of their last words before the waters overwhelmed them: 'we have not lived in vain'. In May 1907 the *Trident* was born. Published by Lothian, the friend of Melbourne writers, price 4d, post free, it was to appear monthly as a journal of modern languages and literature sponsored by the departments of English, French and German in the University of Melbourne. Its editor was Walter Murdoch whose hand may be traced in the 'English' contributions to various numbers of its first volume. It was aimed mainly at teachers and students of the three languages; most of its contributions dealt with problems of teaching and learning; there were a few book reviews and a few reprinted or translated poems. In the number for April 1908 a change of policy was announced. In future contributions in French and German would cease; the result (Murdoch said later) of a Franco-Prussian war. The journal would no longer concentrate on narrowly 'educational' problems, its staff had been changed, and it would be enlarged. It was hoped that it would grow into the 'Australian Review' so long desired, so often attempted, but never established.[5]

So in May 1908 the *Trident* appeared with an elegant new cover designed in *art nouveau* style by the artist Blamire Young, and in a much improved format. It began with a poem 'Australia Mavourneen' by Bernard O'Dowd; Archibald Strong, the learned literary critic of the *Herald*, and John Latham, the promising young barrister and university lecturer, contributed articles. Robert Garran printed one of his translations from Heinrich Heine. The editor himself wrote the first of a series of articles about the life of H. H. Champion, the gentleman-radical celebrated for his part in the London dock strike of 1890. Cast in the form of reported conversations with Champion, who was now living in Melbourne, they may well have been a brightened-up version of a manuscript written by him. (Later that year Bernard Shaw told Murdoch that the narrative was full of mistakes.)

It was a good beginning for the new management who with some optimism and perhaps at the suggestion of Latham drew up in August 1908 a formal agreement about the division of profits: of nine equal parts the editor was to get three, the agent (Lothian?) two, and the others one each; Murdoch was the editor, and the others were Archibald Strong, Bernard O'Dowd, John Latham and B. A. Levison.[6] Whether there ever was any profit for anybody is doubtful, but they had established a review which did appear at regular monthly intervals for two years, with contributors whose names are not unknown in Australian literature and general history. There were poems and articles by Bernard O'Dowd, Arthur Adams, Enid Derham, Latham, Strong, Arthur Jose, Furnley Maurice, le Gay Brereton, H. G. Turner, Ernest Scott, Vance Palmer, Hugh McCrae and (as editor or anonymous contributor) Murdoch, and by some others who ought to be better remembered, like Frederick Sinclaire and Rodney Alsop.

Murdoch left Melbourne in October 1908 on a visit to Europe, leaving the editorship to Archibald Strong. Its last issue was vol. 2, no. 12 for April 1909, when the *Trident* expired with the traditional last words of such brave ventures. It sank very far beneath the waves. Though Murdoch told Latham in 1933 that he had recently seen an article describing the *Trident* as 'a chapter in the literary history of Australia', H. M. Green did not record its existence in his *History of Australian Literature* (1961), yet most of those who wrote for it are embedded in his pages.

Consider now the Brown Society, a private group first invited in 1907 to meet at the house of Herbert and Ivy Brookes to discuss the works of T. E. Brown, the Manx-English poet and schoolmaster, and to hear musical recitals. The subject certainly had its limitations; Brookes, a serious and thoughtful man whom we shall meet shortly, had somewhat idiosyncratic enthusiasms in literature. But the Brown Society—in effect the various guests invited by Brookes more or less monthly in the years before the war, and then less frequently—survived for more than a decade. It fairly soon became a more general 'literary' gathering, at which the speaker might be Ernest Scott, reading from his 'Life of Matthew Flinders', as yet unpublished, or Garran on Heine, or Murdoch on Shelley, or O'Dowd, reading or rather chanting in his bardic manner from poems seldom heard by groups meeting in the house of a member of the Chamber of Manufactures, or Alfred Deakin, father of Ivy Brookes and prime minister of Australia, who lived next door, reading from Wordsworth, or recalling the books of his childhood.[7]

Here we meet some of the same names again, though as guests rather than organizers, in yet another group concerned with the discussion of literature. Murdoch had been introduced to Brookes by Alfred Deakin, and that brings us to the friendship that in some ways affected him more powerfully than any other of his early years.* Deakin had been the most active and eloquent Victorian advocate of the federal union of the Australian colonies, one of the most

---

* For an account of the relations between Murdoch and Deakin, and for their correspondence, see J. A. La Nauze and Elizabeth Nurser (eds), *Walter Murdoch and Alfred Deakin on Books and Men* (Melbourne 1974).

prominent figures in its realization, and the senior colleague of the
first prime minister, Edmund Barton. In March 1905 Murdoch
published a strong defence of George Meredith as a novelist, in
answer to criticisms made by his colleague Tucker in the course of a
discussion in the *Argus* about 'great novelists'. A few days later he
received a warm note of appreciation from Deakin, to whom since his
youth Meredith had been one of the greatest of artist-heroes. They
met soon afterwards, and continued to meet or correspond fairly
frequently until Murdoch left Melbourne in 1913, when the tragic
decline of Deakin's memory had already begun. Their correspondence soon came to an end, but the friendship, in various ways that
will appear, affected Murdoch until his own last years.

It was a friendship based on books. Though Deakin was generally
known to be a well-read man, Murdoch soon found that this conventional description was quite inadequate, for Deakin seemed to
have read 'everything' in English literature and to be better
acquainted with modern French literature and criticism than
Murdoch himself; moreover he could talk about literature with
great resource and charm. The letters, almost entirely about books
and writers, reflect a certain deference on both sides. Clearly Murdoch felt a little flattered by the relationship itself, though there was
no flattery in his comments on Deakin's opinions or suggestions about
old or new writing; there they were conversing as equals. On Deakin's
side there was a certain wistful desire to show to a professional student
of literature that what meant most to him was reading and con-
templation; that though politics was the sphere into which the
chances of life had forced him, since youth his dream had been to live
as a writer and philosopher. Conversing with Murdoch, a man
altogether outside politics, he could briefly suppose that the dream
had not been absurd. '. . . many will miss you and I myself specially',
he wrote in his last letter, and he may be believed; by then he knew
too well that his brief reference to his 'abated faculties' was not a
passing jest.

This friendship led to another. Deakin's son-in-law, Herbert
Brookes, some years older than Murdoch, was an engineer and
businessman, a devoted reader of 'serious' books, a sincere admirer of
cultivated men whose minds moved more quickly than his own. He
was given to private acts of kindness, and easily moved by 'sentiment'
in the eighteenth-century sense. After his move to Perth, Murdoch
continued to write to Brookes for fifty years. They had been
acquaintances in Melbourne; their correspondence, carefully
preserved by Brookes, gradually made them intimate and affectionate old friends.

In October 1908 Murdoch sailed for Europe on his first venture beyond Australia since his childhood. He was thirty-four, he had now for nearly five years been a university lecturer, and it was high time that he saw something of people and places outside Australia. The university could not indefinitely leave vacant the chair of English. Its finances had improved, new chairs in scientific subjects had been created, and the turn of Arts, the poor sister, must come soon. Murdoch's claims to a chair of literature could only be strengthened by a visit that had as one of its professed objects some observation of the state and methods of the teaching of English in its mother country, though in fact this was a matter likely at that time to be less instructive than a lay member of an Australian selection committee might suppose.

It was a short visit of a few months. Violet Murdoch could not go, and (if family legend can be believed) the sophisticated Elzevir, whose articles confidently put the most celebrated writers of the day in their places, actually became homesick—a condition not unknown in other such cases. Moreover it was winter in London; I suspect that he was trying too hard to be economical. His nephew Keith was also in London, preparing for a journalistic career. It was as well.

W.M. to C. E. Sayers, 25 February 1966

> . . . I had what I thought was a heart attack, and was rather frightened about myself. [Keith's] aunt, as it happened, had married a doctor . . . They had lately come to London to live and he had set up as a heart specialist; so Keith insisted on us both going round to see him. The specialist told me that there was nothing wrong with me, except that I had not been eating enough; and he took me upstairs to have supper with the family. Then Keith and I sallied forth to our respective hotels; on the way a very delectable aroma from a restaurant tempted us to have a second supper of grilled steak and onions. (I hope I shouted on that occasion). It seems a trivial thing to remember across the years; but one does remember small things![8]

He had taken with him various letters of introduction to English writers and scholars. He saw professors of English: Oliver Elton at Liverpool, C. H. Herferd at Manchester, Israel Gollancz in London, Walter Raleigh and A. C. Bradley at Oxford. In Cambridge, Lowes Dickinson hoped to get G. C. Macaulay, lecturer in English, to meet him but confessed that they didn't 'do' much 'here' in the way of English literature; perhaps he really meant that in King's they only wrote it.

Visits to academics were proper and might be useful but Murdoch or at any rate Elzevir found more interest in meeting some who were not great scholars and graduates of Oxford, with honorary doctorates

and fellowships. H. H. Champion's letter introduced him to John
Burns, now a cabinet minister; Bernard Shaw told him that the
prosperity of the Scots in Australia, as elsewhere, was the necessary
consequence of the early intellectual sharpness engendered by an
education in the Shorter Catechism. The great experience of the visit
came from Deakin's introduction to George Meredith, as somewhat
earlier it had similarly been for one of Murdoch's students, Katharine
Susannah Prichard. As soon as possible after his arrival in London
Murdoch wrote off to Box Hill, and a few days later listened entranced while the sage, sitting crippled in his wheelchair and very
deaf, talked brilliantly about everything under the sun from Australian wine to Napoleon's ascendancy over the French. Murdoch
had read 'Love in the Valley' and *Richard Feverel* when he was young
and in love; he had now seen Shelley plain.[9]

He was astounded by London and, like Deakin on his first visit in
1887, appalled by its contrasts of splendour and misery. There were
then no travel grants for research. If there had been, Murdoch would
hardly have qualified for one. He met people, he walked in streets, he
looked around, he lingered in second-hand bookshops, but it is
doubtful whether he spent any time in the Reading Room of the
British Museum. Turning homewards, he was entranced with Italy
and above all Florence, though when he boarded his ship at Naples
he was 'rejoicing to feel myself on aqua firma once more', for the
whole city had hourly been expecting destruction like that which had
overwhelmed Messina a few days earlier.

In February 1911 the University of Melbourne was after nine years
at last in a position to invite applications for the vacant chair of
English language and literature. In August it was announced that the
council had appointed R. S. Wallace, a graduate of Aberdeen and
Oxford, and at the time assistant to the professor of English in
Aberdeen.

In universities of the English type, where senior positions are usually filled by advertisement, few teachers holding professorial chairs
have not at some time in their careers applied unsuccessfully for
positions for which they believed themselves to be qualified. There
can be no profit in a fruitless retrospective contest with a long-for-
gotten selection committee. If we look briefly at the case of Murdoch
in 1911, it is because it differed, in ways that affected his whole life
and work, from a situation familar enough in universities of a later
age. I have said earlier that in his time it was not possible to talk
seriously about an academic 'profession' in Australia, which an intelligent undergraduate with scholarly interests might suppose he
would eventually enter. A chance conjunction in the affairs of the

university had unexpectedly provided an opportunity for Murdoch to become a lecturer in English, but there was a place for only one university teacher in that field and there were no apparent opportunities elsewhere. Hence if Murdoch were not appointed he would be out of work.

Applications for the chair had been invited in Australia and Britain. With his obvious qualifications, Murdoch was asked to apply directly to a committee in England which would make recommendations to the council of the university, with whom the final decision lay. The report of the highly respected academics who comprised the English committee, dated 19 June 1911, went first to a committee of the council consisting of Alexander Leeper, the warden of Trinity College; E. H. Sugden, the master of Queen's College; Tucker; and Theodore Fink, a lawyer and businessman who some years earlier had been the chairman of an important inquiry into the Victorian educational system.

Writing to Deakin, Murdoch had said, 'If they get a really good man from Oxford, I am not so irrational as to grumble; but what I do grumble at, and what I have chiefly to fear, is Dr Leeper's view that *anyone*, no matter who, from Oxford or Cambridge, is quite certain to be an improvement on a local man'.[10] I do not know what justification he had for this opinion but perhaps he had had Leeper in mind when he wrote earlier that year, 'whenever I meet an Oxford man I am conscious of an impulse to take off my hat; and his manner implies that I ought to do so'.[11] His actual application revealed some anxieties on other scores. He took some space to explain that his complete responsibility for the courses in English for the past six years had left little time for 'original' work, deliberately he had not attempted to teach 'language' earlier than Chaucer, believing that to deal with both 'language' and 'literature' would end up with mere dabbling in one or the other, and he referred in passing to his journalism which (he said) he had kept up because his tenure at the university was uncertain.

In the event he was right to suspect that the more important hurdle would be the local committee, though he may well have done some injustice to Leeper. The report of the English committee was decidedly impartial, though he could not know that. They had considered fifteen applicants, and of those known to them, R. S. Wallace 'seems to be best suited for the post, and to have the strongest qualifications in both language and literature'. But, they added,

With regard to Mr Murdoch, who is in Australia, the Committee was impressed by the testimony before them as to his character and literary ability, and was convinced that in him the University has a

scholar and writer of high distinction. He differs from the other
candidates named in their history and in the predominance of the
literary over the linguistic qualifications. The Committee was
particularly impressed by the evidence of the valuable work he has
done as Lecturer in the University. The Committee could not of
course have the advantage of seeing Mr Murdoch, and therefore
decided not to attempt to choose between him and Mr Wallace.
Either gentlemen appears to the Committee to be admirably
qualified for the position.[12]

The Melbourne committee reported to the council on 7 August
simply that they had decided to recommend the appointment of
Wallace, the pressmen were asked to withdraw, the discussion was
not recorded, and the council resolved to accept the recommendation, though (it seems) by a very narrow majority. It was not a
question of 'scholarly' publications, for neither candidate yet had
any. Murdoch supposed in old age that his journalism had counted
against him, but in fact, in writing about him in 1912, various
members of the council regarded his *Argus* articles as testimonials in
his favour. He was told in 1939 that Fink's opinion had been influential, and this could have been so. Fink was an amateur litterateur,
an after-dinner speaker much in demand at bookish gatherings.
Wallace's linguistic qualifications—Old and Middle English, the
history of the English language, 'a little' Gothic and Icelandic—
looked impressive, and in line with the stress on 'language' which
in English universities had been introduced to make the study of
English look respectable in the face of classics. A layman with some
little learning may have felt that he should be the champion of
'scholarship', whereas any educated reader—himself, for example—
was qualified to talk about Shakespeare or Dickens. Ernest Scott, who
knew all the men involved, suggests that there was some such division
of opinion.[13] But further guessing is unprofitable.

An interesting, perhaps unprecedented, public fuss followed. It was
not directed against Wallace, who was unknown to anybody in Melbourne, but against the university council as an obsolete body whose
rule, it was suggested, was 'no Australian need apply'. Students and
graduates wrote to the press, the matter was brought up in Victorian
parliament, the council was asked for documents. To Murdoch, no
doubt, it was gratifying to read the high opinions of his ability
expressed by his students and by well-meaning laymen, but he would
not have supposed that public fusses could or should be the means of
making university appointments.[14]

It was a black moment for him. He was at this time erecting a
prefabricated holiday cottage at Dandenong, and used to walk to it
from Croydon to go on with the work.

W.M. to Catherine King, 31 August 1966

. . . it happened that before I started the registrar of the University (who had been at school with me and was a great friend) rang me up to tell me that my job at the University had been given to another man. I fancy the news must have driven me off my chump (temporarily, I hope) because I fancied all the world knew about it and was laughing at me, and as I passed through the little village of Montrose, half-way up the hill, several dogs barked at me in a nasty sneering way that told me they too knew. When I got home in the evening Mum cheered me up and restored me to comparative sanity, and three days later I had a position on the Argus—which they would not have given to a lunatic, with the competition so strong!

'. . . my job at the University'—and of course it was true, in the sense that Wallace's appointment meant the loss of the lectureship, at least after the end of the year. It is not clear whether Murdoch sought, or was offered, the position on the *Argus*. He may well have felt, as he put it long afterwards, that as the university had rejected him, he would reject the university, but in fact, unless the university should create an additional position, he had no alternative.

He had no animus against Wallace. How could he have had? That charming Scot, in the event, made little impression on the study of English in Australia, and spent nearly the last twenty years of his career as vice-chancellor of the University of Sydney. But he did publish, in collaboration with the versatile Tucker, an elementary textbook of English grammar.

Murdoch's last term at the University of Melbourne could not have been his happiest, though at least he could face the commiserations of friends and students with outward calm, since he had the position with the *Argus* in his pocket. He must earlier have given some thought to what he would do if he failed to get the chair. Deakin's letter of sympathy, written before he could have known of the *Argus*'s offer, had said that possibly Murdoch might do his 'appointed work' better as a free lance, as if that had previously been mentioned between them, and of course the connection with journalism had always been partly an insurance against the uncertainty of the university lectureship. His academic colleagues expressed their sympathy in the most practical way, by appointing him as evening lecturer for 1912 at a salary of £100, but by February 1913 he had realized that the pressure of his other work would not allow him to undertake the duties, and resigned.

The engagement with the *Argus* was that of 'leader writer and book reviewer', and Murdoch was described as a member of the 'literary staff' when he left the paper. He seems to have been paid a salary which could cover his leader writing and a good deal of anonymous reviewing. The 'Elzevir' articles which in 1912 appeared more or less monthly and his satirical verse in the composite column 'The Passing Show', would have been paid for separately. No doubt the prospect ahead had induced him, some time in the later months of 1911, to set to work again on the school textbook first projected in 1900, *The Australian Citizen*. Published in 1912, it was for its time a better text for the amorphous subject 'civics' than most of those which were to follow it.

He had no claims to be regarded as an expert on politics, though any journalist must learn to be an authority on anything, if required, but as far as one can tell from familiar touches of style, he was required by the *Argus* mainly to provide leaders on literary and general subjects. Some of these can be identified. It could only have been Murdoch who pounced on the 'new and simple test of literary greatness' propounded by the lord mayor of Sydney to a deputation from the Shakespeare Society of New South Wales, 'All works of great authors are ponderous'; who devoted a first leader to Thomas Hardy; who wrote thoughtfully on a dog's privilege of biting at least once. But there is no gain in further pursuit of one of the various anonymous voices of the *Argus*.

Since a journalist must daily meet deadlines, and at short notice, Murdoch had little time to write except for his paper. One article for another publication, under his own name, did create a certain fuss. It appeared in a special issue, *Australia To-Day*, of a commercial periodical, the *Australasian Traveller*, intended for immigrants and tourists. In a peculiarly thoughtful and critical article for such a medium, the Murdoch of later years is momentarily visible as he writes about the 'quality' of Australian citizenship. 'I do not wish to adopt the tone of a preacher, but it is almost impossible not to assume a rather didactic air when one is speaking from a profound conviction . . .' And he went on to discuss Australian youth:

> It is when we come to the mental and moral qualities of our young men and young women, our boys and girls, on whom the future of our nation depends, that one begins to feel a certain disquiet. I may be succumbing to one of the infirmities of middle age, but I confess I contemplate without enthusiasm the young Australian as I see him (or her) in railway trains, at the theatres, in the streets, at his pleasures, and at his work. He is conceited, he is bumptious, he is ill-mannered, he is smart and superficial, he is flippant. Perhaps it would be unfair to accuse him of having no reverence for what is higher than himself, seeing that he does not believe there is any-thing higher than himself anywhere in the universe . . .

But he gave the 'other side of the medal', 'a sense of organic oneness' or 'mateship', a 'respect for manhood apart from all considerations of wealth'. He thought there was hope for Australia, but looking to America, with its scandals of national and municipal corruption, to England in a year of vast industrial unrest, to Germany and the recent Navy Act, he thought democracy was in danger: 'if we are spared the harsh discipline of war, all the more reason to impose on ourselves the discipline of peace, and deliberately and sternly to set ourselves to the task of cultivating citizenship'.[15]

This was a tone of voice that would often be listened to in later years, though by then after more beguiling introductions to his special kind of sermon, and equally it would arouse the indignation of the sort of people who had no taste for home truths. There was a question about it in the Victorian parliament: it was a slander upon Australians, criticism better confined to ourselves than sent abroad. The curious point about the short discussion was that both the questioner and the premier W. A. Watt, who defended Murdoch, were agreed on his high standing. After referring with regret to the university council's error of judgement in not appointing him to the chair of English, Watt added a strange sentence: 'I believe the time is not far distant when the reputation and ability of Mr Murdoch will be recognized in the highest possible way by his fellow country-men'.[16] A politician of some personal distinction, he was generally regarded at that time as the most likely successor to Deakin as leader of the Liberal party, though he had not yet entered federal politics. Perhaps he had been talking to Deakin himself about Murdoch, whom he knew personally, but what he said was certainly indiscreet, for he was presumably anticipating an appointment not yet determined.

When Murdoch at the age of thirty-seven 'lost his job' at the University of Melbourne, he would probably have known that something was happening about the foundation of a new university in Western Australia, but whether there would be a chair of English in it no one could yet know. Though he could earn his living as a journalist, under an editor who believed that 'we have not had a writer for the press in Australia during the last thirty years who has commanded so wide a circle of eager readers', he could not regard his banishment from academic life with equanimity. He had inherited the Scottish tradition of respect for learning; to have been a univer-sity professor would have been an appropriate vocation for a son of the manse, and in the eyes of relatives of his own generation. Violet Murdoch's family were intelligent and educated; her father, her brother William, her sister Annie, were gifted schoolteachers. The presence of Mr Walter Murdoch of the University of Melbourne on speech-days at Fintona, Annie Hughston's successful school in Camberwell, had added prestige to the occasions. In a circle of friends and acquaintances who were concerned with literature and education he had, by virtue of his position, been a leader.

The principal moves for a university in Perth had been made by Winthrop Hackett, the proprietor of the *West Australian* newspaper, a graduate of Trinity College, Dublin, who had spent the early years of his Australian career in Melbourne. In May 1910 a royal commission had recommended that a university be established, and early in 1911 a University Act had been passed. At that time Murdoch's concern had been with the chair in Melbourne; now he observed with some interest what was happening in Perth. Given the probable predominance of 'practical' interests in that remote city, the study of English literature was likely to be subsumed under modern languages or thriftily combined with some other field, perhaps history. But in June 1912 the first senate of the new university decided that English should be one of the original chairs. Murdoch did not hesitate about what he would do. He explained long afterwards why he was prepared to contemplate a move from Melbourne to the uttermost bounds of civilization in Australia:

> The gist of the story is that I suffered from an inferiority complex at a time when that evil condition hadn't yet received a name. I was very unsure of my capacity to teach students anything worth their learning; and I had a silly desire to show [Violet Murdoch] and her brothers and sisters that I had the goods. I suspected myself of being a nobody and I wanted a chair as evidence that I was a somebody. I am more sensible now, but it's easy to be sensible when one's old.[17]

His anxiety may explain one puzzling, even silly, move made at that time. He enquired whether the faculty of Arts in the University of Melbourne would permit the submission of his three books in place of a thesis for the degree of Doctor of Letters. Even by the standards of 1912 the request seems astonishing, for they were elementary textbooks. It would have made more sense to follow the suggestion of one indignant supporter in the fuss over the Melbourne chair, that he should have put together his 'Elzevir' articles as evidence of his fitness for a doctorate. The faculty very tactfully resolved, while recognizing the value of the books, that the terms of the university regulation required work of a different order.[18]

Murdoch had friends to press his claims. Deakin and others wrote to Hackett, or sent testimonials directly, and by late August Hackett had been so impressed by the opinions of 'a host of good judges in

Melbourne' that Murdoch's hopes must have been high if Deakin told him what he had heard. To support the formal application, Leeper, that advocate of Oxford and Cambridge men, wrote enthusiastically about Murdoch's exquisite taste, his rare gift of expression, his delightful humour; there were powerful testimonials from Tucker, Harrison Moore and Laurie, and from various members of the university council. Murdoch himself placed greatest stress on the fact that for years he had actually performed the work of the professor of English in Melbourne, and he added that his narrow failure to obtain the chair in Melbourne was 'now generally acknowledged ['assumed' would have been more accurate] to have been due to the fact that [he] was an Australian graduate'.

Applications in England were still being considered by a London committee as late as November. But on 21 December the senate of the University of Western Australia met to appoint its first six professors. By 13 votes to 2 Walter Murdoch, M.A., was elected to the chair of English. The press had the news before Murdoch received his telegram. The Christmas vacation had begun; it must have been Monday 23 December 1912 when the daily help 'Mrs Rose came and told us, before we were up, that we were going to Perth'.[19]

At his seaside cottage Deakin, 'dead beat . . . tired out', was bracing himself to tell his family that he must resign from parliament immediately if he were to save some fragments of his disintegrating memory, but there was no reflection of this mood in the letter that closes our account of Murdoch's life in Melbourne:

> Congratulations of course—but am very sorry Melbourne is going to lose you—Still under the conditions no friend would keep you here if he could—The West is fortunate & will be easily conquered if you will only 'let yourself go' to the students as you can very easily if you put your modesty out of Court—There is no room for it when poetry or true literature are afoot & still less when they are a-wing—You will have more leisure to take your own way & I am sure it will be a highway—you will make it one for many others in the more familiar sense—Again very really selfishly sorry that you are to flit so far & yet again! 'Io Paean'!! that at last you have found your Kingdom.
>
> No reply[20]

5

PROFESSOR OF ENGLISH

AFTER THE EFFORTS of private citizens had secured a legal blessing and some certainty about the necessary funds, the found-
ing of a university in those days was only a matter
of the appointment of the first teachers. By Christmas 1912 the first
six professors of the University of Western Australia were chosen:
the professor of history and economics was named early in January
1913 and the professor of agriculture at the end of May. The telegram to Murdoch had asked him when he could begin duty; on
Christmas Eve he replied that he could begin early in February. No
preliminary year or more of academic planning; no earnest and
endless meetings about the interrelationship of 'disciplines'; no
preparation of eloquent brochures about educational aims. A lay
body, the interim 'senate', had determined what the first fields of
study should be; it remained only for the teachers to arrive and to
begin at once to teach. Of course they would need some place in
which to teach, and some students as an audience. But lectures did
in fact start in March 1913, at the beginning of the normal Australian academic year.

In the midst of his hurry Murdoch, with his family, was able to pay
a last visit to Deakin at the seaside; he would see him once again, but
it would not be the Deakin he had known. The last of the Elzevir
articles to be written from Melbourne, appropriately enough a review
of his friend Bernard O'Dowd's poem 'The Bush', appeared on 25
January 1913. On the same day some sixty friends gave a dinner in his
honour at Scott's Hotel, price 7s 6d, wines extra. Some of their names

reflect what he was leaving behind—friendship, literature, the company of interesting and able men like Harrison Moore, Henry Laurie, Frederic Eggleston, Archibald Strong. Cunningham, the editor of the *Argus*, presided; Frank Tate, the great man of state education, proposed 'Success to the Perth University' in the presence of its chancellor, for Hackett was visiting Melbourne. Within the week, on board the *Omrah*, Murdoch and his family were proceeding smoothly across the Bight in company with a party of Labor politicians including Andrew Fisher, the prime minister, who were to attend the turning of the first sod of the transcontinental railway from Kalgoorlie to Port Augusta. They would soon be returning to the 'East', and to the atmosphere of Parliament House in Melbourne, while Murdoch would be beginning to learn what the term 'Eastern Stater' meant to Western Australians. On 12 February he formally reported his arrival in Perth and his ability to take up his professorial duties immediately.

At thirty-eight, Murdoch stood between the oldest of the original professors, the chemist N. T. M. Wilsmore who was forty-nine, and the youngest, the historian and economist Edward Shann, who was twenty-eight. They seemed to him 'a very decent lot'; those were early days. Hackett gave them a reception, and they heard the great Sir John Forrest tell them that while he welcomed them personally, their university was in his opinion many years before its time. 'Everything is chaos to date', wrote Murdoch ten days after his arrival, 'and we find it exceedingly difficult to get anything carried through the numerous boards and committees and subcommittees and other lethargic bodies which stand in the way'.[1] Thus do universities begin, and thus do they continue.

Murdoch was to be associated with the University of Western Australia for well over fifty years, as one of its first professors, as chancellor, and in a prolonged and alert old age as a kind of patriarch emeritus. The history of the university itself in this period has been written by his colleague Fred Alexander in almost unexampled detail;* it would be pretentious to attempt to encapsulate it in a memoir of one of its first professors. Moreover, Murdoch's death in 1970 meant to three overlapping groups of Australians, apart from

---

* Alexander's *Campus at Crawley* (Melbourne 1963) may well be the most thorough and detailed history of the first half-century of a 'minor' university ever written. It is a fascinating record to anyone like the present writer, who was a student and graduate of the University of Western Australia at a time when many of the people originally concerned in its foundation, government or academic work were still alive and active. I have myself followed Alexander's tracks through the university records, so far as they concern Murdoch directly, but much that I take for granted was unknown or forgotten until Alexander recovered it and set it out in an orderly narrative.

his family and personal friends, that what had seemed to be a fixed feature of their various worlds had vanished. These groups were his students and colleagues at the university, the people of Western Australia in general, and the host of his readers throughout the continent. If they reflect aspects of his life and work which in fact were intermingled, it will be useful, and indeed almost necessary in any account of his long life, to disentangle them to some extent. I present him here as a grave and responsible figure, the professor of English in the University of Western Australia. But first let us see him and his family settled in the pleasant city of Perth.

They lived first at Mosman Park, towards the coast, in a big old stone house with verandahs and a large garden, and Murdoch would travel to Perth by train. When that house was sold to the Defence Department in 1916 for use as a hospital, they went temporarily to Subiaco, nearer the city, until they moved in 1919 into the new house which they had decided to build in South Perth, a suburban peninsula almost dividing the two extensive lake-like stretches of the Swan River known as Perth and Melville Waters. The brick, red-tiled house, with a good deal of timber panelling in the interior, overlooked Perth Water to the north, the ground falling steeply down to the water-level. Murdoch's study, lined with full bookcases to the ceiling—he was a competent amateur carpenter—looked south, along a gravelled drive bordering a tennis court, now the site of a pleasant 'wilderness' of shrubs and trees. It was as well, for the view to the north, across the water, was superb and distracting. When the house was first built, there was a verandah on the river side, but about 1930 this was partly dismantled, and one large picture window inserted in the long, rather narrow sitting-room behind it. The view of the mile-wide river, and beyond it the changing skyline of Perth, became part of the legend of Murdoch to those who made their way to see him for some forty years. The house was named Blithedale, after Hawthorne's novel which was much in Murdoch's mind at that time. It stood and stands (1976) in what was then called Suburban road, to the amusement of local people who in the 1920s read Murdoch's fierce denunciation of the 'suburban spirit . . . the everlasting enemy'. Across that road was the fence of the Zoological Gardens, 'the Zoo', where at weekends the crowds came from Perth, disturbing the village calm of South Perth, otherwise unbroken except for the occasional roar of a lion, the howls of hyenas at feeding time, or the high melancholy calls of flamingos on moonlit nights.

They may well have chosen South Perth on the recommendation of Murdoch's colleague, Shann, who was already established there. It was a water-surrounded, village-like oasis, then reached from Perth only by a roundabout journey by road or by ferry across the river, for the bridge that was to span 'the Narrows' where the peninsula approached most nearly the city side of the river was far in the future, and South Perth's isolation protected it from the hazards of traffic and the greed of developers. Yet it was then close to the university on its original site in central Perth. A few minutes' walk to the ferry, a pleasant ten minutes on the water, another easy walk to the university shacks (I cannot say buildings): there was much to be said for living in Perth—that is, until one contemplated the university itself.

Although it was some six years after their arrival before the family settled in South Perth, I have looked ahead so that we may see Murdoch as he always seemed to have been as the generations passed, a Western Australian known to all Australia, living unostentatiously in a quiet suburb, a part of the Western Australian scene. But he had not easily been reconciled to that lot. For years he still looked back with nostalgia to Melbourne, where he had grown to maturity and where his talents had made him someone; in Perth, as a professor in a small community, he was someone by definition, whether or not he exercised his talents, and that was not the same thing. Violet Murdoch must have known this, but the two children were growing up contented in their new environment, and their youngest and last child Anne, born in 1916, knew no other.

A week or so after his arrival in February 1913 Murdoch wrote to Herbert Brookes from a house in Claremont, near the river: 'We are living in the most beautiful place we have ever seen. I am writing at an open window looking out at a wonderful stretch of blue water, with twenty yachts in view, all moving gently before the lightest of cool breezes'. His next letter to Brookes was written nine months later from 'The University, Perth'.[2] But where and what was that?

Even to the untravelled students of 1913 'The University' must have seemed an odd contrast to the dreaming spires that the word invoked. A few one storey weatherboard buildings had hastily been erected on a site within a few hundred yards of the elegant Town Hall. Others, weatherboard or galvanized iron, were to come in time, some transported from the once-busy scenes of decaying goldfields. It was a slum, a shanty-town set down in the midst of a small city, the more depressing because a stone's throw away, across St Georges Terrace, were the trees and lawns surrounding the pleasant Government House. A rough gravel path, muddy in winter, traversed the site from the tin shed at one end which comprised the Men's Common Room to the tin shed at the other which comprised the Women's Common Room. The scene, as Murdoch wrote, was 'unspeakably the reverse of impressive'. Students who knew Tin Pot Alley in its ghastly

University of Western Australia
Tin Pot Alley, about 1929

prime in the 1920s were inclined in their later years to talk about it with a kind of masochistic affection, but if they had once been joyful there, it was because they were then young. They had no standards of comparison; their teachers, who did, were to remain for nearly twenty years in a setting that seemed to have been devised for the shooting of the walk down the street at the end of a cheap Western.

Buildings are not everything when one thinks of universities, but they are a good deal. On the fiftieth anniversary of the opening of the university, Murdoch reminded those who now worked and played in the most beautiful campus in Australia that somehow the teachers and students of the early years had enjoyed their task, that amid their 'squalid huddle' they had found the realities of university education. So they had; as one of the last generation to know 'Irwin Street', I can testify to it. But when the move came at the end of 1930 to the noble buildings at Crawley on the banks of the Swan River which Hackett's legacy of his residuary estate had unexpectedly made possible, no tears were shed, no wakes were held in Tin Pot Alley. We need not recall here the sometimes passionate arguments of the early years about possible sites for a real university. As the trees grew and the lawns spread around the buildings at Crawley it was difficult to suppose that anyone had ever thought of the university as being elsewhere. But if we are to see Murdoch in the setting of most of his time as professor of English, we must recall his own description of 1920: 'Our University, so far as its outward body is concerned, is a collection of weatherboard and corrugated iron structures, of various shapes and sizes and degrees of ugliness which appear to have some-how got themselves huddled together by some queer agglutinative process, without conscious plan or idea'.[3]

Towards the end of his life Murdoch said that academically he had been the least distinguished of the original band of eight professors. It is true that among them his colleagues had higher degrees, or records of research, or more varied experience than he, but the question would be what they would make of these formal assets in the first generation of the most remote of Australian universities. Though to students they loomed larger in that small community than the most eminent of their counterparts did to undergraduates in large and famous foundations, most of them must have known that Western Australia was then no place in which to enhance their professional reputations. Some of them accepted the situation with more equanimity than others.

Murdoch's closest friend among them was Hubert Whitfeld, the engineer who in 1927 became the first permanent vice-chancellor, a man 'entirely honest, unpretentious and human', a former student of

University of Western Australia
Two views, 1931

classics whose ideals were drawn from the dialogues of Plato, which he was apt to quote to laymen on the university senate who were aware only that it was all Greek to them. Wilsmore, the chemist, probably the ablest of them in his vocation, was to Murdoch 'shy, sensitive, encyclopaedic in his learning, caustic in his wit, intolerant of humbug, impatient of the second-rate, shunning publicity, inflexible and austere in manner, but genial and friendly when you knew him'. The words were carefully chosen; they almost automatically suggested their opposites, which he would have applied to some of his other colleagues from time to time. Third among the men who remained especially in his memory was Shann, the economist and historian, 'young and alive to the finger-tips, witty, nimble-minded, resourceful in argument, eager for the truth'. He was writing in 1947, a dozen years after Shann's too early death. They had differed publicly on various matters, especially when the tone of Murdoch's often teasing scepticism about economics and economists (he would not have expressed any views about chemistry) became serious, even bitter, during the depression years, and might have been assumed by some to be directed at Shann personally. Too late, for Shann's death in 1935 was sudden and unforeseen. Murdoch regretted that Shann himself might have shared that impression, for it was true that he had never concealed his own distaste for the circles of power in which Shann moved after governments and banks began to call in the economists to aid them. 'I seem rather old to be learning lessons', he wrote to me at the time, 'but Shann's death has taught me one; you don't realize how much affection you have for a man until he has gone where you have no chance of telling him'.[4]

If we know little, except by inference, of what Murdoch's senior colleagues thought of him, there is unanimity among those who recalled their experiences as young lecturers, in a university so small that the most junior lecturer might find himself temporarily a member of the professorial board as the sole representative of his field of study. As venerable septuagenarians or octogenarians, men such as Alexander, Fox and Shearer who remained to spend their academic careers in Perth, or Hancock and Arrousseau who moved elsewhere, agreed about Murdoch as they had known him in the early 1920s. They remembered him as the special friend, and if need be advocate, of the young teachers, quietly helpful, courteously treating them as equals in a hierarchical society, a conciliator in the meetings where academics are likely to make great issues out of small matters, 'a reassuring person to have about'. He remained until he retired, and indeed beyond then, the particular champion of juniors with real or imaginary grievances; he never believed that even an exasperating personality was a sufficient excuse for what he took to be injustice. But those who knew him in his later years, including some of the young lecturers now seniors themselves, were not so readily inclined to stress his role as a conciliator. A quick wit cannot always restrain itself, most meetings *are* boring, and in time most agenda are *déjà vu*. Criticism can become a kind of game. Alexander has described feelingly what it was like to see a set of academic proposals sunk without trace by Murdoch's verbal torpedoes. There was one layman, a member of the senate, who would never learn that it was impossible to win in verbal controversy with Murdoch. Some of their exchanges in the press during the 1930s have passages of high comedy, yet they read a little sadly as the decent but damaged boxer staggers up for further punishment. Though Murdoch was not an indiscriminate shooter, he could sometimes be tempted by the solemnity of a critic into demonstrating his skill. His irony was generally provoked when he had some cause of his own to defend or expound; he was by nature a peaceful animal, but when attacked he defended himself.

Some academics like administration and meetings; a few are sincere when they say they do not. In a small university the seniors had little choice; decisions had to be made, and there was no one else to make them. So they must meet about large and small affairs.

> You get a queer impression of pettiness [wrote Murdoch in 1928] when you come back to this little university and its politics after being out in the world . . . it's like looking into a glass case in which a lot of insects are stinging one another, and going away and finding them still at it hammer and tongs. The damnable thing is that I'll be going back to committee meetings next week and will soon be in the glass case myself—you get immersed in the paltry business. 'God forgive us all' is what I feel inclined to say after meetings.[5]

Murdoch had recently returned from a year's leave in Europe and was not the first or the last to write or think in that vein. But the fact was, as he knew very well, that he could not with a clear conscience avoid meetings. There were too few academics for any one of them to leave committee work entirely to those who liked it, and besides, one's 'subject' might be unrepresented, or (on the senate) academic matters might be decided entirely by a body of butchers, bakers and candlestick makers. So, grumbling, he took his share of committee work, and his turn at various times as dean of Arts, or chairman of the professorial board, or vice-chancellor in the years before 1927 when Whitfeld was appointed permanently to that office. He had no obligation, however, except during his two years as vice-chancellor, to sit on the senate. That he did so from 1916 to the end of his academic career in 1939, and after his retirement until 1948, could indicate a peculiar humility in accepting the opinion of others that his presence there was essential, or it could indicate that he already held the same opinion. Certainly some of his colleagues, and all students, felt that so long as he was among the curious group who governed their destinies, matters important to them would not be decided by a Higher Power as a result of deliberate misrepresentation or mere misunderstanding, at any rate without protest.

When he arrived in 1913, Murdoch said the right things to the reporter from Hackett's newspaper, the *West Australian*. Upon the work of the first professors would tradition be based. 'Western Australia has to decide whether she is to have a real University or just a sort of glorified technical school ... the university idea should be insisted upon from the very start ... on our work our status will depend'. It would be a vital mistake to begin with too low a standard. Murdoch looked back to the University of Melbourne where the 'Science branches had grabbed all the money'; that, he believed, would not happen in Perth. He saw his own duty as the spreading of a knowledge and love of literature, combined with teaching the use of the English language: 'there is no such deadly enemy to slovenly thought as the correct use of language'. He would even like to see English made a compulsory subject in the science course; the benefits of 'clear, lucid, forceful, accurate expression' were inestimable. He said a good deal more about entrance standards, and relations between the university and the schools, but his main theme, in various forms, was a kind of motto: 'a love of reading and a capacity for clear expression'.[6]

He very naturally began with courses in English much like those he had offered in Melbourne, and in form they did not, indeed could not, vary much over the years, though their contents, the texts and writers particularly to be studied, could change from time to time. One man, later assisted by a a lecturer, was necessarily in such a university constrained to offer general 'survey' courses covering fairly long periods if he were to feel, as Murdoch did, that his students should emerge with some experience of the range and richness of English literature, so that (he hoped) they would not stop reading when they graduated. In his time the courses did not go beyond the end of the nineteenth century, except that in his last years, when he had partly retired from teaching, a lecturer was able to introduce 'modern' poetry and 'practical criticism' in the mode of the 1930s.

English composition and expression were taken seriously and expounded, with awful examples of their abuse, in introductory lectures. Murdoch's aim, as one pupil interpreted it, was to induce students 'to seek purity of diction and simplicity of style, flexibility of thought but exactitude of expression'. Something did stick. It is not likely that a Murdoch man would have written the sentences that his teacher once quoted from a published legal opinion:

> The law, however, does not distinguish, for instance, between the case of a burglar who attempts to stifle the screams of the occupier by putting his hand over his mouth (and who as a result dies because of his condition) and the person who, with the intention of inflicting grievous bodily harm, unintentionally kills that person. Both are guilty of murder.

'Surely not', said Murdoch. 'The burglar is obviously guilty of suicide . . . We then pass from the unfortunate burglar to "the person who kills that person". What person?' To those whose sentences in class essays or formal memoranda or public statements were disdainfully examined as if they were stinking fish, it was irritating that his own prose did exemplify his own rules; one could not reply in kind. But he sometimes caught himself out. He wrote to me on a Christmas Day:

> Your letter—received yesterday—gives me an excuse for sending you and yours all the good wishes appropriate to the day. If you ask me why this should need an excuse, I can only reply in the words of a classical anecdote I seem to remember, 'There you 'ave me.' Obviously I wrote 'excuse' because the right word didn't come into what now tries to do duty for me as a mind. This is senility.[7]

Murdoch's lectures were remembered for what they tried to convey rather than for their manner. There were no musical overtones to his voice, and he gave rather monotonous emphasis, at regular intervals, to the principal word of a phrase or sentence. As a formal speaker he was at his best on special occasions, as a guest at meetings of societies or at dinners, where his mastery of a dead-pan manner kept his audiences in a state of expectation, or on more serious occasions, when his deep feelings were aroused, and personal involvement gave impressiveness to his emphases. But in mere exposition his performance was uneven, at least by his middle years: with a favourite writer his own evident interest was stimulating; with one whom he discussed as a matter of duty the lecture could be as flat as he felt the subject to be, but some unevenness is almost inherent in the nature of general survey courses. What most students gained from his lectures over the years was the impression that literature was there to be enjoyed, where 'enjoyment' could range from good fun to the sombre aesthetic experience of tragedy. One of his earlier Western Australian students wrote of his lectures as 'characterised by a strong sense of an appreciation of literature that was never subordinate to scholarship'—an odd but deliberate description. Murdoch had sufficient scholarship as students understood that term, but he did not assume that they were concerned with English literature so that they might in future write footnotes about it. His job was to expose to them the range and variety of books that they might wish to go on reading.

When survey courses went out of fashion, and there were sufficient experts, or 'specialists' as Murdoch called them, in university departments to allow more intense concentration on narrower fields, when English literature became a 'discipline' rather than a subject, there were no doubt both gains and losses. There is little or no logic in direct comparisons, for the students who alone could make a real comparison are not the same students. One student of the old regime can only say, after many years among those of later generations, that he is grateful for two features of the old courses which appear largely to have disappeared from the contemporary treatment of English literature. The first was the sampling of several centuries of literature, giving a sense both of continuity and of the different tones of different periods, which enriched many aspects of other historical studies. The second was the necessary reading of some of the best of English non-fictional prose, other than that of the critics, Sidney, Dryden, Johnson, Coleridge, Lamb, Arnold, which we too read. It would never have occurred to Murdoch that there could be a serious study of English literature, continued over several years, in which students had no experience of the use of the English language in exposition, argument, description, denunciation, satire, reflection . . . , or that they could claim to be educated if they had not read the *Areopagitica* of Milton.

By my time, about 1930, he was at his best in tutorial classes, where students' papers or discussion of them would provoke his own comment and his observations on life and literature in general, where his expression of bemused astonishment could cause eloquent prose suddenly to dissolve into fine writing, and where the stumbler would came to know the difference between a gentle irony which did not hurt and the sarcasm he sometimes met from some others among his teachers. Murdoch's lecturing however was becoming something of a routine duty. It did not reflect the more recent literary criticism which the more adventurous students were reading, and they would have welcomed some discussion of contemporary or near-contemporary writing. They were somewhat disappointed, too, with the brevity of his comments on the essays over which they had sweated. Edward Shann would fill the margins of essays with critical comments in his neat printing script, Fred Alexander, the historian, would fill a page in his execrable handwriting, but on one of my early essays Murdoch simply wrote near the beginning, 'do not use stereotyped phrases, like "crowded years", "excruciating pain" ', which was salutary, and a comment at the end, 'Excellent', which was gratifying. I had hoped, however, not for more detailed criticism, but for more detailed praise. It was perhaps otherwise with my contemporary Alexandra Darker, who wanted to *write* and expected constructive criticism. Maybe Murdoch knew his students, and knew that all that some of them needed was formal recognition of their dazzling talents. But Alexandra Darker's does seem to be the simpler explanation, that when it came to marking students' essays, Murdoch had by our time grown, if not lazy, at any rate bored.

Students in the early years saw Murdoch as a somewhat drooping figure, brown-haired but with a moustache more distinctly 'red'. In the 1920s he was turning grey. Though still in his fifties, he was generally referred to as 'Old Murdie', partly because all grey-haired men seem old to undergraduates, and partly to express a certain pride of possession in 'Weary Wallie', the professor who slouched along in academic procession as if he were not particularly impressed by pomp and ceremony. He did not ordinarily wear spectacles in those days, as photographs of the period testify; the venerable figure with eyes twinkling over his spectacles came later. One of his earliest students, recalling him as he was in 1915, remembered that he already had a special place in the esteem of undergraduates because they felt that he understood and sympathized with their aspirations. In his old age some of his readers may have thought that his frequent championship of youth, and of youthful ideas which challenged established conventions, was something of a pose, just old Murdoch being provocative. It was not so.

In the first innocent generation, and in their unlovely home, students found something that bound them together in university songs, self-encouraging or satirical, as their fellows in other Australian universities had done. Some were modifications of songs from Sydney, probably suggested by Whitfeld. Others, and the best of them because the words were original and their application local, were written at various times by Murdoch, with his deft pen for light verse. One was a kind of university, or at least undergraduate, anthem to the tune of 'Gaudeamus igitur':

> Sing we now our 'Varsity,
>   Youngest Alma Mater;
> Though she's neither old nor hoary,
> And her name's unknown to story
>   She'll be famous later.

And so on. In 1928 half a dozen students, including Leslie Rees, were invited for what Murdoch calls 'an unknown purpose' to an evening at his house. It went well, Murdoch reported to his daughter Catherine. 'I had written English words for "Giovinezza", and also for "The Lass of Richmond Hill", and invited them to send a team over here to practise them . . . they sang the songs over and over again till I was sorry I had written them, but "Giovinezza" went with a great swing.' So it did on occasions when it was sung by several hundred undergraduates:

> Students all, of pattern various,
>   Joined we are and joined forever,
> Some are dismal, some hilarious,
>   All are yoked in one endeavour.
> In our gravity and jesting,
> In our work and play and resting,
> Alma Mater sends us questing—
>   Seekers of the best are we.
>
> Follow after, follow after,
>   Maids and men with song and laughter,
> To the land of fair tomorrow
>   And the great days yet to be.

The fact that undergraduates of all kinds—engineers, scientists, even Arts students—did once enjoy belting out these words, that they did not find them entirely ridiculous, is a reminder that any attempt to recover the past requires imaginative sympathy as well as documents. None of us, I think, realized that Murdoch, recently returned from Italy with an intense loathing of Mussolini's fascism, had seen no reason why the devil should have all the good tunes.

The idea of the 'Richmond Hill' song probably came from an essay Murdoch had once written, 'On Sitting Still':

> Who will may spoil his life with toil,
>   We know a better way;
> We never burn the midnight oil,
>   Nor wear our brains away.
> Our Chancellor, whose word is law,
>   Would earn our right good will,
> If he would please to grant degrees
>   For simply sitting still.
>
> For merely sitting still,
> Devoutly sitting still,
> If he would please to grant degrees,
>   For simply sitting still.

Undergraduates tended to regard Murdoch with general approval because they felt vaguely that he was on their side in life. Although in most material respects they had more reasons for protest about the world than their children and grandchildren were to have, they did not know it; only occasionally, and then rather as a question of high and somewhat solemn 'principle' than as a demand for 'rights' did they clash with those set in authority over them. It is odd to reflect that I can still feel resentment against what we took to be the underhand dealings of one of Murdoch's colleagues who misrepresented us in high places. The records show that it was Murdoch who restrained the important senators who, accepting the misrepresentation, would instantly have shown students where authority lay, and it was he who successfully persuaded the senate that the students' president—at that time one H. C. Coombs—should be invited to attend its meetings. More generally—for such incidents were rare—students saw Murdoch as a man not given to deference. That was no doubt true of most of his colleagues, certainly of Wilsmore. But Wilsmore did not write and speak in public; Murdoch did, and he could speak as students themselves would like to have spoken about humbug, pretentiousness, examples of inspissated stupidity in public life. When his ironies most displeased their elders, students liked him most.

What could we say when an eminent political figure proposed in 1931 that as an economy measure the university grant should be discontinued and the state secondary schools, from which many of us came, should be closed? Murdoch found words for us. In an article for the *West Australian*, with the simple title 'A Bright Idea', he proposed to give that legislative councillor 'a bit of my mind, such as it is'.

> 'Women and children last!' This, as all the world knows, is the cry of all true British hearts when the ship is sinking and there are not enough lifeboats to go round. And the sound practical man, with no sentimental nonsense about him, almost invariably adds, 'Me first!'
>
> In the same gallant spirit, at this moment of economic shipwreck, when every sound practical man is taxing his wits to find some way of making somebody else bear the brunt of the disaster, a number of distracted passengers have hit on the happy idea of making the younger generation suffer for the bad pilotage which has brought us on the rocks . . .
>
> The question . . . concerns the welfare and honour of our country. The honour—because to starve or stunt the minds of the rising generation seems to me the worst kind of default. We talk a good deal about the rights of bond-holders and others; are we to ignore what every civilized country now regards as the indisputable right of every child to grow to its full mental stature? What is the use of

talking grandly about Australia meeting all her obligations if we are going to shirk this elementary obligation—if we agree to listen to the mean suggestion that we shall bilk the young generation of its undeniable heritage? There is no crime more cowardly than the crime of robbing children. We can sink into no lower slough of dishonour than this into which [he] invites us to descend—this of making our young people pay, now and all their lives long, the price of our own follies . . .

He was, so far, simply getting into his stride.

In 1934, at his own request, Murdoch was relieved of evening lectures at some loss of salary; and by 1937 he was talking about premature retirement: 'I have an idea (possibly fallacious)', he wrote to Whitfeld, 'that I can be of more use to Australia, in the not very many years of possible usefulness that remain to me, in other ways than by correcting essays and conducting tutorial classes.' On Whitfeld's urging, he agreed to remain for a while, with reduced duties and salary, but he stressed that the senate must be clear that it really wanted him to stay before it approved such an arrangement:

> I am not prepared to stay on and be an incumbrance to the University because the Senate has a kindly feeling towards an old horse who has worked for it between the shafts for a number of years. You and I know of universities which have suffered from persons who have occupied professorial chairs after they have ceased to be really fit for them and even after senility has set in. I have a horror of being an aged limpet.[8]

When he did decide to retire at the end of 1939, the year in which he reached the age of sixty-five, he could have stayed on for some years if he had wished to do so, for the senate would certainly have approved this course as it did for some others among the first professors. But, he wrote at the time, 'I am retiring because I have lost any driving force I ever had as a teacher.' For many years he had had a good deal, but his teaching of English was not all that he had done towards the making of a university. Consider one example of an initiative which some of his colleagues would have said was typically Murdochian—that is, it was good for others but happened also to reflect his own interests.

W.M. to Catherine Murdoch (King), 29 July 1928
> I am starting an elementary class in Italian this week. I put up a notice on my lecture-room door asking for names of those who wanted to learn. I expected [a few] to join. To my surprise I found the paper next day covered with names, but when I examined the names I found some surprising ones—e.g. Mussolini, Toti dal Monte, Fisha da Cheap, Staka da Oyst, Garibaldi, Kissa da Gurl,

Maria Spaghetti, & others. But about 40 names were put down seriously before these ribaldries began.

In that irreverent atmosphere began a pioneer venture in the teaching of Italian, long before the inflow of Italian immigrants after the war made the comparative neglect of that language and its literature in Australian universities something of a scandal. Murdoch's own Italian had been acquired after his university days. He was often to argue, to the irritation of 'language' teachers who then were invariably teachers of French (and occasionally German) that Italian should have preference over French if there had to be a choice. It was easier to learn, and to speak, it gave access to a great literature, and few children derived much advantage from the French they had studied at school. In 1929 he was able to secure a small sum from the university to employ a part-time, temporary teacher for 'Elementary Italian', he nursed the subject through the vicissitudes of the depression by appealing for voluntary subscriptions, and his baby survived until in the 1960s the university was at last prepared to recognize that one of the world's great languages was worthy of a permanent and adequate establishment.

The temporary teacher was also a friend. Francisco Vanzetti had come to Western Australia in the 1890s from the neighbourhood of Florence, with some training in architecture but no academic qualifications. His career had been varied—draftsman, clerk, struggling farmer in the hard years of drought and then excessive rain after 1913, adviser in the Agricultural Department, an able writer on farming methods whose theory was better than his practice. At some time in the mid-1920s he heard Murdoch lecture on Florence; much impressed, he spoke to him afterwards, and they became friends.

When Murdoch secured Vanzetti's appointment at the university in 1929, there may have been some hostile comment by those of his colleagues who knew something about his gentle methods of getting his way. But in fact as they or their successors found for more than thirty years, the Italian lecturer was a widely cultivated man with the inestimable advantage (as it was put when he was awarded an honorary degree in 1962) of speaking 'both his own beautiful language and the language of his adoption with perfect mastery'. Before long there was a weekly 'day' when Vanzetti would visit Murdoch in South Perth. At first they would talk Italian and English alternately, and in the later period of their twenty years' 'tutorial' would read Dante together, now for enjoyment rather than instruction.[9]

In January 1931 Murdoch told Herbert Brookes that he was busy translating into English an Italian book on Socrates and would send a copy when it was published. Later that year he wrote for the *Argus* a glowing account of the wise and witty writings of Alfredo Panzini, praising especially his 'romance' *Santippe*, which Australian readers could not enjoy because they had not learned Italian. Whether this was a preliminary 'puff', or a regretful glance at a labour performed in vain, I do not know. At any rate the translation, though completed and prepared for publication, never appeared. Evidently a product of those regular meetings with Vanzetti, it remains today in the Murdoch Papers as a fair copy, ready for the press.[10]

I propose to say nothing more in detail about Murdoch's purely academic career, his formal professional occupation for all but one of the years since 1903. There is more about it in Fred Alexander's book, in the university archives and in student publications over the years, and more still in the written recollections of old students and colleagues. He was a good academic man for the time, the place and the circumstances, a 'figure' in the university despite his ostentatious lack of bustling energy or flamboyance, and he will be seen by historians of local cultural history as an important and civilizing influence in the arid intellectual environment to which he came in 1913. But this is not why 'Professor Murdoch' came to be known throughout Australia.

If years were to pass before Murdoch could contentedly accept his lot in Western Australia, it would nevertheless be misleading to present him as an academic in the mould of a sterner generation, a scholar by inclination, frustrated in the pursuit of his true vocation by poverty of resources and impossible distances from other men of the kind, as perhaps his colleague Wilsmore was. Murdoch, if we are to believe him, did once 'make a feeble attempt to become a specialist'. He thought there was a place for a concise, complete and accurate book on the sources of Shakespeare's plays. In London (this must have been in 1927) he consulted a friendly publisher.

> He knew [wrote Murdoch] of various scholars who were working on the same subject; he showed me that if I were to do the desirable research I should have to live for a year within walking distance of the British Museum; and finally, most useful of all, he counselled me to ask myself if I were sure the subject mattered very much; would any living soul be the happier for knowing exactly where Shakespeare found the plot of his worst play? I had to admit that the absence of my book wouldn't eclipse the gaiety of nations.[11]

So, Murdoch says, he had to accept his lot as a 'Professor of Things in General', like Carlyle's Teufelsdröckh.

This may well be true exactly as he relates it, though I suspect that his idea was to produce a useful, lucid textbook for university classes, a collation of work on the subject already in print, rather than to undertake the kind of original research which the publisher's man seems to have assumed that he meant. By 1927 he was as deeply involved in weekly journalism as he had been in the old days of Elzevir of the *Argus*, and he must have known that he did this kind of thing too well, that he valued it too much as an educational pulpit, to exchange it for long periods in research libraries. If a textbook on Shakespeare's sources were to be done, 'twere well that 'twere done quickly. What a relief to be allowed to go on enjoying books and enjoying writing!

Yet no pupil of Murdoch's should end on this note even a brief impression of him as an academic, as a professor paid to study and to teach English literature in the first generation of a new university. It would be a note not merely ungrateful but false. He earned his salary. On that particular subject, for example, he knew and knew well what scholars, up to his time, had discovered or conjectured about the sources of Shakespeare's plays, as the notes to his editions of some of them sufficiently demonstrate. If his circumstances in Perth and his own temperament and interests meant that he was happy to be relieved of the burden of 'specialism', he was soaked in his English literature. I have known a good many literary scholars; some (as Murdoch might have said) have even been my friends. My impression, based rather on examination of the well-worn books in his own large library than on the unsophisticated impressions of an undergraduate, is that in English literature in general, from Chaucer to Conrad, he was as at least as widely read as the 'specialists', and in some fields—for example, the nineteenth-century novel—more deeply read than most of them. The newly founded university, in its relatively raw and utterly isolated community, had been fortunate in its choice of the first professor of English literature. It had appointed, not a second-class scholar, but a first-class man of letters.

6

WRITING THE 'SKETCH'

ONCE THEY WERE settled in the red-tiled villa in South Perth, Walter and Violet Murdoch and their children provided as good an example of the Australian suburban family as one could find, a fact which the enemy of 'the suburban spirit' appreciated very well. The children, before their marriages, lived at home or travelled with their parents when Murdoch had sabbatical leave from the university. When they were separated by distance, their father's letters, with amusing gossip about domestic happenings, private jokes and serious talk, came to them week by week. They probably thought that all fathers wrote to their children like that, in the same fluent prose, and with the same care to write letters to them as individuals with their own interests and characters.

From all accounts, Violet would have given 'home duties' as her occupation without smouldering resentment. 'Home' meant husband, children, garden, as well as housework and, like the wives of most professional men before 1939, she generally had some domestic assistance. She was the kind of employer with whom a maid would stay for years and be married 'from the house'. In Melbourne the Murdochs had had many visitors, for they lived in 'family country', and academic and literary friends would call at weekends. In Perth Violet had more formal duties in this respect. Until World War II the mail-steamers on the Suez route arrived at Fremantle without fail, coming and going once a week. Visitors to Australia almost necessarily saw something of Perth in the days before the regular air routes to Europe took them directly to or from the Eastern States, and

78

'university wives' almost necessarily came in for a good deal of entertaining. Violet was a good hostess, competent, friendly, but not over-impressed by literary or artistic reputations. In her common-sense way she was apt to prick bubbles of pretension, even those blown by her husband. Outside her 'home duties' she had, it seems, an enduring concern to be useful. If there were illness or trouble of some kind in a family, a young university wife would find her at the door with practical offers of help, and she was closely concerned for many years in active work for kindergarten and other child-care movements.

To Murdoch she was the touchstone for his writing. He sought her opinion on his articles before they were sent in, and valued her not always flattering comments, perhaps (some thought) too highly. Likewise he relied upon her in practical affairs, though the task of making him look relatively neat and respectable, as professors were supposed to be in those days, must sorely have tried her patience. She saw to it, at least, that he observed the social proprieties. Thus he wrote in some shame to explain to his daughter Catherine, who had become engaged in England, that her mother had returned from an outing just in time to prevent his committing a grave solecism. He had written a letter to her fiancé, but 'luckily' had not yet posted it, since, as he was very firmly told, 'the young man has to write first to his prospective father-in-law, who then may reply'.

It is at least tactful for a writer to dedicate one of his books to his wife, but some may feel that the dedication of the first of Murdoch's collections of essays, 'To V.C.M. "Till a' the seas gang dry, my dear." ', would have been more dignified if he had omitted the quotation. He never did care much for his dignity. His rule for writing was 'say what you mean, and say it clearly, precisely, and unambiguously'. In this case, for a Scot brought up on Burns, what he wanted to say had already been said, and there was no reason why he should try to improve on it.

Their only son William (Will) had first tried his hand at journalism about the time (1919) that his father was resuming his own regular writing for the *Argus*. After some early setbacks Will had secured for himself the position with the *West Australian* which he held throughout his life. He made himself into a good professional journalist who could turn his hand to most tasks required of a pressman. With his diverse interests he wrote frequently, under various pseudonyms, for the literary page of his paper. From his childhood he had been plagued by ill-health, and in his thirties tuberculosis left him with a damaged lung. He seems always to have attracted the affection of his colleagues on the paper—'a lovable man', as two of them told me twenty years after his death. In his later years he became a specialist in court reporting and earned tributes from chief justices for his accuracy and tact. He married Jean Virtue, a South Perth girl, who became to Walter Murdoch 'as dear to me as my own children'.

Catherine Murdoch had her first schooling in Melbourne, inevitably at Fintona, her aunt's school in Camberwell. After her first day she returned home in deep disappointment, for she had been told that when she went to school she would learn to read and write, and here she was, still illiterate. But as her father said over fifty years later, 'she

Will Murdoch

Catherine Murdoch (King)

began to be a chatterbox before she could walk, and has never been silent since, except in her sleep'.[1] After schools in Perth and a last year at Fintona when her parents were in Melbourne in 1921, she went on to take her B.A. at the University of Western Australia. In 1927 when her parents returned from England and Europe she stayed behind to take a Diploma of Education in the University of London. There she met a young man, a recent Oxford graduate, Alexander (Alec) King, who was similarly pursuing the study of 'Pedagogy'. Her somewhat apprehensive parents received a cable in May 1928 announcing that she was engaged.

Alec had read classics at New College, as became the son of a clergyman, but his interests were diverse. He had probably been more excited by music, in which he was an amateur of some talent, and by his activities in groups such as the Poetry Writing Club which included Cecil Day Lewis (later his brother-in-law), Rex Warner and W. H. Auden. He and Catherine were married in Perth at the end of 1929 before he settled down to what he supposed was to be his profession, schoolmastering. Two years later, like many other junior teachers at that time, he was out of a job. In 1932 he was appointed temporary part-time assistant in the English Department at the university, a very lowly academic job on a salary that reflected the university's own financial crisis. Possibly there was some talk of nepotism; I had then left Perth and would not have known if there were other contenders as well qualified as he. Certainly his students, and his colleagues in other universities whom I knew in later years, regarded him as a fine teacher and critic whose lecturing and writing were illuminated by his varied artistic interests.[2] In due time he was appointed to a readership. Over many years he and his father-in-law found much satisfaction in each other's company.

Meanwhile Catherine, always energetic, had begun her long association with kindergarten and similar organizations. She had her mother's practical bent; unlike her father she actually enjoyed organizing others, and she soon became a positively eloquent public speaker. When Wyndham and Broome in the north were bombed by the Japanese in 1942 and Perth was expecting its turn to follow soon, all kindergartens were closed. Catherine began a radio career of her own, first as planner of a daily session for young children, later as supervisor of women's programmes, which in time made her as well known on the Western Australian air as her father had become.

It must have been at Christmas of 1921 that I read a little book called *Anne's Animals*. The pictures were rather funny, I thought; the verses were very funny. I wished I could make up such rhymes as those on The Elephant:

> This creature cannot climb the trees,
> Nor swing from branch to branch with ease,
> To put it brutally, but shortly,
> His figure is extremely portly.

Murdoch had written the verses for his younger daughter Anne, the only true Western Australian in the family.

There was a wide gap between Anne's age and Catherine's, and Anne was probably right in thinking in later years that she had been brought up fairly strictly and been over-protected. An 'atmosphere of

books, music & dogs & cats, & university people' had some educational advantages, but even dogs and cats were not quite the same
thing as a brother or sister more or less of her own age. When she was
hinting that a horse would be the most welcome of presents—'but
where could we keep a horse?' wrote poor Murdoch—her sister was
about to become engaged. She was with her parents in England and
Italy in 1934, and regularly went shopping with her father in the
Portobello road, among the stalls of his essay 'On a Mean Street',
with their stocks of 'battered brass candlesticks, cracked mirrors,
worn-out gramophone records, pictures without frames, frames
without pictures, old spoons and forks and knives, cracked vases,
rusty bolts and nuts, discarded sets of teeth, doormats, furniture,
electric switches, jewellery, and even books (at fourpence a volume)'.[3]
She had ideas of becoming a kindergarten teacher, but in 1938 went
to Melbourne to train as a nurse. In 1942 she and Guy Vanzetti, son
of Murdoch's old friend, were married. Guy was a farmer on the
property that had defeated his father, on the sand-plain country
towards Geraldton, 170 miles north of Perth. 'We are tremulously
anxious to see how she will like the life', wrote Murdoch at the time.
He need not have worried. Perhaps he had not realized that Anne too
possessed the female Murdoch's urge to make herself useful in
practical ways and now had the opportunity to demonstrate it.

For suburban dwellers in Australia, holidays mean the bush or the
beach. In his earlier years in Perth Murdoch would sometimes take a
fishing holiday with Whitfeld, and during his occasional visits to
Melbourne would stay with his sisters in the familiar hill country
where once he had erected his own cottage with his own hands. At the
end of the 1920s his daughter Catherine persuaded him, out of 'pure
self-interest' as she said, to buy a cottage at Mahogany Creek, deep in
the heart of the bush of the Darling Ranges. This must have been the
scene of his essay 'My Bush Fire', when out of the gathering darkness,
as the fire grew menacing, there strolled up out of nowhere to fight
and repel it, with few words said, that type of Australian who for
Murdoch was more than a legend: 'long, lean, quiet, humorous,
inarticulate, sagacious, easy going, loyal to his own ethical code,
standing on his own feet and facing the world with a good-humoured
imperturbability, careless about economics . . .'[4] When that cottage
was sold in the mid-thirties, three generations of the family could
spend holidays in its successor, a large old house with orchard and
stream, at Gooseberry Hill. There Murdoch spent some of his happiest days, a patriarch with his children and grandchildren in the
sunlit peace of the hills, and there they all retreated for a while when
it seemed that Japanese bombs would soon be falling on Perth.

Anne Murdoch (Vanzetti)

In those days sabbatical leave was granted readily enough by the governing bodies of universities, but it was hardly possible to take it without financial loss, for some contribution had usually to be made towards the provision of a substitute and there was little or no help towards the expenses of travel. In 1921 Murdoch was on leave in Melbourne, working on his biography of Deakin. 1927 and most of 1934 he spent in England and Europe. Many of his best articles were prompted by his own experiences of people and places abroad, but he was not really a 'traveller' as the word is generally understood. He did take short holiday trips to Ceylon in 1924 and to Java in 1939, but otherwise saw Asia only at the ports on the Suez route to and from Europe; he never went or wanted to go to North America. Though he knew American literature well, he knew little of Americans and tended to judge them too readily by his observations of tourists in Europe. His own preference during his visits to Europe was to settle down, at least for some weeks at a time, in places that meant something to him through literature, rather than to see all there was to see. He liked to potter around the streets, to sit in cafés watching people pass, to linger over second-hand bookstalls. England, France and Italy were the countries of his delight. In retrospect, after returning from a year in Europe in 1927, he regretted that he had not visited Scotland. Not until 1934 did he again see Rosehearty, unchanged after fifty years except for 'the motor-bus running through it and a bowser in the market square'. (Motor-bus, bowser, those words of the 1920s—when did they go out?)

These were research visits only in the sense of *la recherche du temps perdu*. Murdoch was not much concerned to visit universities, though duty required him occasionally to be a delegate on celebratory occasions.

W.M. to Catherine Murdoch (King), 24 June 1927
. . . Then we went into the great hall [of University College, London] & had another great function. The big-wigs this time were Prince Arthur of Connaught (who somehow doesn't look quite a gentleman) and his wife. Lord Balfour made a splendid speech. After some other speeches we delegates were called on in turn & went up on to the dais & bowed to the Prince and Princess. My salaam was meant to be very impressive, but unfortunately my hired gown was a bit too long, and as I bowed I tripped on it and fell on to the Prince's knees. Instead of spanking me—as he had a splendid opportunity of doing—he repelled me with royal indignation and with such violence that he shoved me right on to the knees of the Princess, who screamed slightly. I sprang off at once, of course; but by this time my lovely purple hood had come right over my face, and partly because of this and partly because I was embarrassed by the yells of laughter which came from every part of the hall, I walked right off the dais, which was about five feet high. By this time I was quite dazed, but Winston Churchill took me by the arm and led me back to my seat. Afterwards a man came up & told me he represented the Associated Press of London and that if I paid him ten guineas (£10-10/-) the incident would appear tomorrow in every paper in London. I gathered that many people would have paid ten times that sum for such a chance at publicity, but I was very firm about it & said I was not going to give them

excellent copy and pay them for using it; at which he turned huffily away, so I don't suppose you'll see any of this in tomorrow's papers. You're getting first-hand information which the great public will be denied. But I know there will be a lot of talk about me at Buckingham Palace tonight.

If his hired gown had been his undoing on that occasion, beneath it had been what was probably the best-fitting suit he ever wore, long remembered and deeply mourned.

W.M. to Anne Vanzetti [1949]

My dear, I posted a parcel to you this afternoon . . . It contains only fragments of what were once my best trousers, now made into covers for hot-water-bags and a few pot holders. I may tell you I was very fond of those trousers, & much resent their disintegration. I bought them in London in 1927. I was having lunch, at a restaurant near St Paul's, with [a man from] the Oxford University Press. He came here to see me when he was in Australia on business, so when he went to London I went to see him and he asked me out to lunch. After telling me of many curious things I ought to see in London, he looked at me as if I was a curious sight myself and said, 'I can tell you the address of a very good tailor.' The tailor, it turned out, was his uncle. His place was in Chancery Lane, & he really *was* very good though rather expensive. He made me a suit of a then fashionable sort, now incurably démodé—black coat & waistcoat and striped trousers. The Coat & waistcoat are about as good as ever; the trousers, alas, are covers for hot-water-bags! So the earth passes and the glory thereof. The grass withereth, the flower fadeth. Nothing lasts. Change and D.K. in all around we see. A sad world . . .

Murdoch was not much concerned to seek out academics in order to discuss problems of scholarship. With his wife and his daughter Anne he came to Oxford in the summer of 1934. I showed them round the place which by now, in my last year, I assumed I owned. At lunch in my room I doubtless presided with impressive aplomb, though I seem to remember that Murdoch, asking gentle but disconcerting questions from time to time, occasionally smiled as he had done in English tutorials of old. But it had really shocked me to find that he had made no engagements to meet the dons, that he had come to this seat of learning just to *see* it. So I arranged a visit to the 'English' don in my college, and he asked Murdoch to dine in hall that night. Murdoch wrote later to say that he had enjoyed himself. He tactfully said nothing about the food, and nothing that was not polite about the anxious concern of a pupil that he should continue his scholarly education.

In his early years in Perth Murdoch sorely missed many aspects of life in Melbourne. It is easy to understand why he would not have been reluctant to return, given a position that would have afforded him something like his university salary while sufficiently satisfying his self-esteem, for he had felt deeply humiliated by the business of the Melbourne chair of English. One can guess that at the end of 1921, after a whole year in Melbourne amid old friends and familiar scenes, the Murdochs went back to Perth with something less than joyous expectation. But there was no opportunity to move, at any rate to the University of Melbourne, nor was there likely to be. Murdoch turned fifty in 1924, he was a large fish in his small pond, and by now he must have seemed to be well settled in Perth.

Old colleagues (though in the 1920s they were his young colleagues) to whom I talked in 1973 were surprised to learn that in 1925 Murdoch had still been prepared to move, and not to Melbourne but to Hobart, at a lower salary and in the days when the 400 miles between the cities meant a sea journey rather than a short flight by air; moreover, now well into middle age, he had been prepared to risk another rejection in the hope of being nearer to Melbourne. As he lived on and on into the late twentieth century, Murdoch seemed in the end always to have been associated with Western Australia, the old sage who, from his home in South Perth, had benignly overlooked the river and the city before most of its people were born. It was hard to believe that he had ever wanted to live elsewhere.

One factor in his restlessness during the 1920s was undoubtedly the state of his health, affected as he thought by the climate of Perth in summer. One of his students in the very early years recalled that, frequently enough for it to distinguish him from other professors, a notice on his door would announce that illness prevented his lecturing. It was not, as that student thought, a matter of a general frailty. The fact was that after the move to Perth he suffered recurrent attacks of a complaint relatively mild under its common name of nettle-rash, but in the severe form in which it visited him, both intensely painful and embarrassing. In Melbourne in 1921 he had been free of it for a whole year; it descended cruelly upon him as soon as he returned to a January summer in Perth. 'If [my old enemy] is to become an habitual visitor again, I shall certainly throw up my job here and go to Melbourne and try to live on what I can earn by writing', he told Herbert Brookes,[5] after another severe attack in 1924, and when a few months later he decided to apply for the vacant chair of English at the University of Tasmania, the prospect of recurrences of this wretched affliction as long as he stayed in Perth was certainly in his mind. 'It is £200 less than I get here, but when I take into account (a) the aforesaid proximity to Melbourne and all that is therein, and (b) the much superior climate of Tasmania, I reckon the pecuniary sacrifice as a trifle not worth mentioning.'[6] It is not certain that he submitted a formal application. He may, as a manuscript note by his friend Morris Miller seems to suggest, have made it known in writing that he would accept an offer if it were made. But his name was certainly discussed officially, and he was not offered the chair.[7] He had feared that his age might count against him, but there may well have been other reasons for the university's preferring a man not only younger but with more 'scholarly' credentials. Certainly no one would be likely to suppose by then that Murdoch would either abandon his journalism or begin to produce works of technical scholarship.

Though Murdoch was thus prepared, indeed anxious, in the mid-1920s to return to Melbourne or its 'proximity' even if that meant material loss, he would not simply take any position there that seemed outwardly attractive. In 1924 he told Brookes that he would move if he could see his way to earning a steady £500 by his pen—rather rashly perhaps, but at the time goaded by illness—yet in the same letter he said that he had declined an offer from his nephew Keith Murdoch of a five years' engagement on the Melbourne *Herald* at £1000 a year: 'This I refused, not because it was not sufficiently liberal, but because I do not choose to bind myself to serve a member of my own family'.[8] We may notice here that though before 1940 he did write occasional special articles for his nephew's papers, he was not a regular contributor to the Murdoch press until after his retirement from the university, and then, though presumably the income was welcome to him, he was not 'bound', as he would have been as a member of the staff of the *Herald*. He seems indeed to have viewed the entrepreneurial activities of his nephew with a mixture of admiration and apprehension. He admired his iron determination, for he knew more than most men about Keith Murdoch's difficulties as a youthful stammerer, but he was always constitutionally apprehensive about what men of power might do.

The appointment of a younger man to the Tasmanian chair meant the end of any real hope of Murdoch's returning to the East, though it seems that for a while he did not entirely abandon it. In July 1926 he wrote that he had been rather tempted by an offer made to him by the *Argus*. 'If the wages had been just a shade better, or the work proposed a trifle less strenuous, I would have slipped my cable and gone Melbourne-wards.'[9] But I wonder. In the same letter he mentioned the recent astonishing realization that Hackett's residuary legacy might transform the nature of the university, and that was, for a time, a heart-lifting prospect for the slum-dwellers at Irwin street. A few months later he was granted sabbatical leave, and spent the year 1927 in Europe. If, on his return, academic politics seemed as petty as ever, at least he had realized that he could no longer hope to escape from them to some other existence, and he could accept or rationalize the fact. '. . . Athens in the age of Pericles was a smaller place than Perth, & my particular job seems to be to try to help others to make Perth a place more like Athens than it is now—and there is a good long way to go'.[10]

It was his literary and controversial writing throughout the period, and his broadcast talks in the 1930s, that made Murdoch a 'public' figure in Australia between the wars. Before we consider these activities it will be well to look at his experience in the writing of what he later called his 'first *real* book', for that determined his course as a writer for the rest of his life.

When he said that his *Alfred Deakin: A Sketch* (1923) was 'not a success', he was speaking as a professional author. He meant, simply, that it did not sell. It was published by Constable of London in the spring of 1923 and by October 1924 he had ruefully to admit that it was a financial failure. In 1928 Herbert Brookes made arrangements for the stocks to be taken over by a Melbourne bookseller, and at a reduced price the book did sell out over the years. It does seem to be true, as Murdoch thought, that the original arrangements for its distribution in Australia had been defective. Yet neither he nor Brookes seem to have reflected that by 1923 the great gulf of war lay between the end of Deakin's active career and the concerns of the present, and that renewed interest in a once-famous Australian figure still vivid to them personally could be expected only when the years before 1914 had become 'history'.

The reviews of the book had mostly been favourable. Even journalists anxious to show that they themselves knew far more about Deakin, politician and prime minister, than any professor of English could ever know were prepared to admit its literary merits. 'I see the book is mentioned in bibliographies so I suppose that it is a sort of classic in an obscure and dusty way', Murdoch remarked in 1931, and he could still make a wistful reference, some thirty years later, to 'my wretched little "Sketch" ' and describe it as 'the book I took most pleasure in having written, and that I still can look at without shame'.[11]

A second and larger study of Deakin's policies which Brookes and Murdoch had originally contemplated was never undertaken. I cannot regret it (and I do not say so in jest, as one who did publish forty years later a large book on Deakin). In writing that kind of book, I am convinced, Murdoch would have been working against the grain of his talents. The 'Sketch' did have considerable merits, but also considerable deficiencies as an historian would judge it. If it had been a popular success, if Murdoch had been encouraged or induced to spend further years in the field of political biography, we would have lacked a good deal of his best and most characteristic writing for the sake of a white elephant, for the simple reason that much of the necessary material would not be available until another generation had passed. Why did he embark on the project of a biography at all? Out of admiration for the Deakin he had known, no doubt, out of friendship with Deakin's family, and also, I suspect, out of a secret ambition to demonstrate, at least to the academic world, that if he chose to, he could write a 'real' book.

Deakin died early in October 1919. His family, witnessing helplessly the decline of his understanding until it became as the light of 'a small candle in a vast dark room', had from time to time thought about the nature of an appropriate memorial to him, perhaps the publication of some of his literary manuscripts, perhaps the commissioning of a biography. On a visit to Melbourne, Murdoch had been partly drawn into the matter. Probably he volunteered to give an opinion about the manuscripts, for some of them had been sent to him in Perth before Deakin died, and he seems to have agreed at least to consider undertaking a biography. Towards the end of October Brookes wrote that they all wished him to do it. For the next three years there was a large correspondence between them about 'the book' and its progress, fascinating to me who knew them both, though here I refer to it mainly to illustrate Murdoch's problems in the task he had undertaken.[12]

Brookes was intensely, earnestly, almost religiously devoted to the memory of Deakin. From the beginning he contemplated a vast biographical memorial in which he should collaborate with Murdoch: first a shorter biography to enable the general public to realize the greatness of Deakin's character and his work for Australia; then a work in two volumes (he insisted on *two*), to take three to five years, and to provide a full and definitive record for posterity. Almost incredibly, Murdoch seems at this stage to have been undaunted by such a solemn undertaking. His only condition was that the shorter biography must be the work of one author, however closely they might in practice collaborate in the collection of materials. It should not be simply a reduced version of what would appear at length in the monumental biography: 'it would be possible to write a popular book which would not be a summary but a sketch', and hence there would be deliberate omissions.

Clearly he began his task with enthusiasm. What he read in the large collection of Deakin's private papers fascinated him, though when he moved outside them to newspapers, parliamentary debates and official reports he began to realize that writing biography was not always fun. He found, too, that the writing of a commissioned biography, even a 'sketch', had its peculiar problems. When he began seriously to write, in 1922, the drafts of his chapters were regularly sent to Brookes and sometimes shown to the family. In his earnest way Brookes was always appreciative and encouraging but towards the end they could not agree on Murdoch's criticisms of some of Deakin's political ideas and actions. Though Brookes himself would have agreed to disagree, he had apologetically but firmly to tell Murdoch that the family wished him to eliminate the criticisms. Probably Miss Deakin, to whom her brother's memory was sacred, had insisted that Murdoch, unqualified to assess political situations and decisions, should not intervene in the narrative as a judge in his own right. Though Murdoch protested, he did yield, and he did not follow Brookes' suggestion that in the final chapter, written in the first person, he could if he wished make critical judgements of his own.

Such criticisms of Deakin's policies as Murdoch wished to make would really have been very mild. They would mainly have been queries about the evidence for his consistency in certain episodes, particularly the formation in 1909 of 'the Fusion' of political parties opposed to Labor, and he would have liked to express some sceptical views about the sacredness of the 'two-party' system. Deakin still remained for him the most admirable of Australian politicians; he thought merely that no one, in an imperfect world, could be entirely beyond criticism in all the events and decisions of a life of politics. Though he may have had some apprehensions about further family sanctions when the 'big book' came to be written, he was still assuming for some time after the publication of the 'Sketch' that he was morally obliged to proceed with the proposed collaboration. But after the commercial failure of the 'Sketch', the fate of the 'big book' must have seemed doubtful, and it was clearly with relief that he learned from Brookes in October 1924 that there was no intention to proceed with it 'at present'. A year later he was somewhat alarmed when it seemed, through a misapprehension, that the idea was still alive. 'The monumental work would have no sale, and no readers, as far as I can judge', he wrote. He must now have known that he could never again contemplate the composition of that kind of work, though it would have been difficult to have explained this to Brookes, his loyal and affectionate friend. All the same, he was never a man to waste ideas and opportunities. He had spent much time, labour and pain on the

'Sketch', and he now believed that a smaller, not a larger, book about Deakin would find a market. Several times he returned to this idea, but Brookes was not keen about it, and it was finally abandoned in 1932.

Though I cannot precisely document the point, I feel confident from various hints in Murdoch's conversation over the years that his venture among documents rather than books, among politicians rather than writers, had become far too restrictive. At first he had been working mainly on the fascinating personal documents of a most interesting and highly literate man. The prospect of a wilderness of boring political records yet to be explored must have chilled his irreverent spirit. The 'Sketch', followed by the 'big book', might possibly establish his respectability as a 'serious' scholar—or so he thought. But there was no place in that solemn occupation for fun, for fantasy, for wit, indeed for any of the qualities, except the formal writing of good English, that went with the natural expression of his own ideas. And perhaps most limiting of all, it gave no opportunity for what he most wanted to do by writing, to expound the opinions of Walter Murdoch.

The 'Sketch' did remain for forty years the only study of Deakin based on his personal papers. The quality of its writing was evident to students who knew nothing of Murdoch the essayist; those who did, preferred his more familiar, easy-flowing style to the formality, even in places the rhetoric, of a consciously dignified memorial narrative. It would be graceless, and it is unnecessary here, to present a critical assessment of a largely undocumented book which reflected far more hard work than might be supposed by those who could not then consult the sources for many of his statements. If too often the text relied entirely on Deakin's own versions of events, it was valuable for historians by its revelation of the complexity and range of his intellectual interests. And further it reproduced lengthy passages from his unpublished narratives and reflections that would otherwise have been unavailable for many years. These, rather than the opinions of the author, were to be quoted in other books. The 'Sketch' had presented a well-composed eulogy of Deakin but had suppressed all that was most characteristic of Murdoch.

One last experience with the 'Sketch' must further have dampened Murdoch's waning enthusiasm for the project of the 'big book'. In October 1922, with the manuscript nearly completed, he proposed to the University of Melbourne the submission for the degree of Doctor of Letters of a thesis, 'The Life and Work of Alfred Deakin', and his candidature was naturally approved. The examiners appointed were T. G. Tucker of Melbourne and Berriedale Keith of Edinburgh, well known as a student of the constitutional and political development of the British 'Dominions'. A short but enthusiastic report by Tucker recommended the award of the degree, but Keith, while praising the style and structure of the thesis, gave an adverse verdict, based on more or less detailed criticisms of Murdoch's treatment or lack of treatment of various episodes in Deakin's political career. He had been informed that the standard should be that of any of the leading British universities; he was emphatic that it would not qualify for a higher degree of Oxford, London or Edinburgh. With little resistance Tucker deferred to Keith's judgement, his own original verdict (he said) being based on the literary qualities of the work, while Keith must be regarded as the authority on the actual argument. But in any case the faculty had no option but to reject the thesis, since acceptance required favourable verdicts by both examiners.

Murdoch was hurt and indignant. He told Brookes that he would have withdrawn his candidature had he known that Keith was to be an examiner, for he regarded him as a hostile witness who had bitterly attacked Deakin in his books on imperial affairs, and writing to Ernest Scott he set out at some length his answers to Keith's particular criticisms. Above all, he objected to the examination of a biography, of an attempt to give a picture of a very complex character, as if it were intended to be a formal history of the events in which Deakin was engaged. At first he thought of appealing against the verdict, but in the end made only a formal protest.[13]

It would be fruitless, and indeed improper, for me to traverse the arguments about an examination verdict delivered over fifty years ago. Some of Keith's points were certainly valid; so were some of Murdoch's. I need only say that today the work would not have been accepted for a higher degree for a simple and decisive reason unrelated to its literary merits: except in a derisory sense it is completely undocumented. And I think that for similar reasons it would not have been judged to meet the standards of 'leading British universities' in 1923 if the opinion of an examiner other than Keith had been sought. Murdoch had presented a good book but that was not the same thing as a good thesis. I would like to believe his assurance to Scott that he had not lost five minutes' sleep over the matter.

7

COLLECTED ESSAYS

ARLY IN 1943, at a time of some anxiety about other matters, the prime minister of Australia answered a curious query from the high commissioner in London: Who was the outstanding 'literary personality' in Australia? Curtin had sought the advice of the Advisory Board of the Commonwealth Literary Fund before cabling to Bruce that opinion was divided between the names of Walter Murdoch and Bernard O'Dowd, but since 'the public estimate' could not be disregarded, he nominated Murdoch (for what purpose I know not). Thirty years later, discussing Australian literature between the wars, Geoffrey Serle said, 'The best-known "literary man" of the day was certainly Walter Murdoch . . . a famous essayist and popular educator who wrote nearly all his work for newspapers.'[1] I quote these views without comment, simply to establish the point that between 1919 and 1939—literally, as it happens—Murdoch had become a writer known throughout Australia, and was still remembered as such a generation later. How had this come about?

The formal answer is simple: he resumed his journalistic work. In 1919 'Elzevir's' weekly articles for the *Argus* appeared once more, and a few years later 'Walter Murdoch' began a similar series for the *West Australian*. But the *Argus* was only one among Melbourne's morning newspapers, and though the *West Australian* had the field to itself in Perth, the fame of any of its contributors was very distinctly local. Though his newspaper writings were thus already well known in Melbourne and Perth, his reputation as 'the' Australian essayist rested upon the books of selected articles that he began to publish in 1930, beginning with *Speaking Personally*. These were read throughout the continent. In 1938 five of these books of selections were brought together to make one large volume, *Collected Essays*, which in its second edition (1940) included also the essays separately published as *The Spur of the Moment*. He was busily writing for some thirty years longer, but the *Collected Essays* of 1940 contains all the articles that he was prepared to republish, between hard covers, as 'essays'.* Meanwhile his broadcast talks in much the same vein had since 1933 brought him new audiences. His popularity gives no guide to his 'place' (if he has one) in our literary history, but it does tell us something about the Australians of that time. How could the 'essays' of a distinctly old-fashioned professor of English literature be eagerly read throughout the continent? As a social phenomenon the trick requires some explanation.

We must first ask what he meant by an 'essay'. Not, it seems, the kind of articles—reviews of various books, or appreciations of individual writers—that had made his reputation in Victoria before 1914. These, he said, were simply 'articles'. Nor were all prose compositions that were formally called 'Essays' the kind he began to write in the 1920s. Among the texts for study in his English courses were a good many Essays: Bacon, Dryden on Dramatic Poesy, Macaulay, Carlyle, Emerson, Matthew Arnold and others, but these he took to be examples of literary criticism or biography or (in Emerson's case) lay sermons. For him the essayists were Montaigne, Cowley, Addison and Steele, Goldsmith, Lamb, Hazlitt, Leigh Hunt, and he would admit some among his contemporaries such as Beerbohm, E. V. Lucas, Chesterton, Belloc, Robert Lynd. The distinction is familiar, but it needs emphasis. To take Australian examples, Murdoch's 'Essays' and A. D. Hope's *The Cave and the Spring: Essays on Poetry* are in different categories of writing; they cannot be directly compared just because they are described as books of essays. We should notice further that all of his writings which Murdoch would have admitted to be essays were published during some twenty years in a writing career of seventy. These may well comprise the only work of his that will be noticed in a history of Australian literature, but they will be only part of the writings that an historian of Australian popular thought and culture will need to consider.

The essay has vanished from contemporary courses in English literature. I suspect that younger teachers of the subject, after some

* *Speaking Personally* (1930), *Saturday Mornings* (1931), *Moreover* (1932), *The Wild Planet* (1934), *Lucid Intervals* (1936), *The Spur of the Moment* (1939), all published by Angus and Robertson, Sydney.

exposure at school to Lamb or perhaps to some volume of selected essays, regard the form as beneath their notice. In his appreciation of Murdoch, A. A. Phillips wrote in *Meanjin* (1969) that his success (as writer and humanist) 'is all the more remarkable because his chosen form is the essay, traditionally handled, a form from which the modern palate flinches', with its 'deliberated fragility, its mincing egoisms, its parade of an imposed style . . .'² One knows exactly what he means; I am old enough to have read the essayists of the 1920s whose styles, God help me, I admired as a schoolboy and would then have liked to be able to imitate. Murdoch presumably read that number of *Meanjin*, with its several tributes to his work. I imagine that he would have been gratified that his own attempts in a form of writing which he had ceased to practise nearly twenty years earlier were still remembered with affection, and would have hoped that his egoisms (essential to the form, in his opinion) were not 'mincing'. But, he might have thought, should the essay in general be dismissed because one generation of cooks had made the mixture too cloying? And then he might have asked for one of those 'more or less shabby little volumes' from his shelves, perhaps thinking of Hazlitt's 'The Indian Jugglers'.

Was the essay really Murdoch's 'chosen form'? It was certainly a form that he admired and hence, I suppose, would have liked to do well. But he thought it was a very difficult thing to do well:

> Yes, I prized very highly your appreciation of my little books; only regretting that you should waste your talent on so very minor a figure in Australian literature. This is not mock-modesty. I have no illusions on the subject. My books are not built for immortality, but for a life of about, say, three months. [To L. A. Triebel, 1934]

> An essay is a newspaper article, exhumed, reprinted in larger type on thicker paper, and placed, among other articles, between cloth covers. [Preface to *Lucid Intervals*, 1936]

> My later books have not been books at all but collections of newspaper articles, which people called essays. [To Janet Paisley, 1951]

We should take Murdoch seriously, conceding only a little to the academic habit of self-depreciation. In 1934 he knew very well that his first three collections of reprinted essays were still being read, but when he said that they were 'built' for a life of about three months, he meant that they were *newspaper* articles, often prompted by a current event, or a public pomposity or a new publication. He had not sweated long over them. They were written to a deadline, probably during a weekend, to be posted on the Monday.

Again, we must take seriously his warnings that his besetting sin was the vice of 'preaching', that his essays were almost always intended to provoke thought on more or less serious subjects. He tended to put the point somewhat archly, blaming his covenanting ancestors, for he was too old a journalist not to attempt to live up to his image as an entertaining and teasing writer. Yet if most of his reprinted articles were fun to read, they were rarely written simply for fun. He was not as a rule practising the 'art' of the essay, but using its form to expound his beliefs and prejudices about the values of contemporary society.

His own verdict was that 'such success as I have had with my books has been due to the fact that I have a commonplace mind, with a knack of putting into words what other commonplace people have thought but never said.'[3] Commonplace? Yes, in the sense that he was the constant critic, to the point of prejudice of 'difficult' language, and the constant and fiercer enemy of double-talk, of the language of elected persons, of experts who would blind us with science or abstract words or rhetorical inflation.

When Murdoch began, after World War I, to expound his ideas on things in general rather than on literature only, the essay was his 'chosen form' only in the sense that he now thought more carefully about the pattern of his argument and the audience he was addressing; his manner had already been formed. To earn money he had begun as a young man to write for the press. Before long he had acquired by practice an ability to write quickly and well as if he were talking. There is no time for a journalist to practise the artful conversion of a laboured manuscript into smoothly readable prose; there is always a deadline. As Elzevir in his Melbourne years his 'natural' form of writing had become the swiftly written column-and-a-half, complete within itself, by practised skill made palatable from the very beginning to the 'general reader' appropriate to a particular journal. Any other form of writing was likely, for him, to be a chore, a labour rather than a satisfying exercise of professional skill, a suppression of the gifts he had discovered in the practice of literary journalism. True, he wrote textbooks, but there was little fun in these. True, he wrote the 'Sketch' but, though it is well written, it is rather ostentatiously well written, as if he were taking pains with his prose. There is an unnatural solemnity about that book. His manuscripts, like those of most journalists, have gone with the wind, but that the fluent prose of his articles, easy and varied, was his natural style can be seen in hundreds of letters in his beautiful swift handwriting. There are no obliterations, no hesitations; he never wrote a loose, obscure or clumsy sentence. I cannot imagine that after his early years Murdoch would ever happily have written a 'study' of a particular author, or a series of studies in criticism, carefully shaped, after many interruptions to consult the texts. The 'Sketch' was a duty. When he wrote as Walter Murdoch rather than as the biographer of Deakin, his medium was inevitably the article or the essay.

On 17 May 1919 older readers of the *Argus* saw again the heading 'Books and Men, By Elzevir', and read 'I take up my pen heavy with the accumulated rust of six years, not without dark misgivings.' For some time Elzevir *redivivus* was mainly concerned with the familiar business of reviewing new books and discussing old authors, but now with a difference. The new books were not necessarily 'literary'. For example he noticed with enthusiasm Keynes's *Economic Consequences of the Peace*: 'I regard the study of this book as nothing less than a public duty.' Sometimes a nominal review might really be a pretext for a sermon of his own. Before long, though there was usually a 'literary' undertone or background, 'Books and Men' reflected Elzevir's views on things in general as frequently as his opinions of books and writers. He was now writing the kind of articles which, reprinted in *Speaking Personally* (1930) and its successors, were to make his name familiar throughout Australia.

In mid-1923 similar articles began to appear in the *West Australian* under his own name. The date marks his release from the task of writing the 'Sketch'. Earlier he had occasionally written special articles for that paper, which after the war might well have looked favourably on a proposal for a regular series. But by then he had undertaken his biographical labour, and would do nothing beyond it but his *Argus* articles until it was finished.

W.M. to Herbert Brookes, 12 May 1920

> I have already given up an examinership which brought me £50 to £60 per annum, and propose to give up everything but my university work and my article once every three or four weeks in the *Argus*. This brings me & keeps me in touch with current literature, which I do not wish to lose touch with, for the sake of keeping my own soul alive; and—a better reason still—I wish to keep up my connection with the *Argus* because I may some day depend again upon newspaper work for a living. (I mean that I may some day feel so utterly fed up with university teaching that I may have to retire, and I see no prospect of ever having enough money to retire from work altogether . . .).

One article for the *West Australian*, written before he was a regular contributor but when relief from work on the biography was in sight, long remained a legend to Western Australians of later years who could have read it only if they had seen a happily preserved newspaper cutting. Murdoch did not choose to reprint 'Thoughts on a Kerosene Tin' presumably because its occasion and interest were entirely local,[4] but it may be noticed here because it provides as good an example as any of the later essays of his method of beguiling a reader into considering a matter that the author took very seriously.

In the 1920s the 'kerosene tin', universally seen on Australian farms in a vast countryside unlit by electricity, was still a familiar enough object in a city. With its top removed, it was often used as a kind of bucket or waste-can. Prompted by an observation on his daily way to the university, he began his article thus:

> It lies in Barrack-Street, a little below the Weld Club corner, between the tramway and the footpath. When I first caught sight of it, just a week ago, it had fallen over on its side, and some of its contents—including egg-shells and what looked like decomposing cabbage-stalks—had flowed out over the street. Since then the rain has carried the garbage away and distributed it among the various ponds of which that street, at its river end, chiefly consists; but to-day, as I write, the empty tin is still there, for all the world to see and admire. How it came there, whether it dropped unobtrusively from a passing cart, or was mislaid by some absent-minded member of the Weld Club, or was deliberately placed in position by some thoughtful citizen who had decided that this was an eligible locality (to quote the house agents) for a tin of garbage—we can but conjecture; anyhow, there it lies. It is not a remarkable kerosene tin, in any way; but what does strike me as remarkable is that, of the many hundreds who daily go to and fro from the jetties at the foot of the street, no one seems to notice it, no one marvels at it, no one halts to meditate upon it. Is it nothing to you, all ye that pass by?

What was its secret? It symbolized, he argued, the 'pleasant, friendly, free-and-easy, casual ways' of Perth and Western Australia, where in such matters as the cleanliness of the streets, amiable amateurishness was preferred to professional competence.

> When once you have learned the secret, illustrations come flocking. Take our water supply, rather a vital matter, one would suppose, in our climate. When I came back to Perth last summer, I found the suburbs roughly divided into two classes: those where the water was insufficient, and those where it was undrinkable. I happen to live in one of the former. On hot days a thin trickle came through my taps; on very hot days the trickle ceased. Watering one's garden was impossible until near midnight. Still, I prefer this arid region to the suburb in which a Minister of the Crown declared, with just pride, that 'he had tasted the water, and it had done him no harm'. Have we no historical painter to immortalise the scene—the heroic administrator, having swallowed a teaspoonful of discoloured liquid, waiting to see if he will fall down

dead? It would have been a glorious death. Martyrdom in the sacred cause of amateur engineering.

And so to his real theme: the costs of amiable amateurishness in public policies, or the lack of them, whether you considered the use and conservation of the forests, the growing pollution of Perth's beautiful river, or dangers to public health. They were all matters requiring the application, in administration and practice, of trained intelligence and skills. That meant education.

> And so, if any reader has had the patience to follow the argument to this point, our reflections on a kerosene tin have led us to a plea for the University. For what is a university? It has recently been defined as 'the guardian of the intellectual interests of the community.' It is a gymnasium for the training of competent leaders in every field in which competent leadership is needed if a community is to thrive. If we think we are rich enough to prefer incompetence (the costliest of all public luxuries) we shall leave our University housed in the impossible ramshackle where it now lies huddled, and we shall continue to starve it, to thwart its effectiveness, to limit its activities, and to stunt its growth. Higher education costs a great deal of money; but not a millionth part of what it costs to do without higher education. The policy for the University at present is, I take it, to bear up against adversity and do its best to get ready for the time when it will be wanted. It will be wanted when the community wakes up to the ruinous cost of muddle and incapacity and the dear old amateur in general. Arcadia is a delightful country; but only millionaires can afford to live there.

Collected Essays contains some 180 items, less than half of those published in the same period in the relevant journals. Murdoch would have been appalled at any suggestion that all his writings should be searched out and published as his 'Complete Works'. The very phrase daunted him: 'no author's complete works are worth studying', and especially was this true of journalists, even of his much-admired Hazlitt. 'It seems hardly fair to [his] fame that every scrap of his most ephemeral scribbling should be exhumed and republished a century later'. Nevertheless I shall refer to some of the articles that Murdoch was content to leave in 'the dustbins of old periodicals' when they illustrate, better than those he did republish, his assaults on complacency, often prompted by contemporary events or pronouncements, and if a future historian should wish to look at them, he must consult the original newspapers.

In composing the Elzevir articles of 1905–13, which frequently reviewed several successive books, Murdoch would write the paragraphs or sections one by one. For articles in his later manner he liked to have the idea of the whole in his head before he began, he would then write swiftly ahead so that the tone would be uniform, persuading rather than informing. After quoting in the *West Australian*, an *Argus* article describing Melbourne as 'the great plagiarist among cities', he continued, 'Of course, that was not quite just. Melbourne should not have been picked out as if she were the only or the worst offender; I only did that because it happened to be a Melbourne public that I wished, at the moment, to annoy.'⁵ The word 'annoy' is significant.

Though he refused to regard his articles of 1905–13 as 'essays', their manner did have some of the characteristics of his later writing. He wrote in the first person, as if to emphasize that Elzevir's views were those of one man, not a syndicate; he was not always serious; he took some pains to attract the reader's interest in his first paragraphs. But he stuck to his charter: his subjects were books and (literary) men. The change in the early 1920s to writing, when he chose, about whatever interested him at the time marks the emergence of the 'essayist', though at first he was distinctly coy about claiming that title. Thus in 1923 he published an article with the title 'On Doors'. He announces the subject, only to assure the reader that he is *not* trying to pass himself off as a 'genuine essayist' by demonstrating that he can write on anything under the sun. He would not be so pretentious, for he believes that 'the essay, if not the highest form of literature, is the most difficult of all; that a good essay is harder to write than a good novel . . .' Then he does present, in the traditional mode, an entertaining essay on doors in life and literature, concluding, 'Yes, certainly if I were an essayist I should write an essay on doors'.⁶ This was a mocking exercise by the academic Murdoch who might set for the first prescribed essay of the year 'any subject you like'. It was the kind of essay you might write for a bet, and he would occasionally do it for fun, as in his history of King Cole in the manner, respectively, of Macaulay, Carlyle, Dickens, Meredith, Shaw and Wodehouse. But he could never have been that kind of newspaper columnist who is bound always to be 'funny'. In the 'Murdoch essay' of the years between the wars he used the tricks of intimate writing to encourage Australians to clear their minds of cant.

W.M. to Catherine King, c. 1931
   Looking over 'Speaking Personally' (my favourite reading on winter evenings) I see clearly what my particular trick is . . . I see that I always had a concrete peg on which to hang an abstract discussion. Frinstance: I long thought the doctrine of equality, which silly people attacked as if it meant that we were all mathematically equal, which is absurd, or that we were all exactly alike, which is still more ridiculous, could be defended on the

ground of our common capacity for suffering; but since one couldn't write a newspaper article on so abstract a topic, I had to keep the idea in cold storage for years. Then one day the word 'bloke', with all its implications, gave me the necessary peg . . . Another example: I wanted to write an article to the effect that most evil was preventible by human effort, and would be prevented if we had to; the idea of babies refusing to come to earth till it should be made a better place for them came to me suddenly as just the peg I needed. One more: I had often written more or less ineffectively about the self-righteousness of politicians, and had spoken of them as begirt with metaphoric haloes; but when the idea flashed upon me of a real and not a metaphorical halo developing round one of these absurd creatures' heads, behold my peg. The point is, as far as my own method or workmanship is concerned, to get such a peg every time—some perfectly concrete, and preferably some perfectly common and familiar word or thing, and by its means to excite people's interest or curiosity, and so lead them on to what you want to say.

What you want to say, but what language to use?

W.M. to a colleague, 1 March 1940

Your article on humanism is exceedingly interesting to me, who have been reading some of the American humanists. But as I presume you intend to interest people who have *not* read these birds, I shall offer you some candid criticism. I know it is candour and not flummery you want.

In the first place, what sort of people *are* you talking to? University students? Waterside workers? Philosophers or oi polloi?—I take it that you are trying to catch the ear of the ordinary, fairly-intelligent, under-educated newspaper reader. Is that agreed?

A tremendous lot depends, for such a reader, on the start. Your introductory paragraph would not attract him, & should be cut out . . .

Just look at that paragraph. 'Humanism is an interpretation of life', etc. The first sentence bristles with abstractions beyond the reach of the said reader (call him X).

'Interpretation of life' has no meaning for X. 'Adequate to modern knowledge and circumstances'—even that would need some effort on X's part. He would say 'this is prosy stuff', and pass to another article. Your *first* paragraph should require a minimum of intellectual effort, if you are going to induce X to read on . . .

I won't go on with these criticisms which will probably strike you as niggling and pedantic. My *general* criticism is—that though you have unquestionably hit on a good subject & one that needs airing, you have not sufficiently kept in mind the little weaknesses of X. You couldn't talk of humanism without using abstract nouns, but you have given the poor devil too many for his power of digestion . . .

I have said that if Murdoch had not published *Speaking Personally* (1930) and its successors as books he would not have been known as 'the' Australian essayist, even though all his writings in this form would have been in print. Some years earlier he had thought of their publication between hard covers. Fortunately for him, he had had second thoughts:

W.M. to Catherine Murdoch (King), 4 December 1927 (from Naples)
   ... thank you for offering to spend time on finding a publisher for my articles, or a selection from them. You know I brought them to England partly with some such idea, but I didn't act on it. They're not good enough. They're harmless little essays, rather above the average of the 'Argus' or 'West Australian', & they served their purpose well enough in living for one day. To ask for them a longer life is to ask something they don't deserve. None of them is a real contribution to thought or knowledge or fun or anything else. Let them lie quiet in their little graves. Before I die I *may* write something I should like you to remember me by, but it's away at the back of my brain, and I don't know if it will ever come forward.

Why he changed, or was persuaded to change, his mind a few years later I do not know, but clearly the decision to publish in Australia was the right one. Though he did later publish in England a volume of essays selected from the first three volumes issued in Australia, his countrymen surprisingly showed a positive hunger for writings in a form generally supposed to be appreciated only by relatively small numbers of refined people. He neither told a story nor fiercely stressed his Australianism; he just assumed his readers were literate people, mostly living in towns, 'ordinary, fairly-intelligent, under-educated' readers of newspapers, and talked to them about things that interested or worried him, in a way that entertained and challenged them, without sounding either condescending or, in the manner of some later academic-journalists, offensively matey. It was a remarkable achievement in a particular mode of writing; the original sales and the reprints of his essays revealed that there were large numbers of Australians to whom good English actually added to the attraction of humour and made 'preaching' acceptable. And this was the more surprising because his undertone was ironic, rather than sardonic in the traditional manner of Australian comment on life. He is the only Australian writer to have succeeded in using the essay as a means of popular communication.*

Collected Essays was Murdoch's last book of that kind, though when it went out of print, selections from its contents continued under various titles to appear for many years. Until 1945 he continued to

---

* For the figures on sales of Murdoch's various books of essays, see note on p. 177.

write essay-like articles, not republished as books. Then he hit upon a new vein of popular communication which he mined for some twenty years.

As a 'popular educator' (in Geoffrey Serle's phrase) the essayist of 1919–39 had achieved his aim to a degree unapproached by any other literary journalist in Australian history. Like Kipling in another medium, he was compulsively readable, even when you rejected his values. 'I think I have never seen anyone begin an "Elzevir" column without finishing it: indeed I think that I shall hardly live to see that happen',[7] wrote Nettie Palmer in 1930. During fifty years, wrote Arthur Phillips in 1969, Murdoch had 'probably given more pleasure to more readers than any other Australian prose writer'.[8] In a strange comparison his most severe academic critic had to admit that in Australia 'only one essayist, Walter Murdoch, has won a fame equal to, say, that of Paterson or Richardson'.[9]

The extraordinary popularity, for nearly fifty years of the twentieth century, of the journalistic writings of a professor of English is a simple fact of Australian social and (in the general sense) cultural history. Sooner rather than later it will be examined by historians concerned rather with the Australian people than with their political leaders and institutions. If they do their work properly, they will need to search the newspapers where much of his work lies buried, but I suspect that most of them will be content with *Collected Essays*. With these as samples, they may reflect as follows: here is a writer who over an immensely long career talked about literature and expressed his own ideas on the values and attitudes of civilized society. Over two or three generations very large numbers of Australians read his writings and were exposed to his opinions; in the 1930s and 1940s, in addition they listened to his radio talks, undistracted by the counter-attractions of television. And even these samples of his writings and opinions show that they were neither soporific nor complacent, that consistently he was attempting to prick bubbles of conformity.

No one doubts that the education systems of Australia between say 1870 and 1970 had profound effects, good or bad, upon the quality of Australian cultural life. What effects did the writings of this most popular of popular educators have in his lifetime? I cannot answer that question, but I can say something about the types of people who read him, all with interest, most with pleasure, some with disapproval, over many years. There were academics, though they pretended that his work was too popular for their tastes and his dignity, but how would they know unless they read it? There were schoolteachers, pupils in secondary schools, authors, journalists, businessmen, housewives, architects, clergymen, civil servants, members of parliament, plumbers, farmers . . . Some of these were 'high culture' people in Serle's sense; most of them, including those professionally qualified in their own fields, probably were not, but they were literate, they were readers, and Murdoch made them think. There is an area between high culture and popular culture. Perhaps it covers more than half the community; perhaps Murdoch raised its standards a little; perhaps some parents took notice when he said, 'Try to understand that to your children you seem an inhabitant of a world of obsolete ideas, old-fashioned ways, antiquated conventions. If you cannot move with them, try at least to accept the inevitable movement of youth into a new and perhaps for all you know, a better world than you have grown up in.'

These are questions for social historians. For literary historians Murdoch's writings, and in particular his essays, raise different problems. Academic critics were always, and understandably, somewhat uneasy about them. Some academics did indeed write rather lush appreciations of his wit and wisdom, the charm of his holiday talk, 'the air of conversational ease associated with the aroma of the smoke-room after a friendly satisfying meal'—personal essays about personal essays, all very cosy. The judicious H. M. Green, after comparing Murdoch with other essayists and deciding that he was not quite like any of them, said, 'there is no doubt that he is among the leading essayists in English of the present or the preceding generation'.[10] But whether this was high praise depended upon your view of the 'personal essay' (compared, say, with literary criticism) as a serious form of literature.

The uneasiness of academic critics was most explicitly expressed by Cecil Hadgraft. He did not like the tricks, the affectation of simplicity, the coy use of the first person, above all the artful 'writing down' of Murdoch's essays, which presented the author as an ordinary person, just like you and me. The duty of a professor of English was to defend excellence; the price of popularity was the abandonment of that duty. 'Murdoch is not an ordinary person, and his attempt to make his readers think he is has the unhappy result that they feel fortified in an indifference to art and literature'.[11] Did they? In these days I can agree with much that Hadgraft, himself a professional teacher of English literature, said about Murdoch's use of the personal essay, though what he criticized I would in youth have seen as virtues. There *is* something about many of Murdoch's essays, 'the getting on terms with the reader, the affectation of simplicity', which brings discomfort to a mature and sophisticated reader. He does take too much trouble to capture one's attention in his first innocent paragraphs; he does ever so artfully, 'write down'. I would not resist the implication that in the high line of literature these tricks are disqualifications; there you write for your equals.

But Murdoch's tricks were *teaching* tricks. He would not have been anxiously interested in opinions about his 'place' in Australian literature; he was deeply concerned that Australians should read good literature, and that they should clear their minds of cant. He was a cultural moralist, who wrote unashamedly as a teacher, using the tricks of a teacher. It is the test of a teacher that in time his pupils will see through his tricks; meanwhile, perhaps, they will have learned to read.

After Murdoch's death I undertook to appeal through newspapers for documents and reminiscences, though then without any idea of writing about him myself. The replies, mostly from 'ordinary readers', did not lead me to believe that he could be regarded as a cheer-leader for philistines, or that he had encouraged his readers to feel fortified in an indifference to art and literature. Even sophisticated academics were, in their youth, likely to have been in the condition of those whom Murdoch, using his tricks, was mainly concerned to affect. A letter from one such academic may suggest to social historians a generation hence that it would be worth looking again at the essays which by then may have ceased to interest their literary colleagues.

As a schoolboy in Sydney, I had no access to the Melbourne and Perth newspapers in which Murdoch's essays were published. I discovered them in the school library, in the small volumes which Angus and Robertson produced in the 1930s. When I left school in 1938 I asked for his *Collected Essays* among my prizes. I still have it. It cost 8/6d. for 743 pages. Looking at the book again, I find that I can recall the feelings which many of the essays produced in me when first read. It is clear that I owe a good deal to Murdoch for literary introductions: Cobbett, Chesterfield, Trollope and Voltaire first came alive for me in his pages ('One Crowded Hour', on Voltaire, is really a most compelling essay). Also, he gave me encouragement to continue with certain literary interests I had, in the face of current fashion: 'On Laughing at Tennyson' is still, I think, an excellent defence of the Victorians. 'The Balfour-Conrad Question' was, I thought, a final rejection of the Shakespeare-Bacon controversy by means of a novel but convincing argument. 'The Art of Skipping' persuaded me for ever that skipping was the only way to get through many books. Above all, Murdoch made me feel that literary enjoyment was something to be prized, preserved and enlarged. I did not need to be convinced of this, because I believed it already; but Murdoch reinforced a natural belief through his own sense of infectious pleasure.

Murdoch's influence on me was not solely literary, however. It was also political. 'The Pink Man's Burden' is one of the best defences of political moderation that I have encountered. 'A Medieval Interlude' is a sound warning against the plausibility of ideologies. Murdoch wrote as a man of common sense and compassion; the combination of the two was unusual in my reading. When I read political theory in later years, Murdoch's ideas often came back to me. I have not heard anyone else praise him as a writer on politics, but I am quite sure that he made better sense, and provided a better foundation for political study, than many of those with more pretensions in the field. .

Let me end with two further points. The first is that Murdoch's writing style gave me particular pleasure, and may well have had a deep influence on me. It combined ease with eloquence, and was always limpid, while never prosy. Now and then, on re-reading it, I find the Macaulay-Trevelyan tone a little insistent, but I have no doubt that when I read Murdoch as a schoolboy he was one of the best models I had—far better than any of my school teachers or the editorialists I read, and the clearest, plainest prose writer I had encountered until, a year or so later, I came across George Orwell and Robert Graves.

The final point is that it came as something of a revelation to find that Murdoch was writing in Australia. The Sydney in which I grew up did not seem to me to be a cultivated place, and I did not meet cultivated people, apart from one or two of my school teachers, until I went to the university. It may seem silly to suggest that Murdoch showed me that one could have a sense of the widest culture while remaining firmly based in Australia, but I think, on reflection, that this was so.

THE SACRED DUTY OF GROWLING

IN THE EARLY 1930s *Speaking Personally* and its successors made Murdoch's name familiar to thousands of Australians who never saw the newspapers in which the essays had originally appeared. Some of them, perhaps large numbers of them, were unaware that he was writing from Perth in Western Australia. Then in 1933 he began to speak to them directly.

Systematic radio broadcasting in Australia began in 1923. In 1929 the federal government took over a number of private broadcasting stations and in 1932 established the Australian Broadcasting Commission (A.B.C.), with its own officers and staff, to control these 'national' stations. In contrast both to the British and American systems, private or 'commercial' broadcasting continued as a parallel system. Murdoch's friend Herbert Brookes became the first vice-chairman of the A.B.C.

One of the earliest stations (6WF) had been established in Perth. I remember listening with amazement, some time in the 1920s, to the trickle of a small string orchestra through the ear-phones of a schoolfriend's hand-constructed crystal set; it was not very entertaining, but the wonder was that you could hear it at all.

W.M. to Herbert Brookes, 2 June 1932

... I hope the work of the Commission may bring you to Perth soon, though you won't collect any license from me. I had a crystal set once, but never by any chance was there anything worth lis-

108

tening to, and no member of my family ever wanted to listen, so I dismantled the thing. But if you are now really going to see that good stuff is delivered, I suppose I shall have to scrape some money together somehow and get another set ... I am really very glad to hear that you are to be concerned in so vital a matter; for it *is* vital—anyone can see that broadcasting will sooner or later take the place of literature for a vast number of people.

Within a year Murdoch had been persuaded by Brookes, a devoted admirer of his writings, that he should be personally concerned with this new medium of communication. Early in 1933 he gave his first broadcast, a strange experience described in his essay 'At the Mike',[1] though he gives no support to the legend that the odd sounds that punctuated it came from the tapping of his pipe on the base of the microphone. His first reaction was that he need never *write* another essay as long as he lived; his second—when he thought of the awful chasm between what broadcasting actually was and what it might be—was that he should like to see someone start a Broadcasting Reform League.

Henceforth he was concerned with broadcasting in two ways: as a member of advisory committees on A.B.C. 'talks' programmes in Western Australia, and as one of the best-known broadcasters in Australia. A committee giving advice and arranging programmes on educational topics was superseded in 1939 by a smaller Talks Advisory Committee with more general functions. Murdoch remained an active member until the end of 1950.

The minutes of these local committees have considerable interest for an historian of Australian broadcasting, but they need not much concern us here.[2] There was a good deal of discussion of the familiar questions about radio 'talks': should they be instructive, should they be deliberately provocative, and so forth. We find Murdoch pressing for more time for talks, suggesting to Charles Moses, the general manager of the A.B.C., that good speakers as well as musical artists be invited to Australia; pressing for 'Open Forums', criticizing the virtual monopoly of 'national' talks by speakers from New South Wales and Victoria, and—in his last year as a member—characteristically condemning as ambiguous the title of a proposed forum discussion, 'Can the White Races Hold Their Own?'.

Some of these points did come to the notice of the wise men from the East, for members of the A.B.C. occasionally visited Perth for consultations, and the minutes went on to Sydney to be seen by the highly intelligent Molesworth, from 1937 the federal controller of talks. But during the 1930s Murdoch had in his correspondence with Brookes more direct opportunities to press his views.

W.M. to Herbert Brookes [late 1935]

I am grateful to you for having induced me to go in for broadcasting . . . Surely, surely, we are missing a great opportunity? Consider
the kind of music we get at all hours of every day, and the kind of
music we might be getting. Consider the talks we get. I don't want
the national stations to be highbrow; but I do want them to go on
the principle that the public should be given something a little
better than it wants, or than it thinks it wants. At present I can't see
that the public taste is being raised in any particular by wireless, or
the public intelligence being educated, or the public ideals being
heightened . . . it isn't good enough, my dear Herbert; it simply IS
NOT GOOD ENOUGH. [In red:] It isn't good enough. If I had
another colour I would use it, for the sake of emphasis. Australia
deserves something better.

He was writing before it was possible to listen to alternative A.B.C.
stations in Perth. Certainly in Sydney in the 1940s one could,
throughout most of a day, switch from one good A.B.C. musical
programme to another, until from 1946 one of the stations became
anything but musical during parliamentary sessions.

To the officers of the A.B.C. the problems of trying to please
everybody were difficult enough without the additional burden of
public criticism by one of their most popular speakers. When Murdoch's articles from time to time attacked their standards, he
appeared to be biting the hand that fed him, and his defence, that
'the best way of defending [the commission] against the charge of
being too high-brow is to charge it with being, on the contrary, far too
low-brow' may well have seemed ingenuous.[3]

In September 1939 Murdoch was concerned with issues even more
serious than the dreadful pot-pourris of music such as the 'collection
of phrases from Chopin, strung together like a necklace of odd stones
and queer shells and bits of bone and nuts and things',[4] which he had
denounced earlier that year. The A.B.C.'s principal commentator on
foreign affairs at that time was 'The Watchman'. I still recall with
distaste his throbbing tones, the pretentiousness of his pseudonym.

W.M. to Herbert Brookes, 17 September 1939

I am sorry to say I think I shall have to attack your friend 'The
Watchman' publicly and violently. I think he is poisoning the
public mind. All that super-heated eloquence—all his daily hymns
of hate—must hurt all who wish Australia to go into this war with
dignity and understanding of the issues at stake.

From remote Western Australia, observing the battles of the
A.B.C. with the politicians, and the personalities and policies of the
Commission and its officers, Murdoch began gradually to admit that

there were among them people who were striving to create and defend standards in broadcasting. When he came to know W. F. Cleary, the chairman, he found that he liked and admired him despite his 'loquacity, his egotism and his pontifical attitude'.[5] He was scandalized by the appointment of an utterly unqualified Western Australian to the commission, critical of another from Victoria, but 'as for the Queensland grazier, Bower or Boyer or whatever his name is, my only objection to him is that I have never heard of him'.[6] Again, personal acquaintance caused a revision of his original opinion that all the new commissioners were intellectual nonentities. 'Boyer strikes me as a thoroughly good chap', he wrote in December 1944, not long before the 'Queensland grazier' had entered upon his long and distinguished chairmanship.

When Murdoch gave his first radio talk in 1933, he was a year or so under sixty. He was last heard on the air in 1968. His main years as a frequent radio speaker were the 1930s and 1940s, that unique era before broadcasting was relegated to 'steam radio'. In very old age he was occasionally heard and seen on television, rather as an ancient sage, a piece of living history, than as the teacher who had induced his listeners to think about the values of Australian society, and reminded them of their duty, the 'sacred duty of growling'.

He soon learned the tricks that Jerry Portus, another 'professor of things in general' and an experienced broadcaster, expounded to me in Adelaide in the 1930s—the relatively informal English, the variation of speed and emphasis, the occasional deliberate feeling for a word. But these were the tricks of exposition. Murdoch was a good radio speaker because he was able to convince his unseen audience that he believed what he said, and that he was speaking to each of them.

There were some excellent 'regular' broadcasters in those years: W. J. Dakin, for instance, on science, and Lindley Evans on music. Murdoch sometimes gave a series of talks, generally on 'literary' themes, as in his 'Three Popular Prophets—Wells, Shaw, Chesterton' (1935) or his 'A Library for a Fiver' (1940), advice about books to buy which (I was interested to hear recently) laid foundations for one of the most learned men I know. More often he was heard in single talks on diverse themes. Almost from the beginning, before the days of land-lines, he was recorded in Perth for rebroadcasting in the eastern states. Though his was not a mellifluous voice, and what he said often made listeners uncomfortable, the officers of the A.B.C. soon realized that in this field he was a 'natural'. It could seem an affectionate exaggeration for his former pupil Leslie Rees to write in 1940 that Murdoch was 'the household philosopher of a thousand homes; his cool, even, slightly burred, slightly metallic voice is eagerly listened to from Kojonup to Magnetic Island, from Nimmitabel to Rum Jungle'[7]—that is, throughout the continent—but Rees was then an officer at A.B.C. headquarters and moreover had actually visited these four corners of the Australian world. In 1943 Molesworth was asked to comment upon a complaint about the infrequency of national broadcasts from Western Australia. We need notice here only the beginning of his memorandum:

> In previous years we have broadcast few national talks from Western Australia, chiefly because any such talks had to be recorded and sent to Eastern States for broadcasting. However, we had, from time to time, a short series of talks by Professor Walter Murdoch. We have always been prepared to record Professor Murdoch, and broadcast his recorded talks on the National Programme, whenever he has been willing. It is only on occasions that he is willing. He will never broadcast unless he feels he has something worth while to say.[8]

Though the form was simplified, the subjects of his talks were essentially similar to those of his articles: books, men, values, the problems of the time, the tyranny of words and labels, Australian society and culture as they were and as they might be. His radio talks and his writings were both, in different media, exhibitions of his 'vice of preaching', his everlasting campaign against the 'suburban spirit'. And that being so, it is not surprising to find that there were some who were troubled by the broadcasting of his dangerous opinions.

W.M. to Herbert Brookes, 4 October 1934

> ... Our friend Basil Kirke [local manager of the ABC] is getting rather worried about me—people tell him I am a red-hot communist & shouldn't be allowed to be on the air. As it happens, I hate communism like poison—at least, the Russian variety—and I think I'll have to say so some day in a public way.

W.M. to Herbert Brookes, 4 July 1940

> It will interest you to learn that Mr C. G. Latham, Leader of the Opposition in our State Parliament, tells me that he regards me as a fifth columnist and my utterances as treasonable, and that he is asking the Commonwealth Government to forbid me to write articles or talk on the radio till the war is over. He has got it firmly fixed in his head that I am a communist of the most subtle and deadly kind, the kind that pretends to be something else. I had an interview with him but entirely failed to convince him that I dislike communism.

In the manner of Murdoch's first literary enterprise, when as a child he was encouraged to classify the persons of the Bible as 'good' and 'bad', one could list his likes and dislikes as reflected in his essays and broadcasts. Of course it is necessary for a humorist to have recognizable quirks and oddities. When from time to time he wrote blasphemous words about 'imperial cricket', about mechanical gadgets, about crooners, about golf, he was saying what a middle-aged 'character' ought to say; readers would smile and say how 'whimsical' he was. But a good many of them, I suspect, did see the main message of his preaching as Nettie Palmer saw it: 'to laugh at pompous shams: to make loud, angry noises at bad plays, and pictures, and books and ideas: to "loaf and invite the soul" '.[9]

Some themes were clearly more than quirks: his denunciation of examinations, or at least of formal external examinations, his railings against prevalent methods of teaching English, his remarks about unimaginative and stodgy headmasters, his view that after their forties men were unfitted to hold positions of creative responsibility. These were the more irritating because he seemed to be letting down his own side, the teachers. Still, though his views might be perverse, they were matters on which a professor of English literature was entitled to have opinions. More controversial were his ventures outside his professional province, his ironies and side-swipes at the expense of people who felt, and said, that he should stick to his last. Thus he often criticized the social passivity of churches and churchmen in the modern world, and the comparative irrelevance of their doctrinal differences; that meant trouble. He was positively angry about exponents of eugenics and about 'psychological experts', but here perhaps most readers in the 1920s were on his side. And then there were politicians and economists.

Politicians, traditionally fair game, themselves expect to raise laughs by referring to their occupation. Even the Western Australian politicians of 1930 might have smiled at Murdoch's comment on an examination answer on the cause of the death of Lord Castlewood in Thackeray's *Henry Esmond*:

'The basic cause of death of Lord Castlewood was the series of unfortunate events leading up to the fatal death of that nobleman.' A boy, I say; it must have been a boy; no girl, however talented, ever wrote such a sentence, so solemn, so oracular, so entirely devoid of meaning ... Obviously, the boy who wrote that wonderful sentence is cut out for a political career. Perhaps, being a prodigy, he will die young; but if he lives nothing can keep him out of Parliament. If he can say this kind of thing while he is yet a boy at school, to what heights of eloquence will he climb when he is a man and a member of the House! With what consummate ease will he answer disconcerting questions such as, 'What is the cause of the present bad times?'[10]

Australia has an outstanding tradition of merciless journalistic representation of politicians, a good deal of it, as in the Melbourne *Age* in Murdoch's youth, more unscrupulous than the most despicable of politicians could conceivably be. He was not a competitor in this personal game but he did tend to say more about the vast empty spaces of politicians' minds than was comfortable to those who reflected that the finance of universities depended upon the goodwill of elected persons. Certainly there were some grotesque examples of political unwisdom in Australia in the 1920s, but his deep-rooted scepticism of politicians' intentions and abilities seems to have been based on more than distaste for the awful self-confident localism of the 'absurd creatures' around him. There was a kind of shudder in his remarks on the revelations in the diary of Colonel Repington, reviewed in 1921, of politicians 'in their game of scheming, plotting, shuffling, intriguing, blundering, while men were dying at the front'.

It was the pompous self-righteousness of politicians that roused his ire, whether he was describing an imaginary example, so invariably virtuous in all his dubious dealings that he literally developed a halo, or whether he was embellishing the fatuous comment of a minister of the Crown about Perth's undrinkable water. There was an obvious comment: if politicians were not to be taken seriously, why had he spent some years in writing about one of them?

In 'A Plea for the Politician' he attempted to reply.[11] Parliament, he wrote, that dreary wilderness of insincere verbosity has everywhere fallen into contempt; that can be taken for granted. Still, he believes that the picture of the politician held by the man in the street is inaccurate: he is not, or not generally, 'a person who has sold his soul for a mess of pottage, a person of brass mouth and iron lungs, who spends his days in making promises which he will never perform, in proffering statements which he does not believe, and in drawing wages which he has not earned; a person without a vestige of veracity or a rag of honour'. Far from it. He himself had spent some years 'in writing the biography (and the eulogy) of an Australian politician'. His conclusion was 'that while the politician of the baser sort is among the least attractive of created beings, yet it is in the ranks of the politicians that we shall find the most public-spirited and the least selfish of our citizens'. But they do have a bad reputation and must know it. How can they come to be regarded with respect? By ceasing to be victims of the party machinery.

> We cannot be expected to feel any veneration for a cog or a crank or a lever; our respect is reserved for men. The country is crying out for men—men of courage and conscience, men who will guide us and not merely flatter us, men who have opinions and the courage

of them, men who will sacrifice their convictions neither to party machines nor to popular prejudices. If our present political system makes it impossible for us to put such men in power, so much the worse for us.

I don't suppose that politicians were much affected by the opinions of a popular writer about their profession, though some of them certainly read him. He could be amusing enough, but had no understanding of the real world. It was no use engaging in controversy, for with his damned fluency you could not win a verbal battle with him. But I guess that when his name was mentioned they were apt to think of him in those years as a bit of a nuisance, a 'stirrer' in the language of a later day, an academic who would not stick to his last but would say clever things about public affairs beyond his competence. So from time to time some important figure in Western Australian politics, perhaps a Country Party member, would denounce him as a public danger and make noises about the necessity of disciplining university professors. And he would write an imaginary sermon on the text, 'In the midst of life we are in Perth'.

Among the 'experts' whom Murdoch occasionally denounced were economists, but readers of his reprinted essays, which are neither dated nor complete, would not altogether understand his antagonism in the 1930s to a species surely *a priori* no more objectionable than eugenists or psychologists. It was not specifically personal. Murdoch sometimes criticized his colleague Edward Shann in private letters, but after his too early death in 1935 no one else wrote about him more vividly and affectionately, on various occasions during the next thirty years, than Murdoch. Indeed, one of his early jibes about economics has a joking reference to Shann: 'Walter Bagehot said somewhere that no one has ever shed a tear over the death of an economist; but the statement seems a trifle severe. I know one economist who (when you can keep him off economics) is quite bright and amusing; and there are probably others!'[12] I doubt whether, at that time, he knew any other of the very few 'economists' in Australia, and the reference to Bagehot probably came from Shann himself.

In his occasional sallies about economics in the 1920s he was concerned with the impenetrability and uncouthness of its jargon, carefully picking peculiarly horrible examples from books he was unlikely to have read. I suspect again that Shann, who himself wrote with style, showed these to him. Murdoch might express some fastidious distaste for the concentration of economics on those aspects of life which had no place for beauty, emotion, love. But he was not really preaching *against* anything. His serious concern in this decade, when he was president of the Western Australian branch of the

League of Nations union, was with war, the dangers of renewed international conflict, and the public apathy about these matters. Suddenly, in the early 1930s, he began to attack 'economic experts'—not their jargon, or the dismal nature of their subject, but their claim to any professional competence at all. He was not now teasing but denouncing them as incompetent, blind, prejudiced, and that was his tone for years to come.

In an article originally published in November 1930 he suddenly launched into the theme of 'poverty in the midst of plenty': 'some people speak of the present bad times as an economic crisis; but it is not really an economic crisis, but a money crisis'.[13] Then in April 1931, in an article beginning, lightly, with reflections on the game of 'Fly Poker', he suggested that the reader would be angry if a dabbler began to write about economics. I well remember that some of us did read what followed with astonishment and dismay, for in a paragraph *not* included when he republished the essay he wrote:

> If I asserted (1) that our present monetary system is all wrong, and that the projects so far put forward by our various political parties are at best palliatives and not cures, none of them going to the root cause of our troubles (2) that anybody who poses as an economic expert without having mastered the proposals of Major Douglas and his disciples is a bit of a fraud and (3) that while we are learning what has to be done—say, for the next two years—Australia should make a magnificent demonstration of true comradeship, and allow no one to draw from the common pool more than the basic wage—If, I say, I were to make these assertions (all of which I do most powerfully and patently believe to be true) you would be very angry and say I was mad ... [But the reader need not be worried. In future he would leave the present distresses] to be dealt with by persons more competent than I—to the experts, in fact. Heaven help us![14]

As students we were little concerned with his third point. My own 'income' was £32 per year and the 'basic wage' of about £4 a week would have been a fortune to me. But the second point worried those of us who were also students of economics. It was as if Shann, in the course of an article on public finance, had diverged from his theme to announce his conviction that Bacon wrote the works attributed to Shakespeare, and that any professor of English literature who did not master the literature on that theme was a bit of a fraud.

I do not know precisely how Murdoch became convinced that in the doctrines of Social Credit, as expounded by C. H. Douglas in the 1920s, lay not only the immediate remedy for the world economic depression but the blueprints for the future prosperity of mankind.

Certainly he read for himself some of Douglas's books, for they were in his library. And being Murdoch, once he was convinced of their relevance and importance, he was not likely to refrain from announcing his conversion because he might shock many of the readers to whom 'Douglas Credit' meant heresy. The directors of the *West Australian* would certainly have been among these. Murdoch's regular semi-literary articles ceased abruptly, and though his articles on public issues—for example, on the question of 'Secession' from the Commonwealth—were published from time to time during the 1930s, he practically ceased to be a contributor to that paper until the end of the decade. In his articles in the *Argus* and in a new series in the *Australasian*, which began at the end of 1931 as if in compensation for a loss of remuneration from the *West Australian* (he was shrewd in these matters), he did not directly mention Major Douglas, though often enough he aired his own views on the monetary system and continued to berate 'economic experts'. Not that he wished to give the impression that he had changed the beliefs announced in 1931. He wrote for the *New Era*, a Social Credit journal, and would speak in favour of that cause at meetings of its supporters. In the preface to *The Spur of the Moment* (1939), his last volume of reprints published before the war, he reiterated that he was 'a believer in sane finance—which means, for me, some form of Social Credit'.

Minority movements tended to appeal to Murdoch. The Douglas Credit enthusiasts claimed to have isolated a central and continuing cause of malaise in any complex money-economy. Their proposals were not revolutionary, nor party-political; they were based on their diagnosis of a chronic defect in the modern economic process—that purchasing power sufficient to meet the prices required by producers' money-costs of production did not come into the hands of consumers. This could be remedied by a series of monetary devices which need change nothing—except the paradox of poverty in the midst of potential plenty. The Social Crediters were, he thought, earnest and selfless; their critics, who seemed to have no answer to the massive unemployment problem of the times except the message that we must tighten our belts, were either 'experts' who told you to stick to your last (always a red-rag to Murdoch) or members of a conspiracy of bankers and financiers controlling credit in their own interests, or at best their own institutional interests.[15]

His remarks on 'economic experts' became increasingly sarcastic and even offensive, particularly, I think, after he had been rebuked by D. B. Copland, the most prominent of the economists of the 'Melbourne school' who were frequently read and heard on the problems of the depression:

... the economist has his uses in the world, and one use in particular ... The true use of the economic expert is to refute other
economic experts ... He may have other uses, though I, personally,
have not yet discovered them ... My wireless expert did put my set
right; what has the economic expert ever put right?

Behind this tone lay the frustration and anger of a man deeply moved
by the suffering of the depression years, and provoked by what he
took to be the indifference to obvious truths of those who would not
take the trouble to examine them seriously and carefully.

Murdoch's concern with the cause of 'sane finance' in the 1930s
involved what must have been the most thankless course of preaching
that he ever undertook. Though the themes of his *Argus* articles were
still nominally much the same—books, travel, the odd varieties of
human behaviour—he now, too frequently for most readers, con-
trived to refer to the iniquities of the monetary system and to hint
that the remedy was at hand, ready for use when the forts of folly fell.
In these passages the sarcasm of the angry preacher tended to displace
his usual mode, what Arthur Phillips has called 'the art of good
humoured devastation'. Ridicule or rebuke merely confirmed his
faith in 'the sacred duty of growling'.

As a young lecturer in economics in the 1930s I must have been
somewhat concerned about the state of mind of my old teacher, for I
find this reply to a letter in which presumably I had hinted at
something of the sort:

W.M. to J. A. La Nauze, 31 January 1936

... Of course you are perfectly right about my inconsistency in
confessing that I know nothing about economics and at the same
time claiming to know the cure for our economic ills ... But I don't
admit your inference, for practical reasons. We who are not economists are yet compelled to take action in matters which concern
economics; and the best we are able to do is to make up our minds
which of the economic advisers we are going to listen to. I may,
without a six years' study of the theory and practice of medicine,
make up my mind that I am going to have complete confidence in
a certain doctor; especially when his diagnosis seems to me to fit the
facts of my case better than any other doctor's has done. Now I
have chosen Major Douglas as my economic doctor; and my
confidence in him is not shaken in the least by the fact that other
doctors, who know a million times as much about medicine as I do,
call him a quack. I must admit that I attach more importance to his
diagnosis than to his prescription; but the genius he has shown in
getting at the roots of the disease makes me incline to believe that
his remedy is worth trying. I am so far from being an orthodox
Douglasite that I don't feel confident that his remedy will effect a

cure; but as no one else seems able to suggest any remedy at all except one that would, to my mind, be worse than the disease (e.g., communism), why, I say, let us try the Douglas medicine.

After all, there *is* something in the old tag, that 'outsiders see most of the game'. Yours is a dreadfully intricate subject, and some of you—not you, I hope—get so tangled up among the undergrowth that you fail to see the stark and simple facts that stare us outsiders in the face. After all, there must be a remedy possible for the present state of affairs, and I have so much faith in the English language that I believe there must be a remedy which could be stated in plain and simple terms.

Well, yes . . . but in fact 'the' remedy (as it was to seem for a generation) must already have been in the post, for Keynes's *General Theory* had just been published. We are told (1976) by the prime minister of Australia that Keynes has nothing to say to us now, but at the time perhaps even Murdoch could approve of an economist who argued that 'the characteristics of the special case assumed by the classical theory happen not to be those of the economic society in which we actually live, with the result that its teaching is misleading and disastrous if we attempt to apply it to the facts of experience'. But Keynes also demoted Douglas from major to private in 'the brave army of heretics'.

There was not much fun in all these preachings. Murdoch could prick pomposity lightly; his touch was heavier when he grew indignant about bankers. But even on that grim theme he managed sometimes to write a sentence that one would not willingly let die. In London in 1934 he saw 'a humble painted board with the words "Bank of England, temporary office". Behind that door, I reflected with a kind of thrill, Mr Montague Norman may at this very moment be sitting making a mistake about the gold standard, a mistake that will affect the lives of men and women in Kamchatka and the Andaman Islands.'[16]

In 1927 Murdoch spent some five months of his sabbatical leave in Italy, divided between the beginning and the end of the year. His articles despatched to the *Argus* were confined to the familiar topics of travel writing, entertaining enough because he had something to say beyond mere description, but in these he said nothing about Mussolini's fascist regime, nor did he mention it in numerous letters to his daughter written during his second visit. He was back in Perth in January 1928. On 25 February Elzevir's article for the *Argus*, 'Italy To-day. The Mussolini Regime', was published. 'It is not . . . of the tourist, but of the Italians themselves, that I wish to speak in this article—which, I may say . . . is my last on Italy. After this outbreak I shall return to my usual mild and inoffensive themes. But this last word I really must be allowed to say.'

It was a remarkable article for its time, at any rate for the Australia of its time. For most Australians, Italy was a land of famous scenes and cities and buildings. If Mussolini's regime had brought some discipline to a cheerful but inefficient populace, it would do them no harm, and the trains would run on time. But unlike most tourists, Murdoch could read and speak Italian.

> ... unquestionably a reign of terror is in full blast at the present moment in that unfortunate country ... You must take what I have to say not as ascertained fact, but as mere impressions—the impressions of a person, who when in Italy, did not live among the Americans at expensive hotels, who kept his eyes and ears as wide open as he could, who spoke with as many people as he could induce to talk, who accepted nobody's opinion as necessarily correct, and who was gradually driven to certain conclusions. To put these conclusions in a nutshell—I have an immense liking and admiration for the Italian people, and an utter loathing and abomination for the present Italian Government and all its works and ways ...

> Many good men and true, men of fine intelligence and high patriotism, have been kicked or clubbed to death by bands of young blackguards of the Fascist militia ... Others have been lucky enough to escape into England or France. Many thousands are to-day herded with criminals in those horrible Italian prisons; and many hundreds are eating their hearts out on two small islands near Sicily, which are kept as a limbo for opposition politicians ...

> My detestation of Fascism is not based on a mere question of political machinery. It is based on my observation of the moral and spiritual state into which Fascism has brought the country. All those vices now thrive in Italy which have always thriven in lands where liberty was destroyed. Suspicion, spying, whispering, tale-bearing, sycophancy, hypocrisy, are the natural fruits of the Fascist revolution ...

> I do not know any better way of proving your fitness for freedom than by dying for it; and the Italians shed their blood abundantly in the great cause. And the fruit of all their travail of soul and agony of body is—a country in the grip of a merciless tyranny; a sorry anti-climax! I have too much admiration for the Italian people not to feel assured that the overthrow of that despotism, though it may be long in coming, is bound to come.

This anti-fascist blast from the Antipodes attracted some attention in wider circles than Victoria, for in the May number of the *Contemporary Review* Wickham Steed quoted it at length in his article 'Fascism and Liberty'. He was reviewing books by two well-known refugees from Mussolini's Italy, Luigi Sturzo and Gaetano

Salvemini.[17] Forestalling the inevitable charge of bias, he quoted at length the 'recent and entirely independent testimony' of Murdoch's article, which he wished that 'every public-spirited man and woman in this country would read', and promised to reproduce it in full in the *Review of Reviews* (as he did in the May number). As he pointed out, Murdoch could not have read Salvemini's book, which had not been published when he wrote the article, though (I would add) it is likely that he had talked to various Italian intellectuals in London between his two visits in 1927, so that during the second he knew more precisely what he was looking for beyond the charm of the tourist's Italy.

Violet Murdoch became alarmed. Catherine would return from London later in the year and had some plans for visiting Italy on the way. Perhaps her father's article would put her in some danger. Though Murdoch pooh-poohed the idea that Mussolini or his agents would be troubled by any article by an obscure Australian professor, he did advise Catherine not to return by an Italian boat unless she could travel with a 'trusty companion'. More seriously, he asked her to pay a complimentary visit to Salvemini, who after reading his article had sent him a copy of his *Fascist Dictatorship in Italy* 'with a rather absurdly flattering inscription in it, which, in spite of its absurdity, pleased me enormously'.[18]

In the later 1930s there were still people in Australia—I think of some then holding positions in the University of Adelaide—who welcomed the purifying wind of fascism in Europe, though now their admiring eyes were fixed on Germany or Spain. To such people Murdoch's attitude towards the 'Kisch affair' of 1934–5 could only have confirmed suspicions about him, for why should a loyal Australian wish to protest against the exclusion from Australia of a Czechoslovakian journalist, said to be a communist, certainly a communist sympathizer, who came to lecture against war and fascism? 'Australia', said Murdoch, 'had disgraced herself by excluding an author of international repute who was coming here as an anti-militarist'.[19] If most of Egon Kisch's Australian sponsors were more concerned with the danger to Russia posed by Hitler's rise to power than with the problem of war in general, it was still true that his exclusion had about as much sense as the contemporary ban on the import (in cheaper editions) of the *Communist Manifesto*. After he did enter dramatically by jumping to the wharf in Melbourne, the next few months of his adventures provided a lesson in 'the futility of governmental suppression of dissentient opinion',[20] but whether as a result of his presence a single Australian *changed* his opinion on fascism or communism is doubtful.

Though the fact that Kisch had first attempted to land in Western

Australia was the immediate reason for Murdoch's being one of the first critics of governmental timidity, his words on the matter then and later could only show to some how his mild manner could conceal a subtle corrupter of decent Australian values. I suppose he was more often denounced as a communist by stupid people on the right than as a hireling of capitalism by stupid people on the left, though both labels were attached to him. He would assert that he disliked communism and would hate to live in a communist world, yet he would insist that 'the Russian experiment had to be made, and we ought to watch it intelligently, while remaining glad that the laboratory is Russia and not Australia'.[21] Statements like this, together with frequent criticism of the working of the existing economic system, were enough in the 1930s to arouse dark suspicions, since he wrapped them in a manner of writing that ensured him large public audiences.

Indeed it seems remarkable, in retrospect, that he did retain his readers, for in a 'scurvy' period of Australian intellectual life (in Geoffrey Serle's phrase) he did not flatter the wide range of people to whom he became a 'philosopher' and a guide. His repeated injunction was that, as Australians, they should look at the quality of their civilization—and ponder.

In the preface to *Speaking Personally* (1930) he named 'the suburban spirit' as, for him, 'the everlasting enemy'. His original treatment of that theme had in fact appeared years before in an article of 1921, describing the awful sameness of Melbourne's suburban streets, with their red-tiled houses, neat lawns, gravel paths, *Pittosporum* hedges, reflecting a uniformity of spirit, a complacency, a positive fear of originality or difference.

> The social reformer whose work lies among squalid slums will tell you that a city consisting entirely of streets like this is his idea of the new Jerusalem; whereas Nietzsche, I fancy, pictured hell as a place where people live for all eternity in red-tiled villas with trim and tidy gardens around them. It was streets like this—and what they stand for—that drove Nietzsche into a madhouse. But while he was yet sane, he was the standard-bearer of revolt against the suburban spirit in modern life; and until that spirit has been exorcised, his work will remain valuable.[22]

He proposed a Nietzschean remedy: to set apart the Dandenong ranges behind Melbourne for big-game hunting, and to introduce lions, and tigers, and springboks (eked out with politicians) for them to feed on; young men could go hunting at weekends, returning 'reduced in numbers perhaps, but happier and better than the wildest adventure with a lawn-mower could have made them'. (Nettie Palmer suggested, in a letter to the *Argus*, that a better use for the energies of the supermen of suburbia would be ridding of the Dandenongs of foxes.)

Of course Murdoch was himself a suburban man, a townsman, who lived in a red-tiled villa in a road then (as we have seen) actually called 'Suburban Road', but if he had been asked how he reconciled his preaching with his practice, he would have said, 'Well, I protested.' Or as he put it in one of his essays, 'Mankind may be divided into two races, those who acquiesce, and those who growl. I am on the side of the growlers, always and everywhere; because I remember what I owe to them.'[23]

It was not really the villas that worried him. We could say, by extension, that his enemies were the multifarious aspects of the suburban spirit in Australia: the conformism and imitativeness of Australian cities, 'respectability', the texture of national life and the loss of a sense of national purpose, the reading tastes of the general public. the stultifying effects of educational systems, especially examinations, the failure to stimulate and provide for controversy in radio programmes and schools, the aridity of the Australian theatre, the lack in our literature of a first-rate satirist 'to teach us to laugh at what is ridiculous in ourselves'. So one reader, C. N. Connolly, lists a few of his themes. Consider Murdoch's views about one large and depressing aspect of the suburban spirit.

Murdoch was a constant and known enemy of the censorship of imported books, both as a writer and a man of standing who would state his mind to reporters and be widely quoted. His indignant views on that theme were frequently expressed in the years of 'frenzy', as Peter Coleman called them, when Australia and Ireland led the western world in the practice of official protection, at the borders, of the moral purity of their people.[24] And he was prepared to answer the obvious question: would you have no censorship at all? In 1930 there was actually a Customs Department ban on *Moll Flanders*. After dealing with that *bêtise*, he continued,

> Would you not have a censorship at all then? I do not go so far as that . . . I think there are many really poisonous books . . . There are many books which I should be quite glad to see kept out of Australia. But as I do not know anyone whose wisdom I venerate so much that I am prepared to obey him when he tells me what I ought not to read, so, likewise, I do not trust myself sufficiently to want to dictate to other people. The fact is, I am not very clear in my own mind about this matter of the censorship. I fancy that, without some kind of watchdog, our country might be flooded with pornographic literature.[25]

Had he sold the pass? Not at all, for all that he was prepared to concede was that he could approve of censorship by the unanimous vote of a committee of 'six fairly educated and sane persons' *including himself.* His own standards of the 'hardness' of pornography would doubtless now raise some smiles, but if, *per impossibile,* such a committee had been constituted, educated readers in the generation after about 1930 would have had few worries about the insulting absurdities of the Customs censorship. With Murdoch as a member, unanimous verdicts to ban a book would have been few indeed.

Of course he was not alone, but it is no part of my purpose to summarize the shameful story of Australian censorship, and its gradual alleviation by the efforts of protesting bodies, and some growth in the moral courage of politicians. Murdoch's was simply one protesting voice in this dark period, but it was a well-known voice. In the 1970s it may seem incredible that in 1936 a university professor should have thought it necessary to address these remarks to a meeting of students:

> As to our present Australian censorship I consider it both ridiculous and insulting. It is ridiculous because some whipper-snapper in a government department is able, of his profound wisdom and his wide knowledge of literature, to say what books we may not read; and because some of the greatest works of modern literature have been banned by these illiterates. It is insulting because it assumes that we Australians are less able to take care of ourselves than the inhabitants of the British Isles. I don't think we should try to capture too much ground in a single battle. I think we might start by suggesting to the Commonwealth authorities that any book which is allowed to circulate freely in England should be allowed to circulate freely in Australia. If we could secure that reform it would be at any rate a first step.

He knew well enough that before 'literary' works were banned from entry a small advisory board in Canberra was assumed to have been consulted. His reply was that it was a well-known fact that in many cases the opinion of the board had not been asked for.* I

---

* *West Australian*, 3 June 1936. Murdoch's old friend Robert Garran was then a member of this board and in later years, under a somewhat changed system, became appeal censor. In his posthumous *Prosper the Commonwealth* (Sydney 1958, p. 391) he wrote of the system as he knew it in the mid-1950s:

> The Customs Act is ordinarily administered by the Minister of Customs, and under him by the Comptroller-General of Customs. About most of the imported matter concerned, the Comptroller-General and the Minister have no doubts, and they act without asking for assistance or advice. But in border-line cases they often wish to be supported by expert advice, and for that purpose the Minister has appointed the Censorship Board and the Appeal Censor. These individuals have no statutory recognition at all. They are simply persons who, when the Minister asks for advice, give it to him. When the Minister gets the advice he follows it or not as he thinks fit.

Which seems to take us back, in many cases, to the judgement of Murdoch's 'illiterates'.

suspect that Murdoch, a survivor from the Victorian age, would not have been entirely happy to see on open display some of the books which today are available for purchase by any schoolchild who has, perhaps, won a book token as a prize. But his general record on the question of censorship remains: in the dark days he protested.

At the end of the last chapter I quoted a letter from one academic who had learned something about literature and the world from a reading of Murdoch's essays. So did another, whom I now quote. His letter may help to remind us that though the medium is the same, the message may differ.

> You ask me to write about Murdoch. I remember him, and his column in the papers, particularly as a friend of my father's and a person whose work [he] admired much. He had a couple of volumes of essays which he would read aloud sometimes to us as growing children. Oddly, perhaps, I used to enjoy this. Later as a young man I used to read his bits in the papers often enough but not regularly. They had some favourable influence on my political and other notions and, I think, on my English writing style. I think their influence on my father was not quite like that though. He thought Murdoch 'a clever begger' as he did G. B. Shaw. He admired and enjoyed the cleverness and the quality of the writing in both cases but somehow managed to shut out of his consciousness the political and social message, or at any rate the political and social implications of the writing. However, when I come to think of it, I expect the same might be equally true of his and a host of others' reading of Dickens, for example.

RETIREMENT

THOUGH MURDOCH DID NOT formally retire from the university until the end of 1939, for some time before then his hours of teaching had been reduced, and as it happens the close of one phase of his career can be more fittingly marked by several incidents of his personal life in 1938. If 'one phase' seems a somewhat odd description for a man nearing sixty-five, it must be remembered that for nearly thirty years longer he was still to be widely known as a writer, even though he had nearly finished with his familiar mode, the 'essay'.

In the later months of 1937 the Melbourne *Argus* took on what it proclaimed as a 'new' look, with new type and a more vulgar manner of presentation. Soon the weekend magazine section became a glossy 'supplement' with painfully comic illustrations matching the articles. It was the first step on the long road to the everlasting bonfire in which it met its unlamented death in January 1957, though some then mourned the *Argus* that once had been. From the first appearance of the 'new' *Argus*, Murdoch suspected that they would not long be together.

W.M. to Herbert Brookes, 2 February 1938

. . . I suspect the Argus thinks me rather an incubus nowadays, and if they knew how to get rid of me with perfect politeness I fancy they would do it; but they don't like breaking with too many of the Argus traditions at once. They think I appeal to a few highbrows only. The real highbrows think I am a vulgariser of all that is most holy; so I fall between two stools. You and I probably agree in detesting the highbrow, in the sense of the academic and pedantic and we would both be dubbed highbrows by the lowbrows and lowbrows by the highbrows. But that's a digression ...

What, by the way, do you think of the Argus's chances of survival? I don't like the look of things. The paper seems to be shedding its old dignity; it used to be dignified even when it was most wrong-headed. Now it has come down to rival other papers on their own plane, and the other papers do that sort of thing better. However, it may pull through. I hope it will pull through. It is horrid to see an old institution perish from the earth, unless it is a rotten institution, which the Argus never quite was.

In later years he said that he gave up writing for the *Argus* because the editor insisted on illustrating his articles, and he didn't like it. Certainly the horse-laugh line-drawings which began to appear in January 1938 were an insult to the paper's best-known literary contributor, now presented as 'Professor Walter Murdoch ("Elzevir")'. But if this was excuse enough, Murdoch was probably in any case apprehensive for another reason. He intended to retire at the end of 1939, and it was important to him that he should continue to make some income from writing. If he did not care to be seen in the company of the bedizened *Argus*, he also had doubts whether she would continue to find that there was any advantage in it for her. It was time to seek other company, both as a matter of dignity and of plain insurance for old age. The title and contents of his last article, 'A Frivolous Sermon on Today's News',[1] seemed deliberately calculated to reflect the new *Argus*—the contrast of the seriousness of the current world news with the triviality and frivolity reflected in the advertising and social pages of the press.

It is a terrible time; but a terribly interesting time. Australia is mainly interested in Test cricket. The nations are at one another's throats; Australians are at one another's cocktail parties. Australians are calling out—to their Press, to their cinemas, to their Broadcasting Commission: 'Excite us, entertain us, lull us with crooning, amuse us with simple jokes; for God's sake, keep us entertained!'

So that was the end of 'Elzevir of the *Argus*', who had first appeared in June 1905 and, as Walter Murdoch, in 1899. To a senior member of the staff whom he had known for many years Murdoch wrote regretfully:

W.M. to W. P. Hurst, 12 May 1938
    ... the comic illustrations to my not-at-all comic articles in the 'Argus' made me certain that the paper was reaching out after a

class of reader different from—I don't say inferior to—the class with which I had learned to feel at home.

. . . I received such offers from other papers that I was making a financial sacrifice in continuing to write for you people. I should have been quite willing to make a financial sacrifice for the Old Argus; but for the New Argus I saw no particular reason to do so.

And yet—believe it or not—I do feel a wrench in leaving my old home, in spite of the renovations which have made it almost unrecognizable . . .[2]

The 'other papers' meant the Melbourne *Herald*, with arrangements made for his articles to be syndicated so that they appeared simultaneously in Melbourne, Brisbane, Adelaide and Perth. In the past Murdoch had written very little for his nephew's paper, but perhaps he now realized that if out of pride he continued to avoid even indirect dependence on a member of his own family, he might find as Keith Murdoch's newspaper interests grew that few outlets were left for his journalistic writing. He told Brookes that he did appreciate the wider audience which the *Herald*'s willingness to syndicate articles made possible: 'If a thing is worth saying it seems worth saying to more than a handful of people in Victoria'.[3] Also, no doubt, it paid better.

The class of reader 'with which I had learned to feel at home': they, or their children, still showed a remarkable appetite for his kind of writing. In 1938, as we have seen, Angus and Robertson brought together the various books published since 1930, to make Murdoch's *Collected Essays*. With the contents of *The Spur of the Moment* included in the reprint of 1940 it comprised a weighty tome of over 900 pages which by 1945 was in its fifth 'edition'. I suppose that it may well be the last such volume with such contents to be published in Australia.

A second publication of 1938, *The Victorian Era: Its Strength and Weakness*, provided contrasts with this tome in two ways. It was a booklet of about 70 pages, comprising two public lectures given in the University of Queensland, and apart from *Alfred Deakin: A Sketch* it was Murdoch's only 'real book' not consisting of articles or essays previously printed. More systematically composed than his typical essays, and addressed to an academic audience, these were good lectures, with something to say even to readers who might have supposed that G. M. Young had made other booklets on that subject superfluous. If the chances of life had allowed Murdoch to be what he called a 'specialist', this would have been his 'period', but to his pupils the lectures have a particular interest. What he says in pride of the splendours of the Victorian era, and what he says in condemnation of its miseries, amount to an *apologia pro vita sua*.

If the *Collected Essays* gratified one class of reader, a single unfortunate article of the same year caused much offence to members of another class. Murdoch's essays of the inter-war years had not consciously been addressed to his fellow-writers, but he would generally have been regarded with goodwill by those who were themselves attempting to make literature. He was an Australian figure, a 'man of letters' in an old-fashioned sense, who at least taught his large audience that literature was to be respected, that the best interpreters and the best critics of life were poets and novelists. Though it was true that he noticed few new Australian writers, those who saw his articles in the *Argus* would know that he said more about Australian literature than was reflected in his books, for what he wrote on that theme was for the most part not republished, but he did tend to return to Lawson (of the short stories), to Frank Wilmot ('Furnley Maurice') or to O'Dowd when he gave examples of achievements he respected. With rare exceptions he did not review new novels, though he had noticed Davison's *Man-Shy* with enthusiasm.

Younger writers could make allowances for these tastes. By the mid-1920s Murdoch had come to the time when even an obsessive reader might be more inclined to reread old favourites, or (among new books) to look rather for the works of writers already familiar than eagerly to greet new modes and new themes. Certainly this was true of Murdoch's attitude towards the contemporary English literature of the twenties, and it was n t likely to be very different when it came to new Australian writers. His isolation was a further factor. Though he wrote for a Melbourne paper, he might as well have been in New Zealand as in Perth when it came to literary talk and friendships, to knowing what was going on, to breathing the atmosphere of his earlier Melbourne days. So he was now inclined to express impeccable general sentiments, rather than to discuss specific examples—to insist that Australian literature could not be forced, that it would come when it would come, that the second-rate should not be over-valued simply because it was Australian. Of course, but that could be the sentiment of a literary man no longer particularly concerned to read new work or to watch for new talent. It was a pity, but there was no offence in it.

Academic journalists (including today radio or television commentators) have one weakness in common, however varied the quality of their individual performances: they will never refuse to write or talk, no matter how remote or how rusty their acquaintance with the proposed topic. It is probably less a matter of greed than of vanity and perhaps the suspicion that if they refuse they may not be asked again. Murdoch should never have agreed to write the article

on literature for a special Australian supplement of the London *Times*
to be published on the 150th anniversary of the first settlement. Its
inadequacy as a survey appropriate to the year 1938 rightly aroused
the indignation of Australian writers who could scarcely appreciate
the value of his services as a critic thirty years earlier. The reper-
cussions of this unfortunate article were felt for some years.[4]

The major part of the survey was concerned with what by 1938 was
largely 'pre-history': with Wentworth, Charles Thompson, Harpur,
Kendall, Gordon, Marcus Clarke, Rolf Boldrewood. Then, briefly,
Lawson, Furphy, O'Dowd and Furnley Maurice, praise for Henry
Handel Richardson, though she is 'out of touch with the spirit of
Australia to-day', the promise of good drama in the plays of Esson
and Vance Palmer, the lack of good satire. Finally, sympathy for the
lot of the writer in Australia:

> Ambitious young writers are apt to flee to London, where a
> number of them have achieved success—but their talent has been
> lost to Australian literature. All honour, then, to the stay-at-homes
> who are struggling against heavy odds to lay the foundations of a
> genuine Australian literature and to give voice to their country!
> The foundations have been well laid; already there are things in
> prose and in verse which will some day win recognition from the
> outer world—'Few, but roses'.

Well, not much can be done in two columns, but Murdoch had
failed to mention a single writer who had not begun to publish before
World War I. The first protest appeared anonymously in the Red
Page of the *Bulletin*, an article in fact written by Frank Dalby Davison
who still retained his indignation some ten years later.[5] Davison
argued that Murdoch had failed to appreciate the real influence of
the Australian environment in forming a 'cultural reservoir', 'a fund
of story rooted in the lives of the people, not in overseas culture'; he
berated him for his neglect of recent novelists who had 'reproduced
Australian rhythms in terms of Australia, and [had] individually and
in the aggregate, a literary power and standing, of which no country
need be ashamed', and he named a dozen of them* before he went on
to poets, critics and descriptive writers 'whose work has given the race
a common imaginative background'. His conclusion was that if
Murdoch 'intends to speak at home and abroad for Australian literature it's surely time he made good the gap in his knowledge'.

---

* Naming 'a few that come quickly to mind' he listed 'Katharine Prichard, Norman
Lindsay, Vance Palmer, Brian Penton, M. Barnard Eldershaw, Brent of Bin Bin, Kylie
Tennant, Eleanor Dark, Miles Franklin, Martin Boyd, Velia Ercole, G. B. Lancaster,
Seaforth Mackenzie, Leonard Mann'. Murdoch knew some of these personally and
had certainly read some of the works of the others. He must have decided against
giving a mere catalogue of contemporary writers.

There was really no answer to this: whatever the lasting value of the work of a good many of the writers listed by Davison, it was clear that the proportions of Murdoch's survey were gravely distorted. Given the restricted space available to him, what he actually did say should have been compressed at least by half, to allow him to say something to English readers about the state of Australian literature at the time he was writing; either his judgement or his knowledge was at fault. The society known as the Fellowship of Australian Writers (which then existed only in Sydney) was moved to send an indignant protest to the editor of the *Times*, asking for 'amendment of the omissions and correction of the errors' and supplying details for the performance of these operations. Though the letter itself was not published, its receipt was mentioned and its nature (apparently much on the lines of Davison's article) indicated in what amounted to a good-tempered apology in a *Times* leader of 23 April 1938. This spared Murdoch as one who 'may well have felt that the true Australian literature was the literature which time and the English-speaking world has already judged', but handsomely admitted that there was a 'particular reason why the newer Australian literature should demand attention', now that it was shedding the clothes originally brought from England.

This episode of 1938 may well have conveyed to the eyes of some of the younger writers a picture of Murdoch as a chatterer about Australian literature whom they could dismiss even though their seniors like O'Dowd or the Palmers still held him in affection and respect. How far the protests affected him, or whether he even read them, I do not know, but a decade later he would find that his unfortunate article was still remembered.

'I give my very last university lecture in about four weeks' time; and then I am going to make a magnificent bonfire of all my lecture notes, the accumulation of about 35 years. How glad I shall be to see the smoke rise to heaven!'[6] Most university teachers approaching retirement would echo Murdoch's sentiments of September 1939. Not that, generally, they say the same things from the same notes for a generation or more; they keep old lectures as a kind of insurance against emergencies. Still, it is unlikely that the bonfire destroyed any quite recent notes. Murdoch was now eager to retire from teaching, though he did have some anxiety about income. He would have to depend in future 'mainly on my pen for bread and butter. I have so far wasted my substance in riotous living—that is, in travelling about the world which I don't regret in the least; it was well worth while. But it is going to make me rather anxious for safe investments in future'.[7] His superannuation payment from the university would not yield vast sums from investment, and his income from royalties was bound

.to decrease in time. It was therefore prudent to keep on writing, but no doubt he would still have done so if some grateful admirer had presented him with a fortune on the day of his retirement.

Though he had gladly abandoned class-room teaching, he was not yet done with the university entirely. As a long-standing member of the senate, he was re-elected when his current term expired early in 1941, though when he had agreed to stand he could hardly have foreseen the consequences of his willingness to continue to assist the senate to make up, in his own irreverent phrase, 'What it calls its mind'.[8]

Since the university once again had a full-time vice-chancellor in succession to Murdoch's dead friend Whitfeld, it might be supposed that its chancellor should therefore be little more than a ceremonial head. The presiding chancellor, however, not only derived consider-able satisfaction from his position of public dignity, but also took a minute interest in the details of university administration; he clearly looked forward to another period of office after his current term should expire in March 1943. Some members of the senate did not regard that prospect with enthusiasm. There was some consultation among them and some canvassing, though (I have been assured by survivors) Murdoch had no knowledge of it until they had secured the numbers, when on their earnest representations he agreed to be nominated. At the senate meeting of 15 March 1943 there were two nominations for the chancellorship; Murdoch was declared elected.*

W.M. to Herbert Brookes, 25 April 1943

> Many thanks ... for your cheering words about the Chancellor-ship. It seems to involve more work than I had bargained for. I thought a chancellor was only a figurehead, and that a figurehead was more or less a joke, and certainly something a ship could do very well without. But it seems there are all sorts of things the figurehead is expected to do. My chief labour so far has been to get on friendly terms with our Premier, who—entre nous—doesn't see what a university is for, and thinks it a damned costly luxury, and would close it down if he were not afraid of a public outcry. (I don't think, myself, that the outcry would be very deafening; but I don't tell him that.)

At this time the university was awaiting governmental action on the recommendations of a commissioner of inquiry into its affairs and governing structure. When that became, the next year, a matter of legislation, Murdoch found himself a good deal preoccupied with public speaking.

---

* The senate minutes do not give the numbers for the voting. But a newspaper report did give them, with some unfortunate consequences. The majority was sub-stantial.

W.M. to Herbert Brookes, Christmas Eve, 1944

. . . I have for the last two months been overwhelmed with cares of state in the shape of a University Act Amendment Bill which the Government brought in and which we had to fight with any weapons we could find lying about. The Bill went through last week, but we did manage to secure some amendments which made it less objectionable. It is still venomous, and we shall have to fight to prevent the University from becoming just another government department, as wooden, unimaginative, and routine-ridden as the Education Department.

Tact, some manoeuvring, and various personal links and understandings between men in the university, the government and the civil service meant in the event that Murdoch's apprehensions were not realized,[9] though they had then seemed real enough. But even at this time, when he had been busier (as he thought) than a chancellor ought to be, he knew well that it was better for the university that he, with his assured public audience, should be prominent in such arguments only in exceptional circumstances. The vice-chancellor was tactful and able; the proper place of a chancellor was to support and if need be protect his nominal junior.

As chairman at senate meetings Murdoch sometimes distressed those with orderly minds; he seemed not to have mastered the standard rules of debate. His severest critic came to the conclusion that 'he is not a chairman in the ordinary sense at all but just an old University Don conducting a tutorial class or a student discussion group'.[10] Well, so he was, but sometimes, perhaps, there was a method in his maundering. One of the senators of that time has told me that while Murdoch was indeed deficient as a 'business' chairman, he was always alert when matters of principle were involved, and especially quick to seize on points where hasty decisions, in a desire to dispose of the agenda, might result in injustice.

He had no great liking for public ceremonies and formal appearances. By 1946, his life 'crammed with little activities' which had become wearisome, he was talking of resigning at the end of the year, but despite a severe illness he was persuaded to stay on. The end of his formal association with the university came in March 1948 when he retired from the chancellorship and the senate. 'I can find more useful things to do in my old age; but it's a bit of a wrench.'[11]

Apart from his duties as chancellor and his continued writing, Murdoch had plenty to occupy him in retirement; as long as he could read, and remain in reasonably good health, he was in no danger of falling into inactive boredom or querulous self-pity. There is no magic about retirement at sixty-five, but there are joys, anxieties and sorrows which in the nature of things are not likely to be part of the experience of most family men until the decade of their sixties. He could take delight in the company of his grandchildren; he was gratified by Anne's marriage to Guy Vanzetti, and could observe with amused wonder and relief her rapid adaptation to a busy country life; he was proud of Catherine's success in broadcasting. There were sudden anxieties, as on the day in 1947 when, about to leave for a holiday with his wife, Murdoch heard that Anne was gravely ill; her life was saved by the chance that a surgeon from Perth was able to catch a plane to the north. In general his own health remained good but for one interval. Then he nearly died.

In September 1946 he entered hospital for a prostate operation. When it was over, he began to hiccup regularly and violently, affecting the wound, and 'kept on steadily for $8\frac{1}{2}$ days which, I am proud to say, is a record for that hospital'. The doctors were 'gravely anxious', and recovery was slow. 'I should have been sorry', he said, 'to think I was going to die of hiccupping. It seems such an undignified end'.[12]

There were three explanations of his coming out of the hiccupping which threatened his life. He himself told Herbert Brookes that one of his doctors had a small stock of curare, the poison used medicinally as a relaxant drug, and that this did the trick. The others were given to me by two friends of his, men of God, who will not mind my reporting them. Independently, as visitors to his sick-bed, they induced him to pray and, gruffily, to permit them to pray for him. Next day the hiccups ceased. Who knows what frame of mind was necessary to allow the curare to work?

These were emergencies, over when they were over. It was otherwise in Violet Murdoch's case. In 1939, during a holiday cruise to the East Indies, her spine had been hurt when she attempted by herself to move a heavy trunk. This became a permanent trouble, causing much pain and restricting her activities in various ways for the rest of her life. Murdoch believed, perhaps without medical justification, that but for this injury her last years would have been serene to the end. However that may be, he told Brookes at the end of 1947 that he tried to conceal his own discomforts from Violet: 'She has enough worries of her own, of which the chief is her failing memory.'[13] That was a few days after their golden wedding anniversary, and now for some years Murdoch had to witness what he had once lived with vicariously in reading the manuscripts of Deakin's last years, though indeed the steady gentle fading of his wife's memory mercifully did not seem to involve the agonies of Deakin's solitary struggles against his condition. 'Well, I realize that I have much to be thankful for', Murdoch wrote in November 1949, 'an unmarred companionship

The picture-window at Blithedale
Violet and Walter Murdoch, 1940s

of,—counting the years of our engagement,—about 57 years; something to thank God for, even if the closing stage is very different from what I had looked forward to'.

He was a very lonely old man during 1950. His daughter Catherine and her husband were in England that year. Anne, busy with her family and the life and work of the farm, could seldom make the journey to Perth. Violet was only fitfully in command of the realities of the present, but Murdoch was in a sense thankful for that when their son Will died suddenly in October. Violet did come to realize the fact, but, for her, all blows were now softened. Reading letters of condolence with their constant note of personal affection for his son, the old man felt a nagging grief: had he himself ever told him how much he loved him?

I shall not intrude further, but I give as it was related to me one picture of the Murdochs' last years together. They were seen in Mends street, the village street of old South Perth where some of the shopkeepers had known Violet for over thirty years. It was now for her husband to do the daily shopping. Her arm was in his, the shopping-bag in his other hand—'the only time he was without his pipe'.[14] She died in March 1952.

In the years since Murdoch had parted from the *Argus* there had never been any interruption of his journalism. Even in his wife's last years he had continued to write, finding in the performance of his weekly task some distraction from present cares. But during the 1940s the nature of his journalism had changed.

At first it seemed that he had simply transferred his writing from the *Argus* to the Melbourne *Herald*, though syndication meant that he was now widely read outside Victoria. 'Professor Walter Murdoch needs no introduction to Australians who appreciate good writing and good thinking. In him the essay in this country has discovered its most accomplished and graceful exponent . . . from now on he is to be a regular contributor to the *Herald*.' Thus the first of his new series of articles, 'The Drift of Things to Come—on Tin-openers and Other Gadgets',[15] was introduced on 18 June 1938. He began in the old vein, with some reflections on simple gadgets, the extension of the meaning of 'gadget' to institutions, to parliament, the law, the church, as devices for doing certain things, and the need to ask of all gadgets, 'What is it for?'. This was Murdoch the essayist, and the article, with a few others written in 1938 and 1939, was included in *The Spur of the Moment*. But for some years to come the immediate preoccupations, first of the threat and then of the reality of war, were reflected in what are better described as lay sermons than as essays.

As always, any attempt to establish the bibliography of Murdoch's journalistic writing soon runs into complications. It is sufficient to notice very generally the course of his contributions to the *Herald* until they took an altogether new turn late in 1945. At the beginning the articles appeared irregularly, sometimes separated by several weeks, until in the early years of the war they had become more or less weekly features. Murdoch was now again using the familiar 'Elzevir' as well as his own name, and in 1941 a new pseudonym, 'Sydney Cobbett', made its appearance in articles discussing books and writers 'as one remedy for jangled war-time nerves' in contrast to his more usual discourses on the general issues of war. From early 1943 he was writing only once a fortnight, probably by editorial instruction in a time of enforced economies. In 1944, when Violet was ill and Murdoch was struggling with housekeeping and housework, his admiring friend Brookes would too often look in vain for the Saturday articles which he was accustomed to read to his wife on Sunday mornings.

From his early war-time contributions, down to the fall of France in June 1940, came the last volume of new selections Murdoch was ever to publish, though he was to continue to write for the press for nearly thirty years more. This was *Steadfast: A Commentary*, issued by

Oxford University Press rather than by his old publishers Angus and Robertson. Contemporary reflections on the issues of war by non-combatants, read long after the event, seldom make inspiring reading, and even poets at such times (except Wordsworth, whom Murdoch inevitably quoted) can write in ways that are better forgotten. But wrenching my mind back to 1940, I find little in the articles reprinted in *Steadfast* which a generation and more later need embarrass a pupil of Murdoch's.

'I am trying an experiment in condensation, packing what would normally have occupied a column into half a column. I shall be interested to learn what you think of the innovation. It is not only a saving of paper; it gives me a chance of trying a new art. I have been writing column articles for over 40 years now.' Murdoch was writing to Brookes in October 1942. If war had meant a necessary reduction in the size of newspapers, there were other reasons why he found not unwelcome an enforced modification of his long-established practices. Violet was not well; they were both old; it was almost impossible to get maids and he was 'nurse, cook, bed-maker, bottle-washer, man-about-the-place and general factotum ... not conducive to decent work on newspaper articles'. This was generally his lot in the war years. He was grateful to Brookes who regularly sent him copies of the *New York Times* supplement and other American journals. These gave him ideas for articles, and he confessed that for the first time in his life some of his own writings were near-plagiarisms, for the best American journalists such as Dorothy Thompson were saying important things that would otherwise not be heard by Australians. In the early years of the war he had said what he had to say about the values under imminent threat as Germany overwhelmed Europe. By late 1944, on the eve of his seventieth birthday, he had 'pretty well given up writing on public affairs ... I have fallen back on literature for my subjects with an occasional travel reminiscence'.[16]

In the 1930s Angus and Robertson had published a new volume of essays about every two years. In 1941 their *Selections from Walter Murdoch* contained nothing that had not been printed in one or another of these. In 1945 the book was included in their 'Australian Pocket Library', a paperback series of reprints, with titles selected by the Advisory Board of the Commonwealth Literary Fund, and in the same year his *Collected Essays* was also reprinted. 'This is a relief to me', he wrote. 'All my books have been out of print for some time, with unpleasant results to my income'.[17] He must have meant the books of essays, rather than the anthologies and the editions of Shakespearian plays, but there were no suggestions for another book. Perhaps Angus and Robertson felt that since the *Herald* articles were now syndicated, the market for 'a new volume of essays by Professor Murdoch' would not compare with that of the 1930s when the numbers of his original readers were more limited. In any case the war was over. What he had written on current affairs since 1938 could now have little interest to book buyers, and perhaps further essays in the old vein, with their combination of idiosyncracy, humour and 'preaching', would have scarcely more appeal to post-war audiences.

Murdoch had himself begun to think so. He was over seventy, and tired. Whether he hinted as much to the editor of the *Herald*, or whether there were hints to him that the themes of his regular articles were growing thin, is not clear, but in August 1945 he was contemplating the end of the kind of journalistic writing in which he had been engaged for the best part of forty years.

W.M. to Herbert Brookes, 30 August 1945

I think I'm going to stop writing articles for the Herald or any other paper. My mind has grown too sterile. The Herald suggests that I should do a weekly column, called 'Professor Murdoch Answers Questions'—I certainly won't do it under that title, but the idea rather intrigues me. People would write in and ask questions, which would provide me with topics without my having to rack my brains looking for them. If they sent questions which I couldn't answer—which would happen in nine cases out of ten—I'd ignore these and concentrate on the tenth. I'd like to know what you think of the project. Would you send me some questions?

I cannot believe that he really would voluntarily have brought his regular journalism to an end if this new scheme had not been suggested by the *Herald*. He was an incorrigible writer who would have been restless with his occupation gone, but he did need new themes. In October 1945 he spoke again of his tiredness; he was 'taking a month or so off writing. The Editor of the Herald makes no protest; and I want to get some reading done before I write any more.'[18] No doubt, but I suspect that he was also trying himself out at the new form. After all, once readers' questions were invited, it would be some time before they began to come in, and it would be as well to have some sample 'answers' in hand.

On 17 November 1945 the *Herald* carried an article, 'Answering Letters, A Way Out', by Walter Murdoch. He explained that he was an insomniac because unanswered letters lay heavily upon his conscience; the questions he would now answer publicly would be those concerned with broad subjects of general interest. 'Remember that you are addressing your question to a very ordinary stay-at-home Australian who has read a little and thought a little, but whose ignorance is varied and extensive.' An editorial note undertook to send readers' questions on to him. They should be such that discussion of them would appeal to at least a considerable number of readers.

The first of a new series, 'Answers, By Walter Murdoch', appeared on 24 November 1945.

🕮10🕮

ANSWERS

'A NSWERS' MADE a new career for a literary journalist who in one way or another had been before the public for nearly half a century. To younger writers, the venture must have marked the final departure from literature of one whose qualifications for inclusion in its ranks were taken more seriously by general readers than by themselves. That would not have worried Murdoch, who made no claims for himself, but to an historian 'Answers' requires consideration on other grounds that take us beyond the 1940s, the last decade in which he was actively involved in the concerns of high culture. I begin by returning to the time when his regrettable neglect of recent Australian writing had so offended members of the Fellowship of Australian Writers.

Some time in 1937, in the old 'front building' of the University of Adelaide, I listened (in company with J. I. M. Stewart) to Rex Ingamells delivering to an undergraduate literary society a lecture which was the first public manifesto of the Jindyworobaks, 'those individuals who are endeavouring to free Australian art from whatever alien influences trammel it'. A young man of about my own age, he was nervous, intense, terribly earnest. He argued that Australian literature, and poetry in particular, must rid itself of the dominance of European values, even to the extent of discarding language embodying imagery alien to the Australian physical environment. I remember asking him whether he thought that illustrations in books on Australian themes should always be photographs, so that there would be no doubt about the authenticity of their reflection of the country. To this unfair and superficial question, he answered rather nervously that he thought it might be a good idea.

It may seem strange that one so young, so passionately concerned to affirm that Australian literature must be *Australian* literature, should have sought and received spiritual aid and comfort from so old and confirmed a traditionalist as Murdoch. Indeed if he had read the essay 'On Being Australian', he might have hesitated. English reviewers of *Speaking Personally* had remarked that it contained practically nothing reflecting its native Australian environment. Murdoch objected strongly to the implication that this was a fault. For him Australian writing was, or would be, literature of world standard because of what it said, and how it said it, not because it was concerned with 'the convict days, the droving days, our explorers, the gold rushes, the kangaroo, the jackeroo, the emu, the lyre-bird, blackfellows, boomerangs, billabongs, billy-tea, bushrangers, rabbit-trappers, gum trees, dingoes, damper . . .'[1] Though the Jindyworobaks were not quite saying that these were the only proper themes for Australian literature—they were concerned as much with imagery and language—the list could have been somewhat daunting. But Ingamells was a very isolated young man, and South Australia was then a very isolated place. He 'had barely heard of the Palmers and most other [Australian] writers when he launched the Jindyworobak movement', writes Geoffrey Serle.[2] Knowing him a little at that time, I can well believe it. Murdoch, from his anthologies and textbooks, and from his general reputation even in South Australia among literate but not necessarily highly sophisticated readers may well have been the only long-standing 'figure' in Australian writing whose name was familiar to Ingamells since his schooldays.

When Murdoch received the pamphlet *Conditional Culture* (1938) and the letter that followed it, he must have been distinctly touched. In the old days he had regarded himself as something of a champion of Australian literature, but earlier that year, it had been affirmed publicly and not very politely that he knew nothing of its contemporary manifestations. Now here was a young man with a message, who looked to him reverently as an elder and a leader and asked for his blessing.

W.M. to Rex Ingamells, 6 July 1938

Your note reached me this morning. I had already received, and read with interest and pleasure, your pamphlet on 'Conditional Culture'. I don't agree with you that the style is terrible; it seems to me very vigorous and incisive, though here and there it seems to me a trifle incoherent. What you have to say is what Australia needs just now, and I hope you will go on saying it: but I would urge you to say it as persuasively as you possibly can, even though that may mean talking down to people in a manner you may abhor. We want from you and such as you a culture not divorced from our common humanity. After all, Shakespeare did appeal to the whole nation, though only a few may have valued what was finest in him. His was not coterie popularity. Culture in England to-day seems in danger of becoming an affair of cliques. Perhaps you will say that no general culture can grow on our present social & economic soil. But if culture withdraws into a comfortable dwelling of her own, that soil will remain unchanged. I express myself badly.

I don't count myself among those whose autographs are of any value; and it irks me to think of you going to the trouble and expense of posting that book. But of course, if you do post it, I shall gladly do as you ask.

I look forward to the Jindyworobak Anthology.[3]

This was the beginning of some years of friendly correspondence. I suspect that some of the derision with which the Jindyworobak movement was received, if overtly 'almost entirely because of its Aboriginal emphasis',[4] may also have been tacitly a side-swipe at Murdoch; new movements should not look for patrons among old purveyors of chit-chat about English writers of the Victorian era. When Murdoch wrote to Ingamells that he, though unworthy, considered it a great honour to have his name printed on the letter-heads of the Jindyworobak Club, he may or may not have known how he was to be described. There is a letter-head of early 1939 naming Professor Walter Murdoch as 'Counsellor', which is rather touching, but I wonder whether Murdoch himself pointed out that he was more concerned to encourage than to advise, and that there was a better word, completely consistent with Jindyworobak principles. At any rate I prefer the letter-head in use in 1943, which begins:

THE JINDYWOROBAK CLUB

Barracker:
Professor Walter Murdoch

It was a fitting fate for one who had so frequently deplored the fanatical interest of his countrymen in 'imperial cricket'.

The brief but not entirely negligible history of the Jindyworobak movement in the middle years of this century is relevant only in so far as it shows Murdoch in an unexpected role. Despite (perhaps because of) his considerable innocence, and despite some absurdities which aroused derision at the time, Ingamells was trying to say something worth saying, and retrospective references to the movement tend to treat it with a certain gentle respect.* Here I simply note that in Murdoch's epistolary friendship with a most earnest young man the gain (as Ingamells certainly regarded it) was not entirely on one side.

The original *Oxford Book of Australasian Verse*, edited by Murdoch, had been published in 1918, revised in 1923, and reprinted in 1928 and 1936. 'Oxford' had been dropped from the title in 1923, but the book was still published by O.U.P. and, as critics were to complain, would therefore to many readers appear to carry Oxford's authority. In August 1943 Murdoch told Ingamells that he was again revising the anthology, omitting some of the earlier items and adding some more modern poems. He expected to include some from *Meanjin Papers*, the new literary journal then edited in Brisbane by C. B. Christesen; he hoped others could come from the Jindyworobak publications.[5]

The new edition was published in 1945 by the Australian branch of O.U.P. When it was reviewed in the Sydney literary journal *Southerly* late in 1946 a ton of brickbats, hurled by four separate hands, was released at Murdoch.[6] The four assailants—R. G. Howarth, James Devaney, T. Inglis Moore and Kenneth Slessor—were all writers of verse; one was a poet of distinction. They were not angry young men (the youngest was forty) but simply angry men. There were some professions of respect for Murdoch in his other capacities, but as an anthologist with claims to knowledge, taste or judgement he was unanimously denounced. The new edition retained far too much rubbish, the additions were inadequate and unrepresentative, the relative space given to the various poets was inexplicable and ridiculous. The 'English-speaking world' was informed that the collection was a damaging misrepresentation of the variety and quality of Australian poetry.

The 'world' did not read *Southerly*. By 1949, apparently undaunted, Murdoch was preparing yet another revision, again with omissions and additions. Affecting to be little disturbed by adverse criticism in itself, he acknowledged that it had brought to his attention 'some excellent writers of whose work I had hitherto known nothing'. *Southerly*'s reviewer, though still critical, was milder than his predecessors: 'For all the faults which still remain . . . the anthology is greatly improved in its latest edition'.[7] But Slessor elsewhere con-

---

* 'Some amends are due, I think, to these Jindyworobaks. At first I simply did not take them seriously at all. I made the mistake of supposing that if a case is badly argued, there is nothing in it at all. But there was always a suspicion in my mind, an uneasy feeling that I had missed something important in what they were trying to say . . .' A. D. Hope, *Native Companions: Essays and Comments on Australian Literature 1936-1966* (Sydney 1974), p. 44.

tinued to denounce the collection which, in its various forms, had aroused his aversion throughout his poetic life.[8]

Reading again these rumblings of 1946 after thirty years, I feel a certain sadness. They were unfair to the editions of 1918 and 1923, which contained much verse undistinguished in form and content but truly enough reflected the state of Australian poetry at that time. In 1948 Howarth and Slessor, editing (with John Thompson) a selection of twentieth-century Australian verse, thought it worth including only five writers of the early years: Mary Gilmore, O'Dowd, Brennan, Neilson and Hugh McCrae. These were all represented in the first edition of Murdoch's anthology. The real trouble was that the revision of 1923 continued to be reprinted long after it had become unrepresentative of Australian verse in general. What was published in the next twenty years, much of it in uncollected form, spoke a more sophisticated language than that of the earlier versifiers (Brennan apart), and the 'world', if it was interested at all, would truly enough be misled. Murdoch could and did argue that an author (in this case an editor) owed some obligations to his publishers; readers would expect to find some old favourites in an anthology. He had told Ingamells that the revision of 1945 would not be 'by any means the anthology I would publish, if I had to prepare, not a new edition, but a new book'. But what would he have included in a 'new book'? I suspect that by the 1940s it would have been largely what he considered to be a better and more extensive selection from familiar writers, with relatively few new names. He was in fact out of touch with contemporary Australian writing, and such of it as he did know was not much to his taste.

No one need be ashamed, at seventy years of age and more, of some failure of response to new tastes and experiments in the arts, and Murdoch said as much in declining in 1946 to review a recent book of verse. Poets, he thought, were always best appreciated by men younger than themselves.[9] It is likely that the new poems he did include in the edition of 1945 were chosen rather because the younger men had said they liked them than because he himself was particularly attracted by them.

It is difficult for any author or editor to refuse an invitation by his publisher to revise a text still in public demand; few, in my experience, are likely to make such an heroic sacrifice of royalties. Still, the old anthology had served its turn. It would be replaced when there were better alternatives, and in time its main critics did act as they might with more effect and more dignity have done from the beginning: they became anthologists themselves.

No such thunderings and lightnings played around the last

anthology to bear Murdoch's name. *Australian Short Stories*, selected by
Walter Murdoch and H. Drake-Brockman, was published by O.U.P.
in the World's Classics in 1951. With inevitable but friendly niggling
about this or that alternative story that might have been substituted,
it was well reviewed, even in *Southerly*; by 1973 it had been steadily
reprinted fifteen times. While looking to the past, it also brought its
selection well up to the work of those still actively writing in the late
1940s. Is there anything more to say about it here than to notice that
Murdoch's last formal association with high Australian literature was
distinctly harmonious?

Yes, a little. Like so much else to do with his writings or com-
pilations, the history of this volume is complicated. He told Vance
Palmer in 1948 that it had 'been brewing these 20 years'; some time in
the 1930s Milford, of Oxford University Press, made a formal proposal, and for a good many years the Australian branch of the press
was fruitlessly jogging Murdoch's elbow about it. Murdoch was
doing something in 1939 when he asked Palmer whether he might
include one or two of his stories; a year later he was discussing
business arrangements with him and writing, 'You and I, as editors,
will get precious little out of it, but we shall be doing some small
service to Australian writers in displaying their wares in so popular a
series'. A few months later he asked advice about the selection and
listed some sixteen writers whose work he wished to include, but by
the end of 1941, it is clear, Palmer had had enough. He was busy, so
was Murdoch, and nothing was being done. Regretfully Murdoch
recognized that 'it is really my procrastination that has brought you
to the conclusion that the enterprise is hopeless'. It was a pity, but the
book would have to wait a little longer.[10]

It waited until after his very serious illness in the later months of
1946. He began to think about it again, and dutifully to read stories
brought to his attention by Henrietta Drake-Brockman, who had
known him since her childhood and had once been his pupil. It must
soon have been perfectly clear to him that that able and energetic
woman knew far more about younger Australian writers and their
current work than he could possibly know, and in July 1947 he asked
her whether she would care to become joint editor, even though 'you
may very well dislike having your name on the same title-page with
mine, which stands for everything out-of-date'. Already Dal Stivens,
Bernard Cronin, Margaret Trist and Frank Davison had agreed 'with
alacrity' to be included; the joint editor's task would be to select and
write to some ten or a dozen others.[11]

From old affection and from compassion (for his troubles were
heavy) Henrietta Drake-Brockman accepted, and in effect took

efficient charge of the project, as her working papers and correspondence clearly demonstrate. Though Murdoch's part was by no means merely passive, most of the 'business', even with O.U.P., was done by her, and her personal acquaintance with many active writers in the East greatly aided the work.

W.M. to Henrietta Drake-Brockman, 22 July 1948

So that brings us, as you say, to the end of our task. I say *our* task though I am perfectly aware that I have had very little to do with it. You speak very kindly of our collaboration; but I have a suspicion that you would never have undertaken it if you had known how lazy and forgetful I had grown. You must often have found my procrastination almost past bearing. If it had been left to me to produce the book, it would never have been produced. For one thing, my habit of reading a story and promptly forgetting it would have been a fatal obstacle. I count it one of my happiest inspirations when I thought of asking you to join me in the enterprise; but you must believe me that I didn't realise at the time how much of the work was going to devolve on you. If I had, I wouldn't have had the effrontery to make the suggestion.

On the whole I feel sure it will be the best anthology of short stories to appear in this country. I have my doubts about some of the entries, and you no doubt have misgivings about some of them. But we can always blame each other for the questionable ones.

At any rate I don't think it will do your reputation any harm, and that is what matters most. *Mine* doesn't matter at all; it is a battered old affair anyhow. I suppose we'll have made some enemies . . . but to make an anthology is to make enemies of every ambitious person who finds himself or herself inexplicably left out. But we have not created an army of enemies as my anthology of verse did and as my new edition is going to do over again . . . I am sure our book, with its overseas public, will be helpful in a small way to the story writers of Australia.

In fact it was not the end, for complex and irritating problems about the length of the book and about copyright lay ahead. But these too were at last solved by the same kind of collaboration divided between them in much the same proportions.

I suppose that with Murdoch's 'Answers' a serious student of Australian writing would say that enough is enough. The early Elzevir has a place in the history of critical standards in a provincial society, the inter-war essays demand notice in their own right, but with 'Answers' have we not come merely to the hobby of an old man with a gift for entertaining chat which keeps him occupied, and brings in some money? For a history of Australian writing as high literature the answer, no doubt, is 'Yes'. There is more to be said if we think of writing as argument, as an instrument of education, as a link between literature and general literacy. The old man continued to write 'Answers' for nearly twenty years. He was often admired, he was sometimes denounced, but he was read. Never before in Australia had so many people been so long exposed, week by week, to the lucid prose and humanistic values of one educated man.

He began the experiment with some doubts, knowing well what would be said about a chancellor of a university who engaged in such activities. Probably the initial batch of three questions were supplied by himself, the first of them arising from Brookes's friendly reproaches:

Is smoking a bad habit?
Was it immoral to drop atom bombs on Japanese cities?
Is suicide a crime?

Each question would be answered in about 500 words, which any experienced journalist could write pretty precisely without bothering to count. From the beginning the success of the experiment was assured.

W.M. to Herbert Brookes, 3 December 1945

I am beginning to fear I have raised a Frankenstein monster. Letters from Adelaide and Melbourne every mail; 26 this morning. But I fancy the flood will subside presently. There are not only the people who ask questions; there are the more numerous people who protest against the answers already given!

That continued throughout the years. When the substance of an 'Answer' did offend the susceptibilities of groups or individuals, letters of protest sometimes came in shoals, as if sent under instruction. The origin of questions was indicated by the initials and location of the sender. Occasionally, I suspect, Murdoch answered his own questions when he was determined to speak his mind on some issue of the day. As he settled down to a task which, it seemed, would continue for as long as he wished to undertake it, he came to supply the *Herald* in advance with a small reserve stock of 'Answers', so that continuity would not be interrupted by brief illness or misfortune.

W.M. to Herbert Brookes, 23 March 1946

Many thanks for what you say about 'Answers' ... such a lot of people have said or hinted to me that to write such things is beneath my dignity. I explain that I haven't any dignity. Anyhow, these disjointed notes are bringing me into contact with a lot of minds the reverse of academic, and it's doing me good, whether it does *them* good or not.

Nevertheless, he found the writing a strain. In August 1946 he wrote that he would not keep it up much longer, though it had been an interesting experience, a resolution he was again to make in 1951 when his domestic anxieties were very heavy, and again to break. So, as it must have seemed to many who had been reading the column since schooldays, 'Answers' became a fixed feature of Australian life.

At the height of its circulation—for it was syndicated by the *Herald*—the column appeared weekly in one principal paper or another in all states of Australia except Tasmania, and in New Zealand as well. The *Sydney Morning Herald* dropped it in 1948, and the *Brisbane Courier Mail* in 1957—the latter, Murdoch believed, as a result of ecclesiastical pressure—but to the end it was probably the single newspaper feature in Australia most widely read by those whose intellectual interests were of the middling sort. From time to time his persistent habit of answering 'serious' questions seriously, provoked controversies. But before illustrating these, I give an example of an 'Answer' to a more or less neutral question to show what he made of these experiments in compression, 'little essays' as he called them:

Are You a Sceptic?

If I may say so without discourtesy, I don't quite see what concern it is of yours, nor of what interest it can be to any living soul except my own. You would not, I trust, have asked me: 'Are you a dyspeptic?' or 'Are you an epileptic?' These questions are not more intimate and personal than the one you ask.

But, since I seem to detect in your inquiry a note of challenge and since I have a weakness for accepting challenges, I shall answer your question as briefly and plainly as may be.

Yes, certainly I am a sceptic; I have always been a sceptic; and I hope to be a sceptic till I die. If, while still alive, I find that I have ceased to be a sceptic, I shall recognize that my dotage has overtaken me.

For a sceptic is just the Greek name for an inquirer. (My dictionary tells me that the Greek verb 'skeptomai' means 'I look carefully, examine, consider'; and that is what a sceptic does.) The only really old persons are the persons who have ceased to look carefully, examine, consider; persons who have lost the healthy scepticism of youth.

You yourself are a sceptic, aren't you? At this moment, are you not wondering whether my definition of a sceptic is correct, and making up your mind to look up your own dictionary on the subject? Well, that wondering about the truth or falsehood of a dogmatic statement, that impulse to inquire further into the matter, is the mark of a sceptic.

It is a popular fallacy that the sceptic is an irreligious person. I don't say that every sceptic is religious; but I do say that every really religious person is a sceptic. 'Quench not the spirit,' says St Paul; don't stifle your impulse to inquire, to examine, to weigh and consider. 'Prove all things,' he adds, putting into three words the essence of scepticism.

But notice that he appends a further piece of advice: 'Hold fast that which is good.' I am not praising that barren scepticism which forbids you to hold fast to any belief, and warns you that what you believe on Wednesday you may see reason to disbelieve on Thursday. This kind of scepticism reduces the mind to perfect futility.

The scepticism I praise and try to practise is of another pattern. It is the sworn foe to that intellectual sluggishness which closes the mind to new ideas; it makes war on spiritual stagnation, on the common habit of taking the easy way and running along in a rut that others have made.

And that is why I say that every really religious person is a sceptic. His faith is the firmest of all, because it is his own faith; he has thought for it and fought for it and won it. He has not committed the blasphemy of thinking that the reason his Maker gave him is an untrustworthy implement.

I hope I have helped you to an understanding of a much-misunderstood word. From what I can make out a lot of people confuse 'sceptic' with 'septic'. There is a difference.[12]

'Answers' might range from such pieces of mild 'philosophizing' to recipes for composing a ballade or a villanelle, hobbies that Murdoch found useful as antidotes to sleeplessness. If he chose to answer a frivolous or even an offensive question, he would skilfully turn it into a text for a discourse in another vein. Occasionally he grew very serious indeed.

One example was his attitude in 1950 and 1951 to the measures proposed by the government led by R. G. Menzies for the suppression of the Communist party. In 1950 a bill for this purpose was passed through the federal parliament, but on appeal was held by the High Court of Australia to be beyond the legislative powers conferred by the Australian Constitution upon that parliament. In 1951 the government sought to gain the necessary powers by a constitutional amendment, which required a referendum of the people. The great majority of those who opposed the measures had little or no sympathy with communist beliefs. Their objections were either to the principle of suppression, or to the proposed means, which included powers to 'declare' suspected persons as ineligible for employment by the Commonwealth, and originally put the onus of proof that persons were not members of the Communist party upon themselves.

Murdoch's first private reaction to the bill of 1950 was that it was 'entirely damnable and a piece of pure Fascism'.[13] In June, when it was before the parliament, he wrote a strong 'Answer' on his attitude towards it. He would deal with communists by arresting and punishing them for criminal acts, such as inciting violence or betraying state secrets to a foreign power, but repression, spying, secret police, 'may be the way for the Russians, but not for us'. To require proof of innocence by the accused was dangerous thinking in a democracy. Murdoch was not a communist, but how could he prove it? 'Speaking as a believer in democracy, I declare Mr Menzies'.[14]

Similar views were widely expressed by other intellectuals and academics in the public discussions preceding the referendum of September 1951. In the event the government's proposals were rejected by the very narrow majority for 'No' of 52 082 votes in a total of 4 754 589. It has been argued that the result was powerfully affected by the efforts during the campaign of one man, H. V. Evatt, leader of the Labor party. A 'consistent civil libertarian, [he] gave one of his finest performances, and probably tipped the scales against the government'.[15]

Probably, possibly, perhaps? But many of the electors who contributed to that small margin for 'No' must to the last have been sorely troubled about what vote they should cast. Like Evatt, they were opposed to the communists, who in numbers if not in influence were a negligible minority of the Australian people, but in a normal parliamentary election they would have voted against him and his party. Could some considerable number of worried people, in voting 'No', have found some comfort and some guidance in the views of another opponent of the measures whom they did not associate with a political party?

In September 1951 'Answers' appeared more or less simultaneously in the *Herald* (Melbourne), the *Advertiser* (Adelaide) and the *West Australian* (Perth). Their combined circulations at that time were over 700 000. On 15 September the *West Australian* published Murdoch's 'Answer' to the question, 'How are you going to vote at the referendum?'

> ... The Government is asking the citizens of Australia to give it powers which I do not believe that any government ought to possess. Therefore I am going to vote 'No' ... I am going to vote 'No' because I hate Communism and all its works and ways, and because what I hate most in Communism is that wherever and whenever it becomes powerful it does exactly what the Australian Government is seeking the people's permission to do. To suppress Communism it wishes to borrow Communism's favourite weapon—the punishment of heresy ...

A week later, on the day of the referendum, the same 'Answer' appeared in the *Advertiser* and the *Herald*. If we reduce drastically the figure of 700 000 to arrive at the number of people who might have read it, and if we allow also for the fact that the *Herald* was an afternoon paper, we may say that probably, possibly, perhaps, the views of the old 'philosopher' had some effect upon the 'No' vote in the three states in which they were published. He, like Evatt, had some reputation as a consistent civil libertarian.

It was unlikely that the communists would now regard Murdoch and similar public advocates of the 'No' case as anything other than bourgeois liberals whose sentimental concern for civil liberties had proved useful for the occasion. On the other hand some respectable people were inclined to think of him as at least a 'fellow-traveller'. But that was what he called 'the pink man's burden': to be suspect unless he was always pure white or pure red. Thus after denouncing Menzies' anti-communist bill in July 1950 he added immediately: 'However, we must all back him over Korea. There is no alternative. If U.N.O. fails in this crucial test, the last hope of the world is shattered, and we start again on an uphill climb of a thousand years.'[16] And though he never changed his view about the central issue of the referendum of 1951, in some other matters he came to see in a different light the man whose sponsorship and acceptance of the Murray report on universities transformed the prospects for higher education in Australia. His willingness to support the 'Australian Peace Council' founded in 1949 puzzled some people, for here the issue of civil liberties was not involved. That body, though its founders were 'clergymen, writers, intellectuals and some trade unionists, the great majority of whom were not communists',[17] was regarded by its critics as a communist front, and these well-meaning people as communist dupes. The critics were right about the 'front', but whether supporters like Murdoch were properly to be regarded as dupes depends on how far one thinks they were simpletons to advocate any cause also approved by communists. In a similar case, an old friend later asked Murdoch to comment upon a letter denouncing his support of the 'Australian Youth Carnival of Peace and Friendship' of March 1952. He replied:

> As to the carnival, or whatever it is called, I certainly sanctioned the use of my name. Several of the sponsors of the affair are known to me personally, and they are not communists as far as I know. But I don't much care whether they are communists or not; if I believe them to be genuinely working for peace, I will work with them.[18]

Over many years various readers were concerned by what he had to say, from time to time, on religion and the churches. Indeed that theme takes us back to an earlier period of his career as a public 'preacher'. His critics were divided between those who thought he did not say enough and those who thought he said too much.

Though Murdoch used to affirm that a son of the manse, brought up on the Shorter Catechism, and knowing the Bible intimately, could not be expected to leave theology alone, I doubt whether anything he said over the years, considered as a formal theological proposition, was likely to arouse in a learned divine of whatever persuasion more than a weary impatience. Theology as understood by his father, who *was* a learned divine, was to him largely incomprehensible, as he explained in answer to the friendly criticism of a Presbyterian clergyman:

> I was brought up on the Shorter Catechism, and got into the habit of thinking that membership of the Presbyterian body meant agreeing with a number of dogmas I didn't in the least understand—justification, sanctification, adoption, effectual calling, and what not. I would not dream of sneering at these things; but, simply, I have not the kind of intellect to grasp their meaning or even to be interested in them. I quite understand that church membership—so far as this particular church is concerned—does not imply any elaborate structure of doctrine; but even the little which is, I believe, required means more than I find myself able to give.[19]

But unlike many of those who would say the same thing about the formal doctrines of this or any other Christian church, Murdoch was neither indifferent nor hostile to religion.

> I am one of many, I believe, who devoutly believe in Christ's teachings, and who firmly believe that He could be the Saviour of the world if the world would allow Him to save it, but I cannot be a member of a church. I am one of those who would join a church if they could only find a Christian church to join.[20]

What his personal religious beliefs were would be hard to determine. It is unlikely that he brooded as much about them as his friend Deakin did, but he did believe in something more than the Christian ethic regarded simply as a supreme guide to secular conduct. 'I think that all the great changes I have seen have been spiritual changes;' he said in a broadcast for his eightieth birthday, 'their origin is to be sought in the world of spirit, not the world of matter. And I think the most important fact in the world of spirit is religion'.[21] And in one of the 'Afterthoughts' of his last year of writing (1968) he said:

> I believe that no faith is in the long run tenable which involves

anything contrary to reason; but also that the reasoning faculty, by itself, will not give us a faith by which we can live . . . where I part from [the rationalists] is that they seem inexorably opposed to any suggestion of the supernatural; and I do most firmly believe that without elements of the supernatural there can be no creed that can save us from despair.

In fact—this will shock you—I believe in God.[22]

In the 1930s Murdoch's concern had been with the role of the churches in the secular world; he exhorted them to 'put all dead formulas aside' and 'to stand for the determined and dauntless application of the principles of their Founder'.[23] They should denounce the sinister forces that held the world's economic system in their grip; they should condemn the existing distribution of wealth; they should stand for social justice; they should show by positive deeds and words where they stood as between God and Mammon. Though he did not explicitly commend to them his own favoured remedy for the world's economic ills, he begged them to demonstrate that Christian principles required the reconstruction, not the conservation, of the 'present system'. In various forms these pleas were repeated in essays and broadcasts in that decade. It would be misleading to suggest that appeals to the churches to do what he considered to be their duty were a main and constant theme, the obsession of a self-appointed director of religious action, but he was so well known that when he did write or speak about these matters—sometimes by invitation—there were inevitably remonstrances. 'I have now to go and answer some letters from infuriated clergymen', he wrote to Brookes in November 1941. 'It does not occur to them that anyone who criticizes the Church may do it from love, not hatred, of religion'.[24]

He ran into trouble in the 1940s, or at any rate invited attack, because he would 'answer' questions which to Roman Catholics in particular involved very serious matters.* It was not that his tone was offensive, or that he formally attacked the received doctrines of that Church; he affected to give simply his personal thoughts on various doctrines and propositions at least vaguely familiar to anyone who had been exposed to some kind of Christian teaching, and even then only because a reader had asked him to do so. Nevertheless, as a popular writer, he might be taken seriously. Hence, at least to Roman

---

* Murdoch gave 'Answers' over the years to questions on such subjects as evil, religious bigotry, the idea of heaven, the Athanasian Creed, New Testament miracles, the resurrection of the body, suffering, the Gospels and biblical scholarship, the meaning of 'Protestant', sin, sainthood and heresy, baptism, and on 'secular' topics likely to affect Roman Catholic susceptibilities, such as aspects of communism, euthanasia, the Franco regime, totalitarianism, birth control.

Catholics who might or did read him with general appreciation, his lack of qualifications to speculate on matters of faith and morals should be systematically exposed. Such appears to have been the motive for the criticism that came from time to time from two sources in Melbourne and Sydney.

The first was the *Advocate*, a long-established Melbourne periodical with sophisticated literary and intellectual standards, read mainly, it would seem, by well-educated Roman Catholics in Victoria. The second critic was Father Leslie Rumble, who for many years conducted from a broadcasting station in Sydney a 'Question Box' session on matters relating to the Catholic Church and its doctrines.

For some ten years from the beginning of Murdoch's 'Answers' the *Advocate* kept a close eye on him. In leaders and incidental paragraphs he became, sarcastically, 'the genial professor', 'the "Herald's" answer man', 'the old man of the West', 'the venerable sage'. Sometimes he was scolded more in sorrow than in anger: 'he has floundered in a fashion which is very lamentable indeed in a man of his great gifts and real good will'.[25] Sometimes he was attacked directly:

> The old man is tiresomely dated and outmoded. The dust and decay of the nineteenth century rationalism lies heavy between his lines. He has been corrected so often (but has never to our knowledge corrected his errors in his 'answers') that he is developing a paranoic fixation that theologians are after him. The Professor really overestimates himself. We can assure him that professional theologians read his amateur theologising, when they read it at all, much as they read Punch, or Mandrake, or work out a cross-word puzzle—all right for an idle moment or an after-dinner laugh. But as Christian journalists we feel bound to warn our readers against the subtle and dangerous anti-Christian propaganda, which, consciously or unconsciously, the Professor perpetrates every now and then in his weekly 'answers' . . .[26]

Certainly some of the doctrines he discussed were to Christians very serious matters indeed. But looking through numerous extracts in this vein from the *Advocate* of the years 1946–56, I wondered why they bothered. Could old Murdoch's reflections really have constituted a danger against which the intelligent readers of the *Advocate* needed to be warned? It seems that they could, for as late as 1960, some years after he had ceased to be a regular subject for refutation, he ventured to make pessimistic remarks about the 'menace of the birth-rate', and the necessity for its reduction by family planning. The 'genial essayist' was very quickly put in his place; the problem was the development of food supplies, not numbers, and that, as Professor Colin Clark and others had assured us, could be solved.

The context of Father Rumble's radio criticisms of Murdoch was rather different. He had been engaged in the business of Question and Answer for many years. Most of the listeners who sent in questions, one assumes, were seeking not so much his personal views as the correct answer. Thus Murdoch had written about 'religions of authority' and 'religions of the spirit', quoting the arguments of the French writer Sabatier. It was not surprising that he commended a 'religion of the spirit'. Infallible institutions, even an infallible book, whatever their uses to those who needed an external authority to lean upon, automatically aroused in him predictable reactions. Patiently, Father Rumble sorted out the errors.

> If a religion of the spirit is essential to a nation's well-being, then so also is a religion of authority. The two go together. A religion of authority without a religion of the spirit would be but empty externalism. A religion of the spirit without a religion of authority would result in endless aberrations, if it did not evaporate completely ... But Professor Murdoch is out of his depth in these matters. He is not a theologian. He is nominally a Presbyterian layman, whose proper subject is English literature ... It would certainly be fatal to lean upon his authority in matters of religion.[27]

These voices from West and East were not engaged in debate; there never was, nor could there have been, direct controversy. Nominally Murdoch was chatting, as an old man of eighty, about the meaning or relevance to him of various words and concepts familiar in general discourse as well as in specifically religious contexts. Actually he was not unaware that his remarks might irritate some members of the Catholic Church, for old Protestant suspicions in the sectarian atmosphere that had surrounded his youth in Scotland and Victoria had not been entirely dispelled by his experience of the church in action. To his critics these words and concepts had technical meanings within an authoritative tradition of interpretation, and they too were affected by that Australian sectarianism which had so long caused Catholics to see themselves as a beleaguered minority. Murdoch in his bumblings, and his critics in exposing them, were both preaching to their own converted.

It has seemed relevant to illustrate the kind of reaction that Murdoch's 'Answers' could sometimes arouse, since readers so often used adjectives like warm, kindly, humorous, whimsical, to describe their image of their mentor. It is well to notice that he was not invariably regarded as a wise old uncle. Yet he and the *Advocate* could occasionally find themselves (rather to his surprise) in happy agreement. The question 'What is your idea of Heaven?' might have brought forth 'a variety of alarming answers'. Instead, it had provoked Murdoch to 'sit down and write as sound a piece of Catholic theology as we could reasonably desire in his column ... It is an amazing success'.[28]

Why ask me in particular? The world's literature is strewn with descriptions of heaven—some ludicrous, with harp-playing and listening to angelic choirs, or sitting surrounded by enchanting houris—and some noble, as in the 'Paradiso' and the third act of 'Man and Superman'. But since you challenge me to produce for your inspection not Dante's nor Shaw's, but my own personal notion of heaven, I must try; though I know it will be a failure.

I once read a story of a man who died and thought he was in heaven, because he found himself in a position to do all the things he had longed to do when alive. But when presently he discovered that he was fated to do these delightful things for ever and ever, he knew that he was in hell. To look forward to an unending future of monotonous bliss would be to suffer the tortures of the damned.

Heaven—my heaven—is a state in which there is no future and no past, but only an eternal Now. Both time and space have ceased to be; therefore it is impossible in human language to frame a description. My heaven would be to know the truth, to see the truth face to face, not in fragmentary glimpses as now; to love and be loved, unhampered by the senses and untroubled by the fear that shadows all earthly love, the fear of death; and to contemplate the supreme and ultimate beauty of which all the most beautiful things I have known, in nature and art, are but shadows and hints. That, I think, is the only kind of heaven in which I should desire to find myself after what we call death.

※⟨11⟩※

THE SAGE OF SOUTH PERTH

WHEN MURDOCH DIED in 1970 an obituary in the *West Australian* described him as 'a sage who resisted being called an oracle'. In 1960 an interviewer had called him the 'sage of the essay in miniature'. In 1948 a critic had referred sarcastically to 'the sage of the West'.[1] He would at any time have repudiated the word 'sage', but it was a word that others tended to apply to him, for the most part affectionately, as he approached eighty. In September 1954 he gave a birthday talk as the Australian Broadcasting Commission's Guest of Honour', a programme then more typically devoted to the tactful Australian impressions of visiting business magnates or medical specialists. 'It proved to be easily the most popular talk ever given in this series. Requests for copies of the script came from all over Australia . . .', the A.B.C. reported proudly. Murdoch had become an institution; it seemed well in 1954 to record him while there was still time. Fifteen years later *Meanjin* devoted to him a batch of three articles, preceded by Louis Kahan's fine portrait-sketch. Again it had seemed well to pay a tribute to the Sage of South Perth while there was still time.[2]

After the strain and grief of the several years round about 1950, Murdoch had found himself in deep lethargy, little inclined even to leave his own house. He thought sometimes of visiting Melbourne to see old friends, but 'whenever I dally with the thought, something comes along and gives me a sharp reminder that my travels are over', he told Brookes in December 1953. The mood changed, as it seems almost suddenly, with his formal entry into extreme old age. He was eighty in September 1954, and he was in Europe before another year was out. When we heard him lecture on Browning, about 1930, Rabbi Ben Ezra's 'last of life, for which the first was made' meant little to us, for we were young. It must have meant more to a man then approaching sixty, but at eighty Murdoch had answered Ben Ezra's invitation 'Grow old along with me', and until nearly the end he could with a certain grim humour enjoy the inevitable pun: he was living his second last of life. It was now not impertinent to ask him how he accounted for his longevity. 'Well, I suppose avoidance of fresh air and exercise have helped a lot. My smoking has been very helpful too.' In 1962 he was still a match for young interviewers.

In October 1956 Murdoch was writing about a forthcoming visit to Melbourne to see relatives and old friends and to stay with the Brookeses. He had asked whether they could put up two guests, since his 'nurse' would be travelling with him. 'The fact is that neither my doctor nor my daughters think me fit to travel without someone to look after me, and I have had to bow to their opinion, though I think it nonsense.' The Brookeses had already heard from time to time about the trained nurse 'both intelligent and kind', who had cared for Violet Murdoch in the last year of her life, of the 'faithful nurse' who ordered Murdoch to bed when she thought he was getting pneumonia, and during the surprising journey to Italy and Scotland which he had been able to undertake at the age of eighty, of 'the companion of my wanderings, Miss Cameron . . . a highly competent nurse, who has kept me in the best of form'. It is fitting that he himself should tell who she was, but I must first say that her parents were highland Scots, immigrants of the 1890s, that her father had become a pioneer farmer at Watheroo, nearly 200 miles to the north, and that she had had the advantage of an education at the Perth Modern School.

W.M. to Herbert and Ivy Brookes, 4 October 1956

. . . I think I had better explain about my so-called nurse, Barbara Cameron was in her student days a great friend of my daughter Catherine's. When she had taken her degree [in Arts], she surprised everyone by going in for a course of training as a nurse. She nursed in the Perth Hospital for a year or two; then being of an adventurous turn of mind, she went to Hong-Kong for a year, and then to Shanghai for seven years. Coming back to Australia just before Japan came into the war, she joined the R.A.A.F. and nursed at [the military hospital at] Heidelberg [in Victoria]. The authorities saw that she was very good with shell-shocked men, and put her in charge, as sister, of the mental side of the hospital. There she stayed until the war ended. That's enough of her story, except that after she had gone to her family home up-country for a rest, Catherine persuaded her to come here and nurse my wife, which she did very efficiently.

After my wife's death I was rather a physical wreck; and after a spell in Victoria, where she had some relations, she agreed to come back and look after the wreckage. She has taken care of me ever since; and as you know, she made it possible for me to go and see my native land once more, taking Italy en route.

More could be said, for example that the seven years in Shanghai were spent in a responsible nursing position in a hospital in the International Settlement over which the Japanese, developing their greater East Asia co-prosperity sphere, would fire their shells. But it is sufficient here to jump to a later letter to the same friends:

W.M. to Herbert and Ivy Brookes, 5 March 1962

It will, I am sure, interest you to learn that after ten years of close companionship, Barbara and I are going to be married. It seems the logical outcome.

I know you will wish us the happiness which I don't deserve and she does.

They were married on 8 March 1962 at the office of the registrar-general in the Treasury Building in Perth. Only Murdoch's

Barbara Cameron (Murdoch) and Walter Murdoch

children and a few friends had been told, but inevitably in his case, though he was not the culprit, the news leaked out. The name Murdoch was by now almost synonymous with Western Australia. So, as a reporter said the next day, the leakage 'brought newspaper and television cameramen and reporters scurrying to the corridor of the Treasury Building's third floor. There they were joined by what must have been the entire Treasury staff—shirt-sleeved men and girls who crowded the hall and outside balcony and went down afterwards to the footpath outside'. There were 'spontaneous congratulations from the gallery' as they came out from the office to walk to the nearby cathedral, where Murdoch, out of affection for his friend Bishop Brian MacDonald, had agreed to attend a further short ceremony. He told the reporters that on his second marriage, at eighty-seven, he had hoped to make a statistical record, but had been informed that not long before there had been a happy bridegroom of ninety.[3]

Some months later, an old man writing to one even older Murdoch told Brookes that he had 'composed a poem beginning "The old man lies awake and hears/The hoof-beats of the galloping years," but I won't trouble you with the rest of it. I am not afraid of hearing the last hoof-beat; and neither, I know, are you'.[4] At ninety-four, though physically very feeble, Brookes was still mentally alert and anxious to talk to me about the old times which I knew only through documents. He died on 1 December 1963. But Murdoch was still to see Italy again, and he owed that, not for the first time, to Barbara Cameron, now Barbara Murdoch.

In his birthday broadcast of September 1954 Murdoch professed bewilderment at the mystical significance which the age of eighty seemed to have for the public, but he admitted that by now he lived on memories rather than hopes. Perhaps these very memories—for he had recalled his childhood in Scotland—prompted a course of action which earlier that year he would have thought to be now quite impossible.

W.M. to Herbert Brookes, 22 December 1954

> I have often told you that I had resigned myself to the fact that my days of travel are over, and I firmly believed this to be true. You will therefore be surprised to learn that the longing to see my native land once more before I die, if possible, suddenly became so over-powering that I went straight to the shipping people and booked a passage by an Italian boat to Naples. It was probably quite mad. But I did take the precaution of going to my doctor for an overhaul, and got his opinion that a sea-voyage is what I need. My housekeeper—who as I told you is a trained nurse—goes with me. On the whole there seems a chance of my not perishing en route to

Scotland; if I do, I shall at any rate have made the attempt . . . Do you think this a mad project? My friends here do, though they are too polite to say so. They are probably right. But what if they are? It is an adventure anyhow; and there is no fixed retiring age for adventures.

So, with Barbara Cameron as his watchful companion, he departed in March 1955 for Naples, and in Italy for a month renewed acquaintance with things and places seen long ago. They flew from Geneva to London when Scotland could be supposed to have 'warmed up a little', and then journeyed north beyond Aberdeen to Fraserburgh, to take the bus to Rosehearty, still the village—but no longer the fishing village—that he remembered. His only illness was the homesickness which brought them back sooner than he had intended at the beginning. And at Naples he had been witness to a miracle 'without the intervention of St Januarius'. His upper dental plate had broken. Before him lay the prospect of three weeks at sea on a diet of bread and milk or custard.

W.M. to his family, 31 August [1955] (at sea)

Then was seen with what commanding energy Barbara handles a situation, even the most desperate one. She went to the Purser or somebody & got the address of a dentist. I shall never forget the address,—via A Diaz 8. After breakfast—breakfast!—she got a taxi and we dashed away in search of the ivory-snatcher. Luckily via A Diaz is in the centre of the city & he was in! Barbara talked Italian to his nurse—they got on famously together—and she took away the broken bits of denture to show the boss. She came back and dashed our hopes to the ground. The job would take some days. We were due to leave Naples at ten that night. The dentist himself came and saw us, and Barbara interviewed him; I am too deaf to hear the interview, and couldn't tell whether she was wildly imploring him or calmly ordering him; anyhow, he took the fragments away & kept us in suspense for what seemed like an hour, then he came back shouting exultantly 'è possibile!'. I almost fell on his neck, but he dodged me and told us to come back at six. You may be sure we were there on the tick, and there was the maestro with what looked like an entirely new plate, but fitting like a glove. There were two miracles involved; miracle A, Barbara's persuading or compelling the dentist to do the thing; and miracle B, his doing in five hours a job [on] which you could expect a dentist to take a week—Anyhow, here I am, fit to chew cast-iron knobs & copper ornaments.

When Catherine King was in Italy with her husband in 1957, she wrote from Lazise that some day they must all come there together. Her father asked her to reflect. Alec King's next sabbatical leave was seven years away. 'By that time, if I survive, I shall be just 90; and if you think it would be fun to go to Lazise or anywhere else in the company of a doddering, shuffling, wheezing, dribbling old total loss of 90, your idea of fun must be ghoulish'.[5] They were in Italy together in 1964.

Of course there were physical failings as time went on, but for most of the fifteen years left to him after the return from Europe in 1955 Murdoch had no serious illnesses. He could lament that too many of the books on his shelves had been bought in cheap editions in his impecunious youth when he haunted Cole's Book Arcade, for their small print was now indecipherable without discomfort. Yet his letters reflect continuous reading over the years, even some modern novels—or at least one modern novel. In 1962 he wrote to his old colleague Arthur Fox, 'Patrick White's "Riders in the Chariot" . . . shows tremendous power. When I say tremendous I mean tremendous; it knocks you down.'[6]

His hearing, already becoming rather dim in the 1940s, troubled him more than his sight.

W.M. to Noel M. Cuthbert, July 1967

You have inspired my Muse:
> Said the old red cow to the little black heifer,
> 'I am growing daily deafer and deafer!'
> Said the kindly heifer, intent on cheering,
> 'No matter, Mama; there's nothing worth hearing!'

But I don't agree with the heifer, and on leaving your rooms last week, I was very glad to find I heard better, and very grateful to you . . .

He had always ambled; in his eighties, he shuffled a little. Visiting him in his Melbourne hotel in (as I find) September 1961, I found him waiting for me near the entrance. There were half-a-dozen steps to ascend to the tea tables. Expecting him to precede me, I suddenly realized with something of an emotional shock that I was no longer seventeen, and that my teacher was an old man who would not refuse a helping arm. Yet until he was over ninety he still wrote letters in his familiar hand, and even when it began, about 1967, to tremble a little, he never forsook his classical punctuation for the sloppiness of dashes. He had never been a pedant but he knew that semi-colons did have their uses.

In Perth he could get out more frequently than had been possible in his later seventies, for Barbara was an efficient driver of the car, and they could often visit friends, or meet visitors at the airport. He acquired some new habits, such as the evening game of Scrabble

which he much enjoyed, though like many academics more concerned with interesting words than with tactical situations, he was
generally outscored. He was still regularly writing his 'Answers',
though in the 1960s with increasing weariness: 'I only keep that up',
he wrote in August 1962, 'because I have to earn my bread and
butter. The "answer" I have just sent away is number 1934. I have
promised the newspaper people that when I reach number 2,000 I
will cease to bother them. I can almost hear their sigh of relief.'[7]
But he did not reach it; his last 'Answer' was number 1992. Writing to
Brookes in July 1963—the last letter to his old friend that survives—he
mentioned the prospect of 'another little trip to Italy early next year'.
He had consulted his doctor 'and he very wisely asks, "Does it matter
what country one dies in?" '. And so, before the end of the year, the
decision was made.

In 1954, on the eve of what had seemed in his eightieth year to be
the beginning of his 'last Odyssey', Murdoch had, as he thought, said
farewell to the readers of his 'Answers'. He thanked them for their
interest over the years, but the end had come; the consciousness that
he was not going to answer one more question lifted an immense
weight off his mind. He wanted to see Rome once more, and Tuscany,
and some villages in France and Scotland. And so . . . 'no more of that
catechism'. It had been a Melba farewell. The 'Answers' had been
resumed not long after his return but now, in March 1964, as they set
forth once more for Italy, it surely had to be the end. He wrote for the
Herald a formal 'farewell', concluding with an answer to questions of
his own: 'Of what use has it been? Was it worth doing?'

> I have never for a moment imagined that these answers or any
> other writings of mine have any enduring quality. They are bits of
> journalism; and journalists do not aspire to immortal fame.
>   Quickly the night wind sweeps us away, and the traces of us. We
> serve the purposes of the day, and if we have served that purpose
> faithfully, we must be content to be forgotten tomorrow. Yes; but
> have these answers served even the purposes of a day? That is the
> searching question which I can't avoid asking myself. I should hate
> to think that they had been utterly sterile and futile; but what one
> hates to think may be true none the less. That is the reflection
> which sometimes disturbs my slumbers.
>   Well, to sum up: I have come to the conclusion after much
> pondering and many doubts, that actually, taking them as a whole,
> these answers have not been wholly labour in vain. I have tried to
> express in them—even in the frivolous ones—a certain philosophy of
> life which the real philosophers would not admit to be a philo-
> sophy, but which has been for me a star to steer by. And when
> people write to me, as they occasionally do, to tell me that I have

helped them to see more clearly or to face life more courageously, they hand me the only laurel wreath I have ever coveted.[8]

This, I think, is substantially a just verdict by Murdoch on Murdoch. He *was* a journalist, and he did comfort many people. But his 'day' covered much of the twentieth century, and to historians the night wind will not sweep all traces of him away.

He would not entirely have approved of this last sentence. It is a little too solemn, though I believe it to be true. The old journalist was not quite saying farewell, once and for all, for he concluded that if he happened to see anything in Italy that he thought might interest his readers, he would ask the editor for the hospitality of his columns.

On 16 March 1964 the Murdochs were once again en route to Naples. There Alec and Catherine King joined them and went on with them to Rome. They spent leisurely weeks in familiar places, Florence, Siena, Verona (where the heat drove them out to the neighbouring mountains) and Genoa. Murdoch would sit contentedly at a table in an out-door café observing affectionately the bustle of Italian life, though it was no longer easy for him to overhear the spoken language he so deeply loved. His one disappointment, he wrote in July, was that walking about did tire him rapidly—'I came across a delightful phrase in "The Ring and the Book" the other day which exactly describes me; the old Pope speaks of his "grey ultimate decrepitude." '[9] In Florence his grandson Ian (Will Murdoch's son, now living in England) joined them for a fortnight.

'Yes, I love this country, I don't quite know why, but all the same I'm glad to think we'll be home in six weeks, looking out at the river . . .' The sentiment comes sooner or later to most travellers, in one country or another, and whether they think of the rivers or the mountains of home. By early October Murdoch was writing from Blithedale, South Perth, about his 'scheme for air-conditioning Hades, and how apprehensive the Pope was when he heard what I was planning'.[10]

When it was announced in the Birthday honours list of June 1964 that Murdoch had been awarded a knighthood (K.C.M.G.), an enterprising newspaper had managed to track him down in Siena, and to report his comment, 'I must be the oldest and deafest knight on the list'. Congratulations he duly answered by hand; when I heard from him in July he still had over two hundred messages to deal with before he left his 'sweltering hiding-place' in Verona. But some people were a little surprised, not that the title should have been offered but that he should have accepted it. He was not in principle opposed to formal recognition of public services (he had himself

accepted a C.B.E. in 1939, the year of his retirement), but he had
shown no great respect for titles, 'mixing you up with a herd of Lord
Mayors and such like', as he had written to Brookes in 1931, on
hearing a rumour that his friend had declined one, and he was still
writing about 'such gewgaws' in 1949. Presumably it had occurred to
various people that he would be ninety in September 1964, and the
appropriate steps had been taken, for was he not now a legend rather
than an irritant? And at his age it would have been churlish to refuse.

There was now, in Italy, an immediate problem. It was officially
suggested (if that is the right word) that he might appropriately be
invested in London itself, and that meant much anxious concern for
Barbara Murdoch and Catherine King who were with him in Verona
when a decision had to be made. He solved their problem by slipping
out one morning to a post office to send the telegram which, no doubt
very courteously, pleaded age and infirmity. If he had 'to be hit on the
back with a sword', he preferred to endure the ceremony in familiar
Government House near the site of the old university in Irwin street,
Perth.

To Murdoch there was something lacking in life unless he was
regularly writing to a deadline. The habit was so ingrained that
lacking opportunity to exercise it he felt like a smoker deprived of
tobacco. Not long after his return from Italy, his familiar features,
pipe in mouth, were seen once more as a vignette at the head of a
Saturday column in a newspaper. Not 'Answers' now, but 'Afterthoughts'; not the *Herald*, but the *Australian*, a paper recently
founded by his energetic grandnephew Rupert, appearing simultaneously in the capital cities and, in its vigorous youth, rich in
features and talented contributors, if sometimes rather short of hard
news. Whether he had been invited to contribute, or whether he had
suggested that he do so, I do not know, but perhaps he would not have
found himself among the young lions who then wrote the Saturday
literary pages if his name had not been Murdoch.

The first of his 'Afterthoughts' was published on 6 March 1965. He
had rejected 'Last Fruits off an Old Tree' as too obviously stolen from
Landor, forgetting surely that no one now ever read Landor.
'Hangovers' was ambiguous. 'Afterthoughts' was the best he could
do, provided the emphasis was on 'After' rather than 'thoughts';
probably, he wrote, readers would find his writing antiquated, out of
date, old-fashioned and musty.

> Well, I am not ashamed. I am rather fond of old-fashioned utter-
> ances, such as the recent statement of the Governor of the Com-
> monwealth Reserve Bank, that the year 1964 was a period of
> 'exceptionally high liquidity'. With a slight change of date, what

Dr Coombs says today might have been said, and probably was said, by Noah as he felt the keel of his Ark grinding on the stony peak of Mount Ararat. We don't, on that account, call Dr Coombs and an old-fashioned writer. We love his autograph and would fain see it oftener.

Old Murdie was at it again, Coombs would have thought if he read that opening article, and writing a good deal more sensibly than the expositor, years ago, of the mysteries of the monetary system.

The last 'Afterthought' appeared on 7 September 1968. These 'brief papers of mine—these articles in miniature—mini-essays you may call them' had been mostly gleanings from memory, their writer content to look back. There were sketches of incidents and scenes from childhood, from early days after graduation and from travel, portraits of people he had known, reflections on familiar books, no preaching now, no denunciations, though occasionally modest suggestions such as his proposal for the use of portraits of Australian prime ministers on postage stamps. He wrote about new books concerned with men or matters in his own life, as when Michael Cannon's *The Land Boomers* took him back to family disasters in the Victorian bank crash of 1893, or when Rohan Rivett's little book on Herbert Brookes prompted memories of his old friend. One such 'Afterthought' that touched me was his appreciation of my biography of Alfred Deakin. That book would itself be superseded in time, but for the present it was bound to supersede his own 'Sketch'. I was not worried about the verdicts of the professionals; after all, I was one of them and could form my own judgement. But I was anxious to please Murdoch, and was glad to find that I had done so.

When his own grandchildren began to marry (the first of them, Walter King, in 1956), it was time for Murdoch to accept without grumbling the lot of a patriarch, sending messages to his great-grandchildren, or reporting the habits and sayings of those whom in the nature of things he would never know as adults. But one change in the circle of the family, less predictable than its growth in numbers, could still perceptibly affect the pattern of his life. In 1965 Alec King, now sixty and long since a reader in the University of Western Australia, moved to Monash University in Melbourne as a second professor of English. Such an appointment at that age was rare, but W. A. G. Scott, the first professor, knew what he was doing when he secured as a colleague one of the most sensitive of teachers of English literature in Australia while there was yet time for an infant university to benefit from his talents and experience.[11]

For over thirty years Murdoch had been able to talk to Alec about literature, and for longer, about everything that interested him, with

Alec and Catherine King

Catherine. When she had been away from Perth during her husband's periods of sabbatical leave, Murdoch's weekly letters had
reflected the part in his life played by 'conversation' with her. Now at
ninety he resumed that kind of correspondence, with its family news,
its frank impressions of people they both knew, and its recollections of
past years. He wrote cheerfully enough, with a shrewd eye for absurdities that would amuse Alec, like the newspaper headline
' "Heat-wave broken by cool change." What else a heat-wave could
be broken by they didn't say.' But it is evident that he greatly missed
them. Writing to Catherine in earlier years from Blithedale, he had
rarely begun with more than the date, or occasionally 'South Perth'.
Now he wrote 'Home', or even 'Your second home'.

    In a long cheerful letter of May 1967 Murdoch mentioned, casually
as it were, the prospect of an operation. He supposed that at his age he

might not survive the shock, but though he didn't want to live much longer, he wanted to live long enough to settle his affairs, to see Catherine again, and Anne in her new house on the farm. The operation was in the event postponed, and for some time yet, despite occasional recurrences of the pain that had suggested its necessity, he could continue to live a life remarkably serene compared with that of most others of the small band who pass the age of ninety. Despite the physical weakness of extreme old age, he could still take gentle walks and with Barbara from time to time visit old friends. There were, as always, visitors. Murdoch had his weekly 'Afterthoughts' to write. His memory was undimmed, his wit still keen, the flowing prose of his letters, and even his clear handwriting remained much as they had been fifty and more years earlier. As an old academic he looked forward to seeing the volume of Chaucer edited by his grandson Francis King, and he awaited eagerly the publication of Alec King's study of Wordsworth, reflecting (someone had told him) 'the quintessential Alec'. His comment might have been made in his own professorial days—'I hope it's also the quintessential Wordsworth' —but he wrote with proud appreciation when he had read it.

There was one more journey in these last years, a short visit to Melbourne at the end of 1966 to see the Kings, now by chance living in the house he had built nearly sixty years earlier. He was driven around to his youthful haunts, and the hill country where once he had enjoyed long walks. On that visit he made the tape-recording of memories of childhood and his family on which I have drawn in early chapters of this book. I am struck, on rereading the transcript, by the sadness, in a sense the indignation, with which he recalls the ravages of tuberculosis in families of that time. One begins to understand something about the concern of Victorian literature with early death.

Visiting Perth in June 1968, I called one afternoon on the Murdochs. I had not seen Murdoch for some years. He stooped rather more than I remembered, but with faint surprise I noticed how neatly he was dressed and trimmed. Barbara placed me in a chair close to him, to allow for his deafness, and we talked away in front of a bright fire until it seemed time to go. Ceremoniously he opened a new bottle so that we might take sherry. They both came to the door to say goodbye. At the curve of the little drive, before the trees would hide them, I turned, and we waved. I did not see Old Murdie again.

The 'Afterthought' of 7 September of that year was a little essay on parables. If you travel only to return and talk rot to your friends, you might as well have stayed at home; not all the time spent on reading is well spent; reading novels is on the whole the most profitable kind of reading, for more than other kinds of books they can 'lift us out of that

Entrance to Blithedale, 1976
Study window at lower right

lonely island of egoism in which nature has planted us' and 'make us members of a great fellowship'. It was the last thing he wrote for publication.

It would have shocked Murdoch to think that any memoir of him should linger over the last stages of the physical decline of a very old man. But because there is still something to say about the characteristic Murdoch who remained strong in mind and memory to the end, I must tell in brief words why, so suddenly, the voice of the journalist was heard no more. From September 1968 two successive bouts of influenza left him very weak; the last handwritten letters I have seen are dated October, in the interval between these illnesses, and they are in a very shaky script. He could no longer write or type at length. In April 1970, the least perturbed member of his family about the outcome, he made a 'miraculous' recovery from an operation for hernia which could no longer be delayed, only to be tormented in his remaining months by the unpredictable attacks of an agonizing neuralgia, stoically endured.

Yet he remained himself. A note of 10 October 1968 was written on a card bearing his printed name and address. Over the printed 'Sir' of

Murdoch University, Western Australia, 1975

his name he writes 'rot', he goes on to family gossip, assures Catherine that he is 'imbecile but not insane', and concludes, 'Barbara's favourite poem is Softly, softly catch a monkey (by Milton, I fancy). She quotes it whenever I gallop, which if I did, it would be to see you all.'

In the last but one of his 'Afterthoughts' Murdoch might almost have foreseen the situation which was soon to deprive him of a principal solace of his life. Old age, he wrote, is in many ways the happiest period of life, for an old man has had more time than his juniors to accumulate a happy store of memories. One of the 'blessings' left to him was that he could look round his library, take down a dilapidated old book, and 'renew the ancient rapture which was mine when I first made its acquaintance, years and years ago'.[12] In his last eighteen months he could no longer move at will around his study or, in the sleepless hours, pad off to it to verify the words of a line of one of the poems he was accustomed to recall as he lay awake. Though to the end he still read, the small print of his books acquired in his youth tired his eyes, and so in the evenings Barbara would read aloud, accompanied by him, as it were, for he chose what might have been expected from a believer in 'the great truth that a really good book is worth returning to again and yet again'—*Middlemarch, Daniel Deronda, Oliver Twist, Vanity Fair* . . .

He liked to go out with Barbara in the car to quiet places—to the hills, to Bibra Lake where he could feed the black swans, to the fishermen's jetty at Fremantle where the gulls would take food from his hand—pleasant places, much as they had been when he first came to Western Australia, away from the city where now, even in South Perth, as he had written in August 1968, rectangular and singularly unattractive tenements were sprouting and 'the whole district . . . bristling like an unshaven chin'.

A note to me in his last year shows how much he was still the Murdoch of old, despite his bodily weakness. In May 1970 I wrote to him, on behalf of a student, for information about a man he had known in Melbourne sixty years earlier. His reply (typewritten by Barbara) was prompt. He told what he could remember, and had even taken the trouble to pass on my query to a friend who might be able to help. I would not have written at all on such a matter if I had known that in April he had had an operation. I would have written earlier and very differently if I had known further that Alec King had died of a cancer in March. Murdoch said nothing of these things, for he believed in certain reticences.

When the small band of teachers began their work at the University of Western Australia in March 1913, they were effectively opening the sixth Australian university and, as it seemed, the last for generations to come. Yet by the end of the 1960s, four of the six states had two or more universities, and in Western Australia a second university had actively been considered for some time. Such were the remarkable results of the entry of the federal government into the financing of higher education. By June 1970 the time had come for the government of Western Australia to appoint an official planning board to settle down to a task of several years, in comic contrast to the impromptu procedures of one month in 1913.

The membership was approved late in June. On 9 July, at the first meeting, the chairman read to the board and indirectly to the public a letter from the premier, Sir David Brand, announcing the government's decision that the new institution should be named Murdoch University: 'He is a distinguished scholar and a man of letters. His name gives dignity to our new university . . .'[13]

Earlier that afternoon Barbara Murdoch had answered the telephone, and was asked by the under-treasurer to speak to the premier. She had to tell him that he could not talk directly to her husband, for he was too ill that day to come to the telephone. So it was she who told Murdoch that, if he would agree, the new university would bear his name. She was able to tell the premier that her husband was deeply moved, that he felt greatly honoured, and that he would agree. He had indeed said something like that but, reflecting, he had added words which she did not pass on: 'Well, it had better be a good one.' The old man knew that relative immortality had been conferred on his name, though his own end must be near. And thinking about it a few days later he exclaimed, 'What a way to be remembered!'

So much is verified by the newspapers and by notes of Barbara Murdoch's own recollections. But when, why and by whom was the effective decision for that name made, subject only to Murdoch's consent? For some years yet the answers cannot fully be given, but it can be said that historians will not lack an authoritative document that tells them in detail how the university acquired its eponym.

Later in July the Murdochs drove one day to Bibra Lake. Returning, they saw a solitary man walking along the road past the pine plantation where before long a university would rise. Was he, they wondered, the first of the Murdoch professors?

Pneumonia came briefly. On the night of 30 July 1970 Walter Murdoch died at his home in South Perth.

MURDOCH'S PUBLICATIONS

IN PERIODICALS

In his modest note, 'Walter Murdoch Bibliography' (*Meanjin*, vol. 9 (1950), p. 60), Dr C. Craig wrote that 'sooner or later it is certain that someone will attempt a full-length bibliography of Walter Murdoch's published work. The purpose of this note is to assist whoever undertakes this task.' The word 'attempt' was no doubt used advisedly, but I wish that 'someone' luck. Dr Craig's information will help him for the period 1892-1912, and he may now consult a list of Murdoch's literary articles in the *Argus*, 1899-1913, published in La Nauze and Nurser (eds), *Walter Murdoch and Alfred Deakin on Books and Men* (Melbourne 1974). In due course he should also be able to consult fairly complete and annotated lists of Murdoch's contributions over many years to the *Argus*, the *Australasian* and the *West Australian*, compiled by Elizabeth Nurser, Amanda Gordon, J. A. La Nauze and (especially) Christopher Connolly, which will, in time, be deposited in the National Library of Australia.

If these lists were printed in this book they would occupy a hundred pages or more, though still falling far short of a complete bibliography. Murdoch not only wrote articles for other journals, and prefaces or introductions to various books, but in some periods was an anonymous leader writer. Then we have to add 'Answers' (1945-64) in the *Herald* and 'Afterthoughts' (1965-8) in the *Australian*.

As a literary journalist Murdoch was busily writing for nearly seventy years. Of course he wrote too much, too quickly, and he knew it. Even Shakespeare, he believed, 'would be the first to admit that many things he wrote were written in a frantic hurry, to serve the need of the moment'. And coming nearer to the practice of his own kind of writing he said, 'it seems hardly fair to Hazlitt's fame that every little scrap of his most ephemeral scribbling should be exhumed and republished a century later'. Someone, some day, dying in the attempt to compile a complete list of Murdoch's writings, will recall too late his words about 'the great writers' (among whom he did not claim to be): 'All of them who have lived a normally long life have perpetrated much that is—no, I must not say worthless, but not first-rate; and there is so much of the first-rate to read, and so little time to read it in.'

BOOKS AND PAMPHLETS

The following list does not include (a) new issues or editions, with a few exceptions, (b) chapters in books edited by others, (c) prefaces or introductions to books by others, (d) separately printed broadcast talks.

[1903] *The Struggle for Freedom*. Whitcombe and Tombs, Melbourne.

1906 [With T. G. Tucker] *A New Primer of English Literature*. Whitcombe and Tombs, Melbourne.

1907 *The Enemies of Literature*. Lothian, Melbourne.

[1908] *Educational Problems in Victoria*. Whitcombe and Tombs, Melbourne.

1908 [Editor] *Illustrative Prose and Verse: a Companion to a New Primer of English Literature*. Whitcombe and Tombs, Melbourne.

1910 [Editor] *A School Treasury of English Literature*. Lothian, Melbourne.

Loose Leaves. G. Robertson, Melbourne.

1912 *The Australian Citizen: An Elementary Account of Civic Rights and Duties*. Whitcombe and Tombs, Melbourne.

1917 *The Making of Australia: An Introductory History*. Whitcombe and Tombs, Melbourne.

[Editor] Shakespeare. *The Merchant of Venice* ('The Australian Shakespeare'). Lothian, Melbourne.

1918 [Editor] *The Oxford Book of Australasian Verse*. O.U.P., London.

Second edition, 1923, entitled *A Book of Australasian Verse*. O.U.P., London.

Third edition, 1945. O.U.P., Melbourne.

Fourth edition, 1950, edited with Alan Mulgan, entitled *A Book of Australian and New Zealand Verse*. O.U.P., Melbourne.

1921 *Anne's Animals* [illustrated by Mrs Arthur Streeton]. Endacott, Melbourne.

1923 *Alfred Deakin: A Sketch*. Constable, London.

1926 *The Poets' Commonwealth: A Junior Anthology for Australian Schools*. O.U.P., Melbourne.

1930 *Speaking Personally*. Angus and Robertson, Sydney.

1931 *Saturday Mornings*. Angus and Robertson, Sydney.

1932 *Moreover*. Angus and Robertson, Sydney.

1934 [Editor, with Alec King] *Prose Passages*. O.U.P., Melbourne.

The Two Laughters [selected essays, all previously published in books]. Dent, London.

The Wild Planet. Angus and Robertson, Sydney.

1936 *Lucid Intervals*. Angus and Robertson, Sydney.

1937 [Editor] Shakespeare. *The Tempest*. ('The Australian Students' Shakespeare'). O.U.P., Melbourne.

1938 *The Victorian Era: Its Strength and Weakness*. Angus and Robertson, Sydney.

Collected Essays [all previously published in books]. Angus and Robertson, Sydnev.

1939 *The Spur of the Moment*. Angus and Robertson, Sydney.

1940 *Collected Essays* [now includes *The Spur of the Moment*]. Angus and Robertson, Sydney.

1941 *Steadfast: A Commentary*. O.U.P., Melbourne.

Selections from Walter Murdoch [all previously published in *Collected Essays*]. Angus and Robertson, Sydney.

[Editor] Shakespeare. *Hamlet* ('The Australian Students' Shakespeare'). O. U. P., Melbourne.

1947 *72 Essays: A Selection* [all previously published in *Collected Essays*]. Angus and Robertson, Sydney.

1951 [Editor, with H. Drake-Brockman] *Australian Short Stories*. O.U.P., London.

1953 *Answers*. M.U.P., Melbourne.

1956 *Selected Essays* [Foreword by Ian Maxwell, reprints essays in *Selections . . .*, 1941]. Angus and Robertson, Sydney.

1960 *My 100 Answers* [same as *Answers*, 1953, except for Answer no. 18]. News Ltd, Adelaide.

1964 *The Best of Walter Murdoch: 72 Essays* [reprint of essays in 1947 item]. Sirius books, Angus and Robertson, Sydney.

NOTE ON SALES OF MURDOCH'S ESSAYS

The following totals were compiled from detailed figures courteously supplied by Ms Gwenda Jarred and Mr Bob Shankland of Angus and Robertson, publishers. They do not include figures for the 1941 edition of *Selected Essays* and the 1945 edition of *Collected Essays*. Some figures are for numbers sold; others, from which relatively small numbers for review and complimentary copies would have to be deducted, are for numbers printed.

Of the original separately published volumes of 'new' essays, *Speaking Personally* (1930) sold about 16 000 copies to the end of 1950, when it went out of print. Printings or sales of *Saturday Mornings, Moreover, The Wild Planet, Lucid Intervals* and *The Spur of the Moment* (1931-9) were, in total, about 20 000 by 1941, when they were all out of print.

Collected Essays (1938, 1940) sold about 12 000 copies by 1941. Of *72 Essays* (1947) about 11 000 were printed by 1951; about 1300 copies of the same collection, now called *The Best of Walter Murdoch* (1964), were sold.

Sales of the Australian Pocket Library edition of *Selected Essays* (1945) were about 24 000 by 1950, and of the school and the general editions (1965) about 7600 by 1964.

NOTE ON SOURCES

Murdoch's own papers (MS. 2987, A.N.L.), though indispensable to a biographer, are a relatively small collection, largely lacking in-letters. The Brookes Papers (MS. 1924, A.N.L.) have much relevant material, above all the Murdoch-Brookes letters, 1907-63. The Deakin Papers (MS. 1540, A.N.L.) have the Murdoch-Deakin letters, and two volumes of Brookes-Murdoch correspondence, mainly about the 'Sketch'. Many other collections in Australian libraries include letters from Murdoch; these are identified in my end-notes. Originals or copies of letters from or concerning Murdoch, sent to me in response to a public appeal in 1971, have been placed with the Murdoch Papers. These include his letters to his daughter Anne Vanzetti. Many letters from Murdoch have been lent to me privately by their owners; I hope that ultimately copies will, with permission, be placed in the National Library of Australia, though access may for some time be restricted. In particular Murdoch's letters to his daughter Catherine King have been invaluable. Collections of scripts for broadcast talks, not entirely identical, are in the Murdoch Papers and the A.B.C. Archives, Sydney. Files of the various newspapers and journals referred to in the text and notes are in the National Library of Australia and/or the La Trobe Collection of the State Library of Victoria.

Correspondence between Murdoch and Herbert Brookes is in the Brookes Papers, MS.1924, National Library of Australia (A.N.L.), unless otherwise identified. In other cases where no location is given, the document remains (1976) in the possession of the owner.

REFERENCES

1   A SON OF THE MANSE

¹ For Rosehearty, S. Lewis, *Topographical Dictionary of Scotland* (London 1846); Francis H. Groome, *Ordnance Gazetteer of Scotland* (Edinburgh, 1885); 'Parish of Pitsligo', in H. Hamilton (ed.), *Third Statistical Account of Scotland — The County of Aberdeen* (Glasgow 1960), pp. 335-44; Rev. Stanley Hill (Rosehearty) to J. A. La Nauze, 1 May 1973; information from Lady Murdoch, Francis King, Catherine King, A. J. Youngson.

² For Peter Murdoch and his family, detailed information from P. J. W. Kilpatrick (Edinburgh), 1976. Note that in W. Ewing (ed.), *Annals of the Free Church of Scotland, 1843-1900* (Edinburgh 1914), vol. 1, p. 280, the year of James Murdoch's birth is given as 1817, and when he died in October 1884, his age was registered as '65 years'. Both figures are incorrect. His father's name was also incorrectly given as 'Patrick'.

³ For Braco Park and the Garden family, information from P. J. W. Kilpatrick, 1976, and in his letter of 22 June 1974 to Dr Margaret Doyle, in the possession of Catherine King; 'The Late Miss Garden, Braco Park', cutting from *Banffshire Journal*, 15 July 1879, in Murdoch Papers, A.N.L.; Walter Murdoch, tape-recorded by Francis King, December 1966.

⁴ Anon., 'The Church Union in Rosehearty: A Retrospect', cutting from . . . *(?)* *Evening News*, 8 December 1906, in Murdoch Papers, MS.2987, A.N.L.

⁵ *Everlasting Punishment: A Sermon Preached before the Free Synod of Aberdeen at Their Request. By the Reverend James Murdoch, Minister of the Free Church of Scotland, Pitsligo* (Aberdeen 1864). Copies in Bodleian Library and British Museum.

⁶ W.M.'s various reminiscences of his parents and his childhood in Rosehearty are scattered widely in his published writings, in his personal letters, in interviews reported in various newspapers, and in a tape-recording made by Francis King in December 1966. I do not document these in detail, except for special points.

⁷ She was Mary Gray Garden, née Hogg, who edited *Memorials of James Hogg* (London 1895), and wrote the introduction to *Poems of James Hogg* (London 1886) in the 'Canterbury Poets' series.

⁸ W.M., *Collected Essays* (Sydney 1940), p. 434; tape-recording, December 1966.

⁹ The incident is related in 'A French Memory', an essay in W.M.'s *Steadfast: A Commentary* (Melbourne 1941), p. 179.

¹⁰ S. Martin, *A Tale of Two Churches* (Melbourne 1967), p. 27; information about *Potosi* passengers from Public Record Office, Victoria, 10 September 1973; W.M. to C. Murdoch (King), 10 June 1928.

2 SCHOOLBOY TO SCHOOLMASTER

[1] Walter Murdoch, *Collected Essays* (Sydney 1940), p. 356.

[2] I am greatly indebted to P. J. W. Kilpatrick for the details of Peter Murdoch's will. The reference in the Scottish Record Office is SC67/36/31, p. 141.

[3] G. Blainey, *A History of Camberwell* (Melbourne 1964), pp. 71-2.

[4] G. H. Nicholson and D. H. Alexander (eds), *First Hundred Years: Scotch College, Melbourne, 1851-1951* (Melbourne 1952), p. 30.

[5] G. Serle, *The Rush to Be Rich* (Melbourne 1972), p. 273.

[6] Blainey, op. cit., p. 57.

[7] W.M., 'The Money-grubbers' Frolic', *Australian*, 18 February 1967.

[8] Information from Professor S. J. Butlin.

[9] Information from C. J. Mitchell, Ormond College.

[10] Information from Dr G. Oxer, Wittenoom, W.A., to whom I am indebted for copies of W.M.'s letters to his father; W.M. to Mrs Baird, 10 February 1954, files of the *Australian Dictionary of Biography*.

[11] 'Books and Men' by Elzevir (W.M.), *Argus* (Melbourne), 6 January 1912.

[12] W.M., 'Afterthoughts', *Australian*, 27 November 1965.

[13] 'Some Random Memories', by Elzevir, undated cutting, c. 1940, in Murdoch Papers, MS.2987, A.N.L.

[14] Information from Mrs Theodore Beggs and Miss Betty Beggs, kindly sent to Philip Brown, to whom I am indebted for making inquiries on my behalf.

[15] W.M., 'Afterthoughts', *Australian*, 22 July 1967.

[16] Miss Betty Beggs, quoted in letter of Mrs Theodore Beggs to Philip Brown, 10 July 1974.

[17] John Hetherington, interview with W.M., *West Australian*, 17 December 1960.

[18] W.M. to Latham, December 1960, Latham Papers, MS.1009/1/10715, A.N.L.

[19] W.M. to Fred Oxer, 5 December 1896, copy from Dr G. Oxer.

[20] For Johnstone Hughston, letter from Anne Heal to Catherine King, 18 August 1976.

[21] Blainey, op. cit., p. 72; *The History of Fintona 1896-1946* (Melbourne, n.d.), p. [1].

[22] W.M. to Catherine Murdoch (King), 3 June 1928.

[23] W. de Steiger to J. A. La Nauze, 18 October 1971.

[24] 'People We Know', *Punch* (Melbourne), 24 August 1911. My colleague H. J. Gibbney, an authority on pressmen of the period, thinks that Keith Murdoch was the author, and other passages in the article support his view.

[25] See C. E. Sayers, *By These We Flourish: A History of Warrnambool* (Melbourne 1969); and letters between W.M. and Miss Baird, 1963, by courtesy of Miss M. Johnstone, Warrnambool Public Library.

[26] *History Falsified*, nos 71, 79 (Melbourne, n.d. (?1904)), *The Struggle for Freedom: A Review*, no. 84, Australian Catholic Truth Society pamphlets.

3 ELZEVIR

[1] The documents are attached to the minutes of the council of the University of Melbourne for the meeting of 7 December 1903.

[2] The Murdoch Papers, MS.2987, A.N.L. contain cuttings of verses published in various journals, and a fair-copy MS. book of unpublished poems. Most of them can be dated in the period c. 1898-1902.

[3] In the *Quadrangle*, an undergraduate magazine, October 1892, copy in Baillieu Library, University of Melbourne.

[4] 'The Two Faiths', one of 'Two Sonnets' which according to C. Craig (*Meanjin*, vol. 9 (1950)) were published in the *Australasian*, 12 March 1892. His date is wrong, but there is an undated cutting in the Murdoch Papers.

[5] 'The Passing of Love' and 'The Climber', both in fair-copy MS. book, Murdoch Papers, MS.2987, A.N.L.

[6] 'Ave Imperatrix!', *Argus*, 31 December 1900.

[7] W.M. to A. and F. Wilmot, 24 November, 3 December 1903. Frank Wilmot Letters, MSS.4/6, Mitchell Library.

8 One of his stories is included in *Australian Short Stories*, first series, selected by Walter Murdoch and H. Drake-Brockman (Oxford University Press (World's Classics) 1951). It was originally published in the *Argus*, 21 June 1899. Some others are in the Murdoch Papers.

9 'Fiction on Myalong Station', *Argus*, 26 April 1899; 'When the Creek Is in Flood', *Argus*, 13 September 1899; 'Jan Kroetz', *Argus*, 9 May 1900. I thank D. Abbott for identifying these.

10 W.M. to Vance Palmer, 23 December 1941, Palmer Papers, MS.1174/1/6051, A.N.L.

11 10 June 1899.

12 *Argus*, 15 September 1900.

13 There is a list of articles, 1899-1913, in J. A. La Nauze and Elizabeth Nurser (eds), *Walter Murdoch and Alfred Deakin on Books and Men* (Melbourne 1974), pp. 103-8.

14 *Argus*, 13 March 1909.

15 *Argus*, 27 February 1909.

16 Vance Palmer, *A. G. Stephens: His Life and Work* (Melbourne 1941), p. 20.

17 'A Plea for Australian Literature', *Argus*, 4 August 1906.

18 *Argus*, 6 May 1905.

19 W.M. to A. G. Stephens, 22 January 1907, Hayes Collection, University of Queensland Library.

20 W.M. to Vance Palmer, 23 December 1941, Palmer Papers, MS.1174/1/6051, A.N.L.

21 K. S. Prichard, *Child of the Hurricane* (Sydney 1963), pp. 97-8.

22 Palmer Papers, MS.1174/1/72, A.N.L.

4 MELBOURNE FRIENDSHIPS

1 W.M. to J. G. Latham, 28 December 1912, Latham Papers, MS.1009/1/142, A.N.L.

2 For example Warren Osmond and John Docker, in theses still (1976) in progress, and D. Walker, *Dream and Disillusion* (Canberra 1976).

3 I am grateful to Warren Osmond for drawing my attention to the minutes of the Boobooks' meetings in the papers of Harrison Moore held in the University of Melbourne Archives. He has made use of these in his M.A. (University of Sydney) thesis, 'The Education of a Victorian Liberal: Frederic Eggleston 1875-1916' (1974).

4 Lothian published *The Enemies of Literature* (Melbourne 1907). His reminiscences were tape-recorded by Francis King, W.M.'s grandson, who made a transcript available to me. He told the same story to C. E. Sayers; see his *David Syme* (Melbourne 1965), p. 302.

5 Files of the *Trident*, 1907-9, are in the Baillieu Library, University of Melbourne, and in some other Australian libraries.

6 Agreement, in two versions, in the Latham Papers, MS.1009/16/486, A.N.L. B. A. Levison was an able young lawyer who disappeared from the Melbourne intellectual scene in 1910, when he went to London to join a legal firm. (Information from Osmond's thesis, referred to above.)

7 The main records of the Brown Society are held in the Brookes Papers, MS.1924, A.N.L.

8 Keith Murdoch Papers, MS.2823/7, A.N.L.

9 See W.M. to Deakin, 18 November 1908, in La Nauze and Nurser, op. cit., pp. 38-40, and the detailed accounts by W.M. in *Argus*, 6 March 1909, and *Lone Hand* (Sydney), 2 August 1909.

10 W.M. to Deakin, 28 May 1911, in La Nauze and Nurser, op. cit., pp. 55-6.

11 In a review by Elzevir of a book on Oxford, *Argus*, 11 February 1911.

12 The documents are in the minutes of the council of the University of Melbourne, held in the university archives.

13 E. Scott, *A History of the University of Melbourne* (Melbourne 1936), p. 189.

14 Letters to the editor, in *Argus*, 9, 11 August 1911, and *Age*, 10 August 1911; *Victorian Parliamentary Debates* (Legislative Assembly), vol. 127 (1911), pp. 550-5, 593; *Punch* (Melbourne), 24 August 1911.

[15] *Australia To-Day.* Special number of *Australasian Traveller*, 1 November 1912. Copy in A.N.L.

[16] *Victorian Parliamentary Debates* (Legislative Assembly), 21 November 1912, pp. 2980-3.

[17] W.M. to Alec King, 26 March 1950.

[18] University of Melbourne, Faculty of Arts Minutes 1911-18, 19 July 1912.

[19] University of Western Australia, records in registrar's office, file 256[a]; Senate Minutes, Book I (duplicate volume); F. Alexander, *Campus at Crawley* (Melbourne 1963), pp. 55, 58; W.M. to Catherine King, 24 July 1966.

[20] Deakin to W.M., 26 December 1912, in La Nauze and Nurser, op. cit., pp. 64-5.

5   PROFESSOR OF ENGLISH

[1] W.M. to Brookes, 22 February 1913.

[2] W.M. to Brookes, 22 February, 18 November 1913.

[3] In *West Australian*, 19 August 1920.

[4] Tape-recording of radio interview by Catherine King, 29 August 1963, A.B.C. Archives; *Black Swan* (University of W.A.), October 1947; W.M. to J. A. La Nauze, 28 August 1935.

[5] W.M. to Catherine Murdoch (King), 26 February 1928.

[6] Interview in *West Australian*, 13 February 1913.

[7] W.M. to J. A. La Nauze, 25 December 1944.

[8] Senate Minutes, 16 August 1937.

[9] Information from Guy Vanzetti and Catherine King.

[10] Vanzetti's son Guy recalls that it was 'not offered for publication, as someone had already done it'. Colleagues expert in Italian literature tell me that they cannot find in the bibliographies any reference to a published English translation of *Santippe*, though (they say) that is not absolutely conclusive. But it could well be that in inquiring about translation rights Murdoch found that the work had already been done, though his predecessor had not yet found a publisher. I am told by an expert reader that the translation itself is smooth and accurate, creditably avoiding the somewhat mannered style of the original.

[11] 'Afterthoughts', *Australian*, 22 May 1965.

6   WRITING THE 'SKETCH'

[1] W.M. to Brookes, 19 July 1963.

[2] See his *Wordsworth and the Artist's Vision: An Essay in Interpretation*, London, 1966, and *The Unprosaic Imagination*, ed. Francis King (Perth 1975).

[3] *Collected Essays*, p. 610.

[4] *Collected Essays*, p. 119.

[5] W.M. to Brookes, 9 October 1924.

[6] W.M. to Brookes, 18 December 1924, in Brookes letter-book, Deakin Papers, MS.1540/74, A.N.L.

[7] Information from Professor Michael Roe.

[8] W.M. to Brookes, 9 October 1924.

[9] W.M. to Brookes, 15 July 1926.

[10] W.M. to Catherine Murdoch (King), 12 February 1928.

[11] W.M. to Brookes, 13 July 1931; to J. A. La Nauze, 9 July 1964; television interview, 1962.

[12] Correspondence in Brookes Papers, MS.1924, A.N.L., and Brookes letter-books, Deakin Papers, MS.1540/73-4, A.N.L.

[13] Berriedale Keith Papers, University of Edinburgh Library, EUL MSS, Gen. 145; W.M. to Ernest Scott, 4 August 1923, Baillieu Library, University of Melbourne; W.M. to Ernest Scott, 10 August 1923, MS.703/5/2/108, A.N.L.; W.M. to Brookes, 25 November 1924, MS.1540/74, A.N.L.

7   COLLECTED ESSAYS

[1] Curtin to S. Talbot Smith, 1 March 1943, Palmer Papers, MS.1174/1/6304, A.N.L.; G. Serle, *From Deserts the Prophets Come* (Melbourne 1973), p. 124. The members of the Advisory Board in 1943 were S. Talbot Smith, W. A. Osborne, G. Mackaness, Flora Eldershaw, Vance Palmer. I thank H. McQueen for a copy of Curtin's letter.

[2] *Meanjin*, vol. 28 (1969), p. 222.

[3] To Janet Paisley, 1951.

[4] *West Australian*, 11 July 1922.

[5] *West Australian*, 25 July 1925.

[6] *Collected Essays*, pp. 227-30.

[7] *All About Books*, 18 November 1930, p. 281.

[8] *Meanjin*, vol. 28 (1969), p. 221.

[9] Cecil Hadgraft, *Australian Literature* (London 1962), p. 273.

[10] Green, *History of Australian Literature* (Sydney 1961), vol. 1, p. 696.

[11] Hadgraft, op. cit., p. 275, and in more detail in his article 'Murdoch's Mask', *Southerly*, vol. 8 (1947), pp. 20-5.

8   THE SACRED DUTY OF GROWLING

[1] *Collected Essays*, p. 529.

[2] The minutes of the Western Australian committees are in the A.B.C. Archives in Sydney. I thank Miss P. Kelly for her help in making them available.

[3] W.M. to Brookes, 12 May 1937.

[4] W.M. to Brookes, 25 April 1939.

[5] W.M. to Brookes, 25 April 1939.

[6] W.M. to Brookes, 31 December 1939.

[7] *B.P. Magazine*, 1 March 1940.

[8] A.B.C. Inter-office Memo, Talks from Western Australia, Molesworth to Bearup, 24 March 1943, A.B.C. Archives, Sydney.

[9] *All About Books*, 5 December 1930, p. 339.

[10] *Collected Essays*, p. 381.

[11] *West Australian*, 12 April 1924.

[12] *Argus*, 27 August 1921.

[13] *Collected Essays*, p. 401.

[14] *Collected Essays*, p. 143; for the original, *West Australian*, 18 April 1931.

[15] See B. Berzins, 'Douglas Credit and the A.L.P.', *Labour History*, no. 17 (1970), pp. 148-60, and her M.A. thesis, 'The Social Credit Movement in Australia to 1940' (University of New South Wales, 1967).

[16] *Collected Essays*, p. 539.

[17] *Contemporary Review*, May 1928, pp. 545-54.

[18] W.M. to Catherine Murdoch (King), 17 June 1928.

[19] *Argus*, 9 November 1934.

[20] A. T. Yarwood, foreword (p. xx) to Egon Kisch, *Australian Landfall* (Melbourne 1969), first published 1937.

[21] *Argus*, 22 July 1933.

[22] *Argus*, 23 April 1921.

[23] *Collected Essays*, p. 29.

[24] Peter Coleman, *Obscenity, Blasphemy, Sedition* (Brisbane 1962), p. 24.

[25] *Argus*, 30 August 1930.

9   RETIREMENT

[1] *Argus*, 9 April 1938; in *Collected Essays*, p. 811.

[2] W. P. Hurst Papers, MS.6107, La Trobe Collection, State Library of Victoria.

[3] 9 April 1939.

[4] 'The Literary Output' in *Times* supplement (Australian number), 26 January 1938.

[5] *Bulletin*, 16 March 1938, p. 2. Davison to Murdoch, 29 July 1947 (letter in the Drake-Brockman Papers), refers to his authorship of the article.

⁶ W.M. to Brookes, 17 September 1939.
⁷ W.M. to Brookes, 26 May 1939.
⁸ W.M. to J. A. La Nauze, 2 August 1938.
⁹ See F. Alexander, *Campus at Crawley* (Melbourne 1963), chs 5, 6.
¹⁰ Alexander, op. cit., p. 247, quoting W. Somerville.
¹¹ W.M. to Brookes, 7 March 1948.
¹² W.M. to Brookes, 18 October 1946.
¹³ W.M. to Brookes, 26 December 1947.
¹⁴ Related to me (1973) by Monsignor J. T. McMahon, of South Perth.
¹⁵ *Collected Essays*, p. 734.
¹⁶ W.M. to Brookes, 24 August 1944.
¹⁷ W.M. to Brookes, 11 July 1945.
¹⁸ W.M. to Brookes, 16 October 1945.

10   ANSWERS

¹ *Collected Essays*, pp. 331-2.
² G. Serle, *From Deserts the Prophets Come* (Melbourne 1973), p. 134.
³ Ingamells Collection, MS.6244, Box 259/3 (d), La Trobe Collection, State Library of Victoria.
⁴ Serle, op. cit., p. 132.
⁵ W.M. to Ingamells, 23 August 1943, as in note 3 above.
⁶ 'Anthology Anatomized', *Southerly*, vol. 7 (1946), pp. 190-201.
⁷ *Southerly*, vol. 12 (1951), pp. 223-6, review by Kelvin Lancaster.
⁸ See Kenneth Slessor, *Bread and Wine* (Sydney 1970), on 'Anthologies in General'.
⁹ W.M. to Flexmore Hudson, 2 May 1946, Hudson Papers, File 21, Menzies Library, Australian National University.
¹⁰ W.M. to Vance Palmer, 13 November 1939, 4 December 1940, 23 December 1941, 28 April 1942, Palmer Papers, MS.1174/1/5619, 5855, 6051, 6107, A.N.L.
¹¹ Murdoch's letters, and many other documents about the collaboration, are in Henrietta Drake-Brockman's papers, at present (1976) in the possession of her son, P. M. Drake Brockman of Canberra. I am very grateful to him for allowing me to consult them.

I add a note about Davison's 'alacrity' in agreeing, seeing that in fact he was *not* represented and that in the preface to a second series of Australian short stories in the World's Classics (1963) the editor, 'Brian James', had only one criticism of the first series, that 'strangely enough' Davison was omitted. The correspondence on Murdoch's side is in Davison's papers in A.N.L., MS.764/1236-1244, and on Davison's side in the Drake-Brockman Papers mentioned above. Davison accepted, naming his stories; a month later, without explanation, he withdrew. Reluctantly, on being pressed by Murdoch, he explained that he had always doubted Murdoch's claims to have knowledge of, or interest in, contemporary Australian literature; that he had first agreed to be represented on the urging of Vance Palmer; and that his uneasiness was confirmed by the tone of Murdoch's letters. Murdoch in reply cleared up an unwitting ambiguity in an earlier letter, but further offended by remarking that he had always thought Australians needed not more knowledge of each other but a closer acquaintance with the world's masterpieces. Davison replied that world masterpieces were in fact all very regional, and 'if you really think Australians are not in need of knowledge of each other through imaginative literature, how do you make your contention square with your present activity?' Murdoch told Palmer (A.N.L., MS.1174/1/7409) that Davison had 'a contempt for my intelligence and character quite frankly expressed. I like him for his honesty, but I can't change my spots at my time of life!' If Murdoch had been a little more careful about his first letters, the curious exchange would not have arisen, but on the issue as he understood it Davison said some salutary things. He would not, later, change his mind in answer to a personal appeal by Henrietta Drake-Brockman.
¹² Answer 96 in *Answers*, a selection published by Melbourne University Press (1953) reprinted as *My 100 Answers* by News Ltd, Adelaide, 1960.
¹³ W.M. to Catherine King, 7 May 1950.
¹⁴ *West Australian*, 24 June 1950.

[15] Robin Gollan, *Revolutionaries and Reformists* (Canberra 1975), p. 268.

[16] W.M. to Brookes, 7 July 1950.

[17] Gollan, op. cit., p. 260.

[18] W.M. to Herbert and Ivy Brookes, 9 April 1952.

[19] W.M. to Rev. Dr John Mackenzie, 25 October 1939.

[20] Address to the Presbyterian Assembly, reported in *West Australian*, undated cutting (?1935).

[21] *Broadcaster*, 13 November 1954.

[22] *Australian*, 20 April 1968.

[23] *Collected Essays*, p. 528.

[24] 18 November 1941.

[25] *Advocate*, 16 January 1946.

[26] *Advocate*, 26 February 1948.

[27] Rev. Dr Leslie Rumble, M.S.C., *That Catholic Church* (St Paul, Minnesota, U.S.A., 1954), an extract kindly supplied by the author. In a letter of 14 October 1973 Father Rumble courteously explained that his criticisms were concerned only with the *religious* implications of Murdoch's reported words, but he did think that in this instance Murdoch was contending that *some* deep-seated religious acknowledgement of God was a nation's best defence against the rise to power of an essentially Godless communism.

[28] *Advocate*, 29 October 1947.

11   THE SAGE OF SOUTH PERTH

[1] *West Australian*, 31 July 1970 (Athol Thomas), 19 December 1960 (John Hetherington); *Advocate*, 26 February 1948.

[2] *Meanjin*, vol. 28 (1969). Articles by Louis Triebel, Mary Durack and A. A. Phillips.

[3] *West Australian*, 9 March 1962.

[4] W.M. to Brookes, 20 August 1962.

[5] W.M. to Catherine King, May 1957.

[6] 4 April 1962.

[7] W.M. to Brookes, 20 August 1962.

[8] *Herald* (Melbourne), 7 March 1964.

[9] W.M. to Catherine King, 24 July 1964.

[10] W.M. to Catherine King, 9 October 1964.

[11] See, for example, Alec King's *The Unprosaic Imagination: Essays and Lectures on the Study of Literature*, ed. Francis King (Perth 1975).

[12] *Australian*, 31 August 1968.

[13] *West Australian*, 10 July 1970.

INDEX

Set in 10 point Baskerville on 11 point body